THE MANAGEMENT OF POWER

THE MANAGEMENT
OF POWER

PAUL G. SWINGLE

UNIVERSITY OF OTTAWA

LAWRENCE ERLBAUM ASSOCIATES, PUBLISHERS
1976   Hillsdale, New Jersey

DISTRIBUTED BY THE HALSTED PRESS DIVISION OF

JOHN WILEY & SONS

New York   Toronto   London   Sydney

Lawrence Erlbaum Associates, Inc., Publishers
62 Maria Drive
Hillsdale, New Jersey 07642

Distributed solely by Halsted Press Division
John Wiley & Sons, Inc., New York

Library of Congress Cataloging in Publication Data

Swingle, Paul G
   The management of power.

   Includes bibliographical references and index.
   1. Organization.   2. Power (Social sciences)
3. Organizational change.   4. Bureaucracy.   I. Title.
HD38.S8477   658.4   75-45316
ISBN 0-470-15030-0

Printed in the United States of America

Contents

Preface

This book started as two separate books that slowly drifted together. The first was a book on revolution. The title of that book was "Plebeian Power," and in it I intended to examine how organizations in our society — governments, industries, universities, churches, or what have you — become senile, arrogant, and stupid gerontocracies. The book was to examine a variety of methods that have been suggested for gaining leverage on bureaucracies, forcing them into a high level of turbulence, and eventually bringing about either change or destruction.

The central part of that book involved a detailed analysis of the concepts of conflict, violence, strategy, and power. I have spent a great many very pleasant hours discussing these issues with students. Some of these discussions have been in the formal context of seminars which I have presented on interpersonal conflict, whereas the most fruitful discussions tended to be with interested students who seemed to enjoy rapping about these issues over coffee or a beer.

The universal concept that these students had about managers, administrators, politicians, bureaucrats, etc., was that they were a group of unthinking, power-hungry, but cowardly men whose entire lives were focused on maintaining the system and gaining greater status within that system. To accomplish this, these people spent most of their time, in the students' view, developing a variety of very sneaky and tricky ways to keep people under control, to get more work out of them, and to exploit them. During these conversations the students spent an enormous amount of time complaining about the Establishment and expressing their general sentiment that things were messed up too badly and the system too strong to do anything about it, and that one might just as well give up; and several of them did. There were a few activists among them, people who organized student strikes for a variety of different reasons, or those who participated in sit-ins, protest marches, and the like. However, even the more active students gave the impression of feeling that by and large the whole enterprise was hopeless but that one could not live with oneself if one did not do something.

One of the more startling features of the activist students was that, recognizing that I had management experience, had taught in a graduate school of business for a while, and was a management consultant (although they considered these to be "dirty" areas, concerned primarily with exploitation of the Have-Nots in society), they sought my advice on methods for launching successful protests, organizing and controlling their own groups, publicizing dissent, etc. In short, they recognized that such organizations required the development of a set of skills that could be utilized for the purpose of keeping the organization effective and efficient.

The second book was to be entitled something like "The Management of Decision Making" and was addressed to managers and administrators. This book grew out of my association with a graduate school of business; much more directly, however, it grew out of my association with managers and administrators, both in the context of special institute courses that I presented and in the course of consulting for industry and government.

I was encouraged to start this book because I was astounded to find that approximately 25% of the managers and administrators with whom I came into contact, who had been out of school for at least 10 years or so, were really extraordinarily angry with the system and were searching for methods to institute change; either that or they wanted out! They had roughly the same definition of their organization and the organizations with which they had to deal as I and some of the angry students mentioned above had. They considered the institutions to be organizationally senile and arrogant, with absolutely no method for accommodating change or being responsive to the needs of society.

In this book I intended to deal with the theoretical issues of conflict, strategy and the properties of organizations that produce senility. I also intended to examine the process of conflict eruption, and I intended to conclude the effort with a system for power sharing. This system, which I refer to as the "overlapping decision center system," is one that I developed several years ago. It is the system that I present in all my institute courses and in my consulting work. Again, I have spent many enjoyable hours discussing the details of these issues with concerned managers both in the context of special seminars I have conducted for management institutes and, again more fruitfully, in the context of having a few beers with managers after the seminar is over.

The results of the discussions that I had with managers, administrators, students, etc., seemed quite consistent with what was happening to my writing of these two books. Mainly, they tended to drift together. I found that I was dealing with global or societal issues, discussing such matters as plurality versus elitism in society, and examining the concept of enhancing the intelligence of government and industry by developing strong and powerful adversaries. The nonbusiness graduate students with whom I discussed these issues seemed most concerned with the global issues and with methods for bringing arrogant bureaucracies to their knees. However, thirty minutes exposure to any one of the student protest groups was an experience in anomie. Virtually everything that went on was chitchat; the potential for launching a successful and sustained protest against any organization was so out of the question it was almost laughable. Few if any of the leaders of these groups had any of the skills necessary to form a powerful organization.

The discussion with managers and administrators, that is, the concerned ones, in contrast, tended to focus on more practical day-to-day issues. "True," they would say, "society is all messed up; true, some of these things may have to be destroyed to be made humane and responsive to society's needs; but I see absolutely no way of bringing these things about. I want to know what I can do tomorrow within my own organization." Much of what I have to say in this book, I have learned from these concerned managers. Their concern, I may add, contributes not a little to the sense of optimism apparent in the following pages.

In short, after discussing this book with a large number of people on both sides of the fence, and attempting to write both books, it became perfectly clear that I had one book on my hands. It is written for those people who feel that organizations should be efficient and humane as well as capable of responding to change in society and being self-regulatory.

This book reflects the thinking of many extraordinary people, those with whom I have personal acquaintance and those I know only by way of their work. It reflects also my association with concerned people who have been willing to listen, and actually seemed to have enjoyed listening, to me talk about these issues and helping to clarify them. A special acknowledgment must go to those arrogant buffoons whose obedience brought them to positions of influence in sycophantocracies with which I have been associated. Without that field experience, this book might never been written.

PAUL G. SWINGLE

THE MANAGEMENT OF POWER

1

Introduction

In the early 1960s, when the United States had unconstitutionally restricted world travel for its citizens, a group of 80 or so American students traveled illegally to Cuba. Cuba lies 90 miles off of the Florida coast but the students had to travel over 14,000 miles, via Czechoslovakia, to get there. That, ladies and gentlemen, is the model of most of our organizations of today. To go 90 miles one must travel 14,000 miles.

This is a book about the science of the future—management. Organizations are a fact of life. They are here to stay. They are inevitable and society cannot survive without them. That many, if not most, present-day organizations are gerontocracies operating in senile, irresponsible, repressive, and downright stupid fashion does not indicate that they have to operate that way. Organizations can be rendered responsive, intelligent, efficient, and humane if only we are capable of harnessing the conflict that normally operates as a derisive and destructive force and using it constructively.

This book is written for managers, members of the Establishment. An increasing number of managers want out of this Establishment. They feel trapped. They feel that they and the people they work with are apathetic because the problem of trying to render their organization more intelligent is too big. They are familiar with the books written by the prophets of doom, which point out in very great detail what is obvious to everybody, that things are pretty messed up. The managers feel that they can do very little but be obedient, that they have no methods for influencing their organization, and they find the stress levels to which they are exposed are becoming totally unacceptable. Alvin Toffler in his book *Future Shock* considers this attitude, man envisioned as a helpless cog in some vast organizational machine, as the most persistent myth that managers have about the future. Although a persistent myth, the attitude is very pervasive among managers and is responsible for a great deal of their depression and personal gloom. We shall examine the source of this attitude and why it is at least unproductive if not totally inaccurate.

I usually start my institute courses with a description of some very ingenious experiments that have been done with rats. The experimental situation is as follows. Rats are placed in a box with a grid floor that can be electrified any time the experimenter chooses to deliver a very painful electric shock to the rat. The rat, having all the food and water that he requires, has only one simple little job to do. That job is to make "decisions." To measure such decision making, the rat is provided with a lever on one end of the box. A rear projection screen, onto which geometric designs can be projected, is located above the lever. The rat is then presented with a very simple managerial decision-making situation: to make "go"–"no-go" decisions. This is accomplished as follows: whenever a circle is projected on the screen above the lever, the rat is to interpret that as a "go" decision. The rat must push the lever within a few seconds after the image of the circle is first projected; otherwise he receives a very painful electric shock. If he pushes the lever within the allotted time, however, nothing happens; that is, he avoids the shock.

The second image that is projected on the screen is that of an ellipse. The ellipse is to be taken as a "no-go" decision, in that when it is projected the animal receives an electric shock only if he pushes the lever. If he does not push the lever, nothing happens. Now, if a very clear circle and a very clear ellipse are used, the rat can live in this environment very happily and very contentedly. That is, the rat eats quite normally, drinks quite normally, and does not display any behaviors that indicate that he is under a high level of stress or anxiety. The rat almost never receives an electric shock as he is simply attentive to the display during the time when he is supposed to work (i.e., when images are displayed).

We now interfere with the rat's happy little world by making the circle more and more like an ellipse. The point comes when the rat can no longer, with absolute certainty, discriminate between the "go" signal and the "no-go" signal. Under such circumstances the rat goes through a condition known as experimental neurosis. He throws himself over on his back, goes into a catatonic state, gives a great many indicators of having a full-blown hysterical attack, and if he is left in this situation he will eventually die.

The rats are not managers, of course, but there is a lesson to be learned from this experiment; it indicates one of the primary causes of stress, the necessity to make decisions based on imperfect information when the cost associated with error is extremely large. We have many prototypes of such stress situations: such jobs as air traffic controller, in which information overload is a serious problem, at times rendering decision making difficult, when the cost associated with error is extraordinarily large; or responsibility for operating very costly, high-speed, automated equipment, in which error, in this case perhaps simply delay in responding to a warning signal, can result in the production of large quantitites of unsaleable items or damage to costly machinery.

At the management level, managers are frequently placed in a position in which they have to render decisions based on imperfect and inadequate information when the cost associated with error is great. With the advent of highly automated information retrieval systems, such as remote access computer retrieval systems, it is frequently not the paucity of information that increases the uncertainty of a correct decision but the relatively new phenomenon of information overload. We are now in a situation in which managers can be provided with more information in 30 seconds than can be digested in 2 weeks. Managers are frequently placed in a position in which they do not have time to simply review all of the available information to determine what information they really want to examine in some detail. They are in a situation in which the costs associated with incorrect decisions are frequently high but in which the information needed to increase the accuracy of decisions is either ambiguous, confusing, or simply buried in unmanageable quantities of other information. The decision maker is caught in a situation of extraordinary stress.

People in stressful situations, like the rat in the box, start developing serious problems associated with the parasympathetic nervous system. They ulcerate; they have coronary complications; they are grumpy and angry and cannot cope with other trivial stressful situations. And we have other indicators, such as alcoholism, high levels of interpersonal conflicts, high divorce or marital conflict levels, high turnoverism, absenteeism, grievances, etc. etc.

It is also enlightening to learn that brain overload may be related to brain deterioration. Ivan Khorol recently reported in a UNESCO publication that improper use and overloading of the brain has brought "the human brain . . . to the brink of ruin." He points out that the twentieth century brain must process more information daily than previous generations would have processed in a lifetime. As an interesting aside, we know that senility is much more prevalent in older males than in older females. Given the male presence in most decision-making situations relative to the female presence, one wonders whether equality in the corridors of power will equalize the senility statistics?

Now, one of the reasons that managers are placed in such high levels of stress is that the organizational structure in which they are involved is hopelessly archaic. The only method that organizations seem to have for responding to inevitable change is that of the major shakeup. Consulting firms have estimated that all organizations experience a major shakeup or reorganization on the average of once every 2 years, and even that seems to be a conservative estimate. Organizations are not responsive but change the way dictatorial governments change. Once things become intolerable then a counter-power group develops that eventually is able to bring about a coup.

The second reason managers are exposed to such extraordinary levels of stress is that the information that they have is old and out of date. A recent television commercial for one of the data communications companies showed a manager sitting behind his desk taking things out of his in-basket, shaking his head, and putting them in his out-basket with the statement "had I known about this yesterday, something could have been done." We very frequently do not receive the up-to-date information required because the burden of providing information does not reside where it should in the organization. Very frequently it is the manager's obligation to find out what the people for whom he is responsible are doing and where they are with respect to specific projects that have been assigned to them. The burden for obtaining information, of course, should not reside on the decision maker.

The third source of stress is that the information obtained by the decision maker is not in the correct form. Often it is buried in copious trivial information that, although important, is not important to the decision maker at that time. Moreover, very frequently the information that is received by the decision maker has been sifted and abstracted, if not "sweetened," by a subordinate who may not be cognizant of the nature of the information required by the decision maker.

As an aside, referring again to animal studies, it is interesting to note that one can create much the same sort of hysterical-like behavior in animals that have been exposed to choices between two positive but mutually exclusive events. Much as the donkey that was caught between two haystacks and starved to death because he could not decide at which haystack he wished to eat, hungry monkeys have been rendered neurotic by offering them a choice between two equally attractive foods. Monkeys frequently forced to choose between equally attractive amounts of, say, cherries and peanuts, in which the choice of one means the loss of the other, become maltempered and develop tics, stupors, and so forth. Again, I am not trying to indicate that managers are rats or monkeys but I am trying to point out that we have very good evidence to indicate that any kind of decision making is stressful business. We are not doing much to increase the life expectancy of managers at the present time and there is some evidence that the life expectancy of middle-level managers is actually declining somewhat.

The fact that many managers spend 60 or 70 hours a week, and sometimes more, doing their jobs points out another immediately obvious problem. Managers spend 70 or 80% of their time doing housework. They are busy fighting "brushfires" or "bailing out the boat" to use some of the common buzz phrases. Everything is an urgent problem and the deadline is yesterday. They spend their time checking on the details of work being done by subordinates and they chase people trying to find out what is going on or the state of a particular job. They are urged to give guidance on issues to relieve others of decision-making stress. They deal individually with people, attempting to encourage them to improve their performance. They waste untold hours in committee meetings that are called not for the purposes of decision making but because somebody is bored or lonely or does not wish to take the responsibility for making a decision. They supervise the efforts of a large number of individuals on a one-to-one basis. They supervise budgetary commitments and sometimes people come to them when they run out of pencils. The point is that most managers spend an incredible amount of time in supervisory activities, which, although a necessary part of management leadership, does not define the main function of a manager. The main function of a manager, as is obvious to every manager, is to anticipate future events and develop systems and processes for accomplishing those future events. That is, the main function of a manager is to avoid brushfires, not to put them out. This requires that managers spend a large amount of their time in planning and forecasting activities and an equally large amount of time developing systems to bring future eventualities to fruition.

The purpose of this book is to review some of the concepts from both polemology (the science of contention) and organizational behavior. It is directed specifically at providing managers with a workable understanding of the situations that give rise to stress as well as the workings of organizations that render the organizations stupid and unchangeable except by major confrontation. As I stated before, the book grew out of my consulting experience and the experience I had offering courses to managers at various institutes. It reflects the comments, suggestions, and concerns of many extraordinary managers; those who are highly concerned with making their old organizations more efficient and more intelligent. It reflects my own experience as a department chairman in a university as well as my experience of attempting to radically force change in hopelessly senile sycophantocracies—and losing. It is written specifically for managers, or bureaucrats if you prefer, because we need good administrators; and if important changes are going to take place in society, I am convinced that it is people on the inside who are going to generate those changes.

To accomplish these things, to reduce your own level of stress, to make your operation more efficient, to start introducing important changes in your organization, you are going to have to become a Sherlock Holmes type of manager. You have to make your management experience into a science. Good managers, like good scientists, like good physicians, like good teachers, are good observers. They collect evidence, they formulate hypotheses, they test their judgment against the available facts and they discard hypotheses, theories, and notions that prove to be inconsistent with the facts. Above all, they collect information. They avoid opinionated guesses or basing their judgments on bias, tradition, or marriage to methods of operation that have proved successful in the past.

We are going to be focusing on the structure of organizations. In particular we shall be concerned with those structural features which generate conflict, affect decision-making processes, and affect the veracity of information. We are not dealing with personalities. It is the basic premise of this book that good managers are intelligent people who understand organizations and the dynamics of group decision making. They are not born with the talent. There are no specific characteristics associated with their leadership capabilities. In other words, the only things that are required to be a first-class manager are smarts and training.

I am writing to you, that is, other managers, as part of the Establishment. I am also writing not as someone who is capable of changing total organizations, which I assume most of you are not. You are caught somewhere in the organization and feel, probably quite rightly, that no matter what you do you are going to have very little effect in terms of the total organization.

In his new book *Something Happened* Joseph Heller (1974) captures this feeling of impotence. The major character, Bob Slocum, a successful middle-aged corporation executive, contemplates disobedience by spindling, tearing, folding, defacing, stapling, and mutilating his neat machine-processed pay check:

> What would happen if, deliberately, calmly, with malice aforethought and obvious premeditation, I disobeyed? I know what would happen: nothing. Nothing would happen. And the knowledge depresses me. Some girl downstairs I never saw before . . . would simply touch a few keys on some kind of steel key punch that would set things right again, and it would be as though I had not disobeyed at all. My act of rebellion would be absorbed like rain on an ocean and leave no trace. I would not cause a ripple.
>
> I suppose it is just about impossible for someone like me to rebel anymore and produce any kind of lasting effect. I have lost the power to upset things that I had as a child; I can no longer change my environment or even disturb it seriously. They would simply fire and forget me as soon as I tried. They would file me away [p. 15].

The basic premise on which this book is written is that, although you do not control the organization and hence cannot change the total situation, you can introduce change within your own area of influence, be that two people or two hundred people. Therefore, rather than trying to change institutions by major confrontation, much like Samson destroying the temple, or perhaps a more appropriate analogy may be Don Quixote charging his windmills, we can attempt to change total organizations by grabbing one pillar and shaking it. If a few do so, the collective turbulence may then be sufficient to force the organization to become responsive or to crumble.

To be a good Sherlock Holmes manager, however, you must have the facts. You know there is conflict. I do not have to tell you that; what I can tell you about, however, is what conflict is, what gives rise to it, how one type of conflict differs from others, what kinds are destructive, and most importantly how it can be harnessed. You know people play games. We are going to talk about different strategies of such situations or interactions and how you can understand what is going on while it is going on, not after all is said and done. You know you make decisions with imperfect information. You know you are gambling. What we are going to talk about are the resources you have and how you can avoid rendering yourself stupid by focusing your attention on the wrong causes or the wrong features in your organization. We are going to talk about how you can be more successful as a manager, how you can develop an organizational structure within your area of influence that permits you to live with inevitable change. For the organization of the future will not be stable: it will be constantly changing and constantly developing. We can hope these changes to be systematic and disciplined as opposed to explosive and destructive. We are going to be talking about how you harness conflict and how you make it work for you. To understand these concepts we will be talking about different philosophies of conflict, the various theories of conflict, theories of power, different kinds of games, myths, and so on. This is not a conservative book. It is based on the assumption that what we are doing today is decidedly not the best model for what we should be doing tomorrow.

I should indicate at the outset that in the last chapter I propose a simple organizational structure that can be used for small departments within organizations which I have suggested to many managers over the past few years. It has been put into effect by many managers in a number of nationally visible companies. It works and it works very well indeed. However, it is not the only organizational system and I wish to stress at this point that this is not a book on techniques, gimmicks, whistles, or bells. There are other systems that work well and perhaps better than the one advocated at the end of this book. What is critical, however, is a full understanding of the dynamics of organizational behavior and group decision making. This understanding will permit managers to modify any system to generate a more intelligent and more responsive organization. Cookbooks are all right for baking cakes: they are certainly not suitable for the training of scientifically oriented managers.

As a final comment, I have been told by several people (never managers) that some of the sections of this book are too abstract and are seemingly unrelated to management. I have come to the conclusion, a conclusion with which many managers concur, that some things are better stated in the abstract. When we have a firm grasp of theoretical content of such issues, applying them to the real case is no trick at all. Concepts too closely related to specific situations are frequently resistant to generalization to other situations that outwardly appear to be different but in terms of the dynamics are essentially the same.

ORGANIZATIONAL CONCEPTS

The Organization

It is probably appropriate at this time to clarify some of the terminology that is used in the book just to make sure that we understand one another. I use the term "organization" or "social unit" interchangeably to indicate any group of individuals acting concertedly to satisfy some consistent objectives, goals, or needs. Hence, companies are organizations or social units, as are governments, universities, church groups, social clubs, etc. Organizations or social units are characterized by recognizable, although perhaps not explicitly stated, rules and goals. Decision-making centers can, potentially at least, be found anywhere within the organizational unit. Specialization of roles or tasks and the capability to organize, rotate, or change personnel also characterize organizations.

Systems

The major problem that one has when writing a book on management is that of excluding variables. Everything seems to be relevant when we talk about the factors with which a manager must be concerned. This book focuses specifically on power, conflict, and violence as they figure importantly in the life and the activities of administrators. Again, it is my contention that sensible and realistic analysis of the causes of conflict and violence and, more specifically, a sensible and rational harnessing of conflict and use of power can render organizations less rigid and more susceptible to systematic and disciplined change.

The concept of systems, although apparently straightforward at first glance, is a very difficult concept for most people to persistently keep in mind. We are so prone to think in terms of linear, cause–effect models. We isolate one or two causes and a limited number of effects and delude ourselves that if we can subject the causes to our influence we can exact some kind of predictable effect. Unfortunately, the world does not go around quite that way and we find that we are constantly surprised that things do not go quite the way we have planned.

There are many excellent examples that can be offered to explain systems, including everything from warehouse allocation, freeway traffic systems, merchandising, and hospital care to marriage and garbage collection. Our focus again, however, is on interpersonal conflict and organizational power. The essential systems concept which is of importance to us is that any event or phenomenon or episode we observe or experience is both a cause and an effect, is influenced by and is influencing a great many factors. We are part of every system we observe or experience and we may interpret systems in a variety of different ways.

Now, it is important to understand that our description of a system affects a great many things. The way we perceive a system affects the way we describe it and, conversely, the way we describe it affects the way we see it. In short the reality we experience is to a very great extent influenced by our predilection to look for various things, which in turn derives from the way we describe the world around us.

Another important consideration is that we must be very careful about the measurements we use, for all things have a tendency to exceed our scales of measurement. Little squabbles end up in violent and brutal murders, hot water suddenly boils, the unfathomable suddenly becomes obvious, etc. In short, there are changes of state within any system that we care to analyze. Sherlock Holmes, in one of his attempts to clarify his thinking about a particular case by relating it to Watson, replied to Watson's protest "but that's impossible" by stating "if it is impossible then I must have stated the facts incorrectly, but the facts are correct." One may have very accurate and precise measures of the various inputs and outputs in a system and yet be completely in the dark as to what is going on within that system. Much of what is in this book is an attempt to point out that simplistic analyses of conflict, power, and violence keep one completely in the dark about the factors that give rise to and sustain conflict and, more importantly, preclude any sensible attempt to harness such conflict.

As a point of departure we can define a system as a set of identifiable factors that are coordinated to accomplish a set of goals (Churchman, 1968). It is important to understand that whenever we attempt to limit a system for the purposes of analyzing it, measuring it, or modifying it we are by definition abstracting something out of a larger whole. Strictly speaking, we can consider the entire universe to be a system. Then we can consider such things as our solar system, our planetary system, etc. In an organization we can think of the total organization as a system and we can think of our particular little bailiwick as being an identifiable system in that a set of purposes or objectives can be enunciated. We can also identify parts that are or should be coordinated for the purpose of satisfying or reaching those objectives or goals.

Conflict derives from a clash of systems in that one person's objectives, goals, and purposes may be at variance or detrimental to the objectives, goals, and purposes of another person who is part of "the" system. Marriage offers a workable example in that husband and wife are part of a system which can be perceived differently by each one of the protagonists.

It is important to enunciate the objectives of any system one is attempting to analyze. However, the stated objectives of a system are frequently at variance with the real objectives. As Churchman points out, university presidents may state, in their public appearances, that the function of the university is the creation of new knowledge and the dissemination of that knowledge to eligible students. If you closely examine the purpose of the president's efforts, however, one can see that the real objective is expansion.

We can ask such questions as what is the stated objective of a system, what is the real objective of a system, and what is the legitimate objective of a system. This casts the problem in three different perspectives because by focusing our attention on each one of these set of objectives individually we come up with a different description of what reality is.

There are several systems approaches described by Churchman. Each emphasizes a particular aspect of the system. Such emphasis, of course, can introduce error, for any fixation on a single feature of a system may encourage us to ignore other factors that are critical to our understanding.

Perhaps the most commonly encountered systems approach is that of efficiency. Those who advocate efficiency contend that systems are to be understood in terms of costs, wastes, production, output, etc. Fixation on efficiency can, of course, introduce errors in judgment. For example, although emergency equipment lays idle most of the time, the cost of maintaining such equipment may be trivial compared with the large costs associated with emergencies that cannot be handled.

The second position is the science approach to defining systems. This approach emphasizes objectivity, the development of models, and the application of formal logic in the form of mathematics and other systematic disciplines, such as economics, behavioral science, etc. As pointed out earlier in this book, one of the great dangers of the scientific approach is that we may not keep in mind that we are dealing with behavioral systems and not physical or thermodynamic systems. Many of the phenomena we observe in every day social situations defy our concepts of additivity, conservation of energy, etc.

The third position is that of the humanists, which emphasizes that systems are people and the approach to systems consists of looking at such human values as freedom, dignity, and privacy. Systems should not impose plans or intervene to the detriment to the quality of human life.

The fourth position enunciated by Churchman is that of the antiplanners, who feel that any attempt to lay out our specific and rational plans is rather foolish or dangerous or downright evil. The antiplanners point out that the appropriate approach to any system is to react in terms of one's experience and not try to change it by means of a grand design.

Now, for our purposes, what is essential in our understanding of these basic differences in approach to social systems is that as a manager you are going to confront people who describe reality in different ways, many of which are similar to those enunciated above. You are going to run into people who resist your attempts at organization presumably on the basis that you are being authoritarian or dictatorial or that you are imposing a grand design which infringes upon their basic human values. You will also confront individuals who will constantly harass you about efficiency. The reason that the efficiency advocates find their position so interminably tenable is that all organizations, all managers, alas, all human beings, are inefficient and inept and careless and savings can, at least in the short run, be very easily found. Similarly, you are going to confront people who feel that any attempt at planning is hopeless because the world is so chaotic, so hopeless that one should simply get along as easily as one can reacting to situations as they arise. Our point here is not whether they are right or wrong, or whether you are right or wrong, but that all of these elements figure into your calculations and to your analyses of conflict. They also figure importantly in terms of your attempts to harness conflict and render your situation intelligent. Recall our purpose in all of this is to create pockets of intelligence within your sphere of influence. We are not out to change the world or even change the organization for by and large that is a hopeless enterprise.

We should also understand that even though we may, in the first instance, precisely and objectively define and describe a system, systems are fluid and turbulent and constantly changing. Hence, because systems do not stay constant our descriptions of systems must allow for such change. There are several very poignant examples that may be offered. Marshall McLuhan, Churchman (1968) notes, points out, for example, that the telephone is now part of the communication system, just as the ear is. It would be almost as difficult to cut off the telephone as it would to cut off one's ear. There are conditions under which one is expected to answer the telephone and frequent refusals to do so generate as much hostility and counterreaction as does standing in a room and not responding to somebody who is attempting to speak to one. Hence, technology of both the hard and the soft variety, that is, both machines and people, as well as machines and processes, constantly change, constantly develop, or are constantly modified and in turn affect the system of which they are a part.

In summary, although we are not attempting to describe the systems approach to management we should always keep in mind that social organizations, managerial systems, and organizational systems are very complicated, highly interactive structures that contain people, resources, thoughts, machines, etc., which influence each other. The interactions and the counterinfluences are all harmonious and the real challenge to the administrator is his ability to see that harmony. Regardless of whether the system is a violent revolution or a children's concert, the entire complex is logical, systematic, and harmonious. The complexities of all systems are understandable; whether or not we understand them is a different matter.

The Bureaucracy

It should be recognized that all organizational hierarchies drift toward oppressive states so that potentially good relationships or organizations become repressive. In general the tendency is for hierarchies to move toward bureaucracy, which is the concentration of decision-making power in a single person or single center. People tend to have negative associations with such terms as hierarchies and, in particular, bureaucracies. However, it should be perfectly obvious that all of the organizations that we are going to be talking about are bureaucratic organizations. In most organizations power is concentrated and, although decision-making prerogatives may be delegated to subordinates, final accountability usually rests on a single individual. The proposals that are made throughout the book are based on the premise that most organizations are in fact bureaucratically organized. Most organizations are structured in terms of a single accountable person in any decision-making center. Whether we feel that is the way it should be or the way it will be in the future is neither here nor there. Present reality is that virtually all organizations are bureaucracies. We are going to be working with the concept that one can increase the total power of an organization and render it more intelligent and responsive by debureaucratization. Forced delegation of responsibility or, more strictly speaking, forced participation in important decision making is the key concept to debureaucratization.

The Establishment

We come finally to the concept of Establishment. When managers talk about the Establishment, they by and large do not know what they are talking about. They are the Establishment and their definition of "Establishment" is likely to be very emaciated indeed compared with the definition that can be offered by the many oppressed groups in our society. However, for our purposes I think it is important for me to point out what I mean by the Establishment. Basically, "the Establishment" refers to any bureaucracy that has become pathological. For example, "the Establishment" refers to a situation in which fiction becomes truth or fact emerges from fiction or fantasy. Racial superiority concepts in any societal unit or organization, for example, is an Establishment concept. Similarly, the meritocracy myth is an Establishment concept.

THE MYTHOLOGY OF MANAGEMENT

Radicalism

Let us do away with some myths. The first, and one that I can speak of from very personal experience, is the myth of radicalism. This myth is based, I think, on the notion that people can play God. It is based on the assumption that if one gets angry enough at a situation and goes in and causes a sufficient amount of disturbance, then all of the other people who are like minded will have sufficient courage to stand up when you stand up, say "yes I also agree and I also will not tolerate the present situation." However, such radicalism is not very efficient; one soon finds that one is dealing with a large number of cocktail party radicals who identify and espouse radical rhetoric on Saturday night but when the chips are down on Monday morning they hide behind closed doors in their offices. The tendency, of course, is to attribute cowardliness to these people who have not stood up when you stood up rather than to attribute stupidity to yourself.

There are strategies for change that work and there are strategies for change that do not work. I am not saying that radicals should stop being radicals. I am simply saying that in order to institute change within your organization, you do not have to set fire to the president's Cadillac. There are radical writers who maintain that one should constantly draw lines between oneself and the boss, should wear bluejeans to work, should glue up politically radical posters, and should be generally disruptive to demonstrate that one does not accept the façade of the organization. However, very few of us are going to do that and, of those of us who have, most have lost. It is also interesting to note that one of the members of the Chicago Seven ran for mayor of a California town and another one accepted an assignment to write for *Mad* or some similar magazine. Saul Alinsky, the very successful radical organizer, always maintained that you work within the Establishment getting one part to work against the other. In short, I think radicalism is a managerial myth, first, because very few of us are stupid enough to do it and, second, those of us who have tried it by and large have lost. Also, evidence indicates that there are more generally efficient ways of introducing change.

Helplessness

If we reject radicalism in management as a myth, however, we must also reject the notion of helplessness. Helplessness very frequently reflects one of two things. First, the belief that what one will not do, one cannot do. If you feel that you are being pressed by a particular person or group of people within the organization, there is nothing to stop you from shooting them all, blowing up their houses, blowing up their Cadillacs, or sending around notices to everyone indicating that you personally feel that they are all a bunch of arrogant bastards. You can do these things but the fact of the matter is that you will not, because they are very costly to do. At a more realistic level, the reason you do not protest against the arrogant use of power is because you quite rightly observe that any protest that you would be capable of launching is likely to give rise to your being thrown out of the organization.

The second feature of the helplessness myth is what I call the "Chief Honcho" error. This is a copout concept that many people have and it runs something like the following: "I'm too weak now in my present circumstance to bring about any important change in the organization. Anything I might do would be very trivial in the whole complexion of things. When I get to be the Chief Honcho then I'm going to do great things. I'm going to change everything." The fallacies inherent in this concept are obvious to everyone: (1) you will probably not ever obtain that level of power; (2) no matter how high you get in the organizational hierarchy, there is *always* somebody on top of you anyhow, either within your own organization or in terms of regulatory bodies; and (3) most important, to get to be a principal administrative officer in a sychophantocracy means that by the time you "arrive" you will be completely sucked up by the system and incapable of recognizing needed areas for change, much less being able to bring them about. I think that we can reject the feelings of helplessness as well as the myth of radicalism as representing two extremes of a dimension. By and large, managers tend to be more sympathetic to the radically oriented person than to the helplessness-oriented person, but that is neither here nor there. They both tend to be rather unproductive points of view.

Stability

The third myth is the stability myth. This is based on the assumption that one can find a system that will work for an organization and that that system will be satisfactory for the organization over a long period of time. As I indicated earlier, companies are constantly going through very major shakeups. This does not even include all of the many minor reorganizations that every company goes through routinely. We are not going to find an idyllic state of affairs, we are not going to find a technique that will be continuously satisfactory. The only state we can look forward to is one of constant change and we had better develop systems for accommodating ourselves and our organizations to that constant change.

The Meritocracy Myth

The most serious myth that we have to do away with, however, is the myth of the meritocracy. We believe, in our society, that rewarding people simply and nondiscriminatively on the basis of merit or achievement reflects true fairness and democracy. This myth leads people to believe that the most capable people will be rewarded for their efforts with positions of greater responsibility, prestige, and money. I am always stunned by the naïveté of people caught in such organizations who accept the myth of the meritocracy as a basic tenet of their modern religion. In all meritocracies someone or some group (even if it is the entire organization) must evaluate achievement and decide on appropriate rewards. The definition of what type of activities have merit then rests with the evaluating person or group. That so many scientists in universities are carrying on government-supported research on the most mundane and trivial of problems while society is crumbling about them offers a good example of the meritocracy problem. If the power structure of a university department falls into the hands of people who spend their lives on trivia, they are likely to define such trivial activities as meritorious and worthy of reward. Scientists desiring to open up new avenues of inquiry or activity then are caught in a power confrontation with the Establishment desiring to maintain its position of prominence. Scientists who accept this path to prominence are likely to spend a lot of time talking about their pursuit of knowledge, or the mandate they have from society to fight on the exciting frontiers of knowledge. They expend enormous energy on trivial research over which the mantle of scientific respectability has been thrown. The contribution of such activities, of course, is a powerful force in the maintenance of the status quo.

We have all, of course, seen the absurdity of such people on countless occasions. Albeit angering and frustrating, persons who feel that positions of power and responsibility endow them with the ability to judge the merit of activities about which they are totally ignorant are a source of constant amusement. That they are buffoons, however, does not mean that they are to be ignored. In fact, such people are likely to be the targets of protest activities. The silent majority are those who acquiesce to the meritocracy and submit themselves to such judgments.

A second aspect of the meritocracy myth that leads to inactivity is trust of the authorities. I am reminded of a woman who during the build-a-fallout-shelter phase, had a telephone installed in her shelter so that she could talk to her friends when she was forced to live there. People who trust the authorities feel that people who gain positions of power must be the most capable, least corruptible, and best able to make judgments consistent with the will of the people. They feel that no matter what the crisis, service will be restored in a few hours.

Although such people usually readily admit that all people are human and make mistakes, they feel that even if the person makes a mistake, the position must be supported. Therefore appeals are made to support a policy or course of action because it is the president's judgment. Trust of high-status people then derives from acceptance of the meritocracy. Persons who get to the top, however that is defined, must have deserved to get there and therefore deserve greater privileges and are mandated to judge the achievements of aspirants.

If one stands back and looks at the meritocracy myth dispassionately, it is really strange that people are so easily captured by it. In any organization, if you have one look at the merit rating scale on which superiors are supposed to rate their subordinates, it becomes immediately apparent that we are dealing with fiction. Superiors are supposed to rate subordinates' judgment, cooperativeness, ability to get along with people, creativity, fairness, decisiveness, and so on (the only essential difference between merit rating scales being the ingenuity of the people who make up the terms). The fact of the matter, however, is that people cannot make these judgments with any degree of accuracy at all unless they are very highly trained and given very specific systems for making such judgments. Such judgments tend to reflect personal feelings, recency (i.e., a person who normally screws up but happened to do a fantastic job the day before his rating tends to enjoy the benefit of the rater's faulty memory), lack of standards against which to rate subordinates, and so on. There is pretty good evidence indicating that more can be discerned from merit ratings about the person doing the rating than about the person being rated. Some people tend to be very lenient, others tend to be very difficult in their ratings. Threatened managers are unlikely to give extreme judgments and hence bunch everyone up around average ratings. Most managers are also unprepared to indicate that someone for whom they are responsible is really completely hopeless, for this undoubtedly can reflect on their own managerial capability.

The point, then, is that the meritocracy myth reflects the belief that people who are in superior positions are bestowed with the capability of making judgments about extremely complex behaviors and issues about which they know next to nothing. Studies on the relationship between supervisory ratings of subordinates and subordinates actual on the job performance indicate little, if any, relationship. Yet organizations constantly avoid collecting firm hard evidence on their employees; instead they rely on the judgment and recommendations of superiors. Most peculiar, but nonetheless a myth.

Now the meritocracy myth is simply an outgrowth of the concept of social Darwinism. Darwinism related to human social behavior reflects the belief that the strongest, most skillful, wisest, and most adaptable individuals are those who reach positions of power and influence. As in the jungles, those unfortunate individuals who have some defect of character, intelligence, or strength are found on the bottom of the social ladder. As social myth, the meritocracy myth becomes troublesome when we find individuals who believe that people at the bottom of the social structure deserve to be there by virtue of some basic defect. This mythology is usually stated in terms of a cultural lie. That lie is that people can always overcome problems. No matter what the problem is, with a little more effort, a little more fight, a little more dedication to purpose, all problems can be overcome. People at the bottom therefore have not tried hard enough, whereas people at the top are those individuals who simply have not given up until a problem is licked. A cartoon that reflects the cultural lie of the meritocracy myth depicts two imprisoned men, chained hand and foot, spreadeagled against a concrete wall. Just above their heads is a tiny little window, not large enough for a mouse to get through. The caption reads: "Now this is my plan."

The meritocracy myth, aside from justifying the fact that those in senior positions deserve to be there and that those at the bottom deserve to be where they are, has another very unfortunate effect. Senior managers who believe the meritocracy myth or find that others believe it find themselves caught in a very difficult situation. They find that by virtue of their positions they are consulted on issues well beyond their experience and expertise. If they do not know and say so, their image is eroded. Lesser persons are expected to have areas of ignorance and within reason are rewarded for indicating their lack of expertise in particular areas. Chief Honchos find that others expect them to know things, otherwise they would not be on top. Coupled with the cultural lie that with a little more effort, a little more fight, or a little more ingenuity all problems can be overcome, the manager finds himself in a very precarious position. He finds that he cannot fail.

Albert Ellis (1973) indicates that one of the prime causes of stress and anxiety is that individuals attempt to play Jehovah. That is, they find themselves in positions in which they tell themselves that they cannot fail, that they cannot make human mistakes. This is, to some extent, reinforced by subordinates who believe in the myth that good superiors should be flawless, they should be perfect, they should not fail. Now, as Ellis comments, anytime an individual says to himself that he must not fail or make a human mistake, the individual goes through the process of awfullizing. In awfullizing, individuals go through magical thinking by which if they fail it indicates that they are a failure. That is, they start to believe that they are their behavior. If they make a human mistake it indicates that they are not appropriate for top-level positions because top-level people do not make mistakes. Hence, managers become extraordinarily anxious about making presentations, about taking decisions, about subjecting their operations to scrutiny, for that simply provides a situation in which they cannot live up to an unrealistic standard.

The problem with respect to bureaucracies, of course, is that this myth leads people to expect the impossible from superiors, superiors expect the impossible from themselves, and then superiors become extraordinarily stressed about normal everyday screwups. Superiors then attempt to seek sanctuary by not rocking the boat. They do not reward initiative, they reward obedience. They do initiate new areas of activity but attempt to keep a very low profile. In addition, they are very careful not to delegate enough responsibility to threaten stability by starting any new area of activity. They keep their objectives unclear so that results can always be justified on a post hoc basis. Hence, the meritocracy myth is very damaging. The inevitable result is the development of a senile bureaucracy coupled with extraordinarily neurotically stressed managers whose energies are directed at seeking sanctuary.

The Myth of Common Sense

It should be obvious why we reject common sense. All one need do is look around at the discouraging chaos in society, hopelessly inefficient government, hopelessly inefficient university administrations, environmentally destructive industries, etc., ad nauseam, to come to the undeniable conclusion that the people responsible for running our societal institutions only vaguely, at best, know what they are doing. Virtually all of our "science of common sense" is a hilarious display of contradiction, which loses its hilarity once we realize that people use these conceptions to justify virtually any course of action they choose to follow. We need not make a big thing of this because it is perfectly obvious to everyone that we desperately need administrators who know what they are doing. Those who understand organizational processes can analyze situations, make decisions, and institute change.

BUREAUCRATIC STRANGULATION

Although we like to think of any organization with which we are affiliated as being an efficient and humane societal institution, be it government, university, industry, or what have you, the fact of the matter is that virtually all organizations are hopelessly archaic, inhumane, and senile. Most societal units, particularly the more established ones, tend to be gerontocracies in which power is in the hands of the aged or sycophantocracies in which power resides in those who flatter and support. To retain their power prerogatives, these individuals establish all sorts of frustrating rules and procedures that serve the purpose of slowing down, if not altogether preventing, any change in the status quo.

As a point of departure, consider the following passage from Kurt Vonnegut's (1970) book *The Sirens of Titan* in which one of the characters of the book, Ransom K. Fern, is attempting to persuade a remarkably lucky man, Noel Constant, that he needs a monstrous organization to protect his earnings from being eaten up by the Bureau of Internal Revenue:

"Mr. Constant," said Ransom K. Fern, "right now you're as easy for the Bureau of Internal Revenue to watch as a man on a street corner selling apples and pears. But just imagine how hard you would be to watch if you had a whole office building jammed to the rafters with industrial bureaucrats—men who lose things and use the wrong forms and create new forms and demand everything in quintuplicate, and who understand perhaps a third of what is said to them; who habitually give misleading answers in order to gain time in which to think, who make decisions only when forced to, and who then cover their tracks; who make perfectly honest mistakes in addition and subtraction, who call meetings whenever they feel lonely, who write memos whenever they feel unloved; men who never throw anything away unless they think it could get them fired. A single industrial bureaucrat, if he is sufficiently vital and nervous, should be able to create a ton of meaningless papers a year for the Bureau of Internal Revenue to examine. In the Magnum Opus Building, we have thousands of them! And you and I can have the top two stories, and you can go on keeping track of what's really going on the way you do now." He looked around the room. "How do you keep track now, by the way—writing with a burnt match on the margins of a telephone directory?"

"In my head," said Noel Constant [from *The Sirens of Titan*, p. 79].

Permit me to state the two major organizing concepts around which I have written. The first is that conflict, although inevitable, need not be destructive; instead, it can be the dynamic property or life force, if you will, of an organization that when properly harnessed can keep organizations responsive. Destructive conflict is generated by organizational and bureaucratic senility.

The second major concept is that the harnessing principle used to make conflict work for the organization, making it responsive and self-regulatory, is the principle of plebeian power. Plebeian power means quite simply that organizations are better off, that is they are smarter, when they have organized and powerful subgroups with which they must deal. Society is better off when constituencies are organized and powerful and organizations are better off when subgroups within the organization are organized and powerful. As discussed in the final chapter, one property of the overlapping decision center system is that managers can expand their power base by delegating responsibility and sharing power, if you will, with their subordinates. Plebeian power then reflects the concept of system regulation based on the principle of strong constituencies. It is the concept that smart government, smart management, and smart administration implies that the governed, managed, and directed or administered people have power in their own right and are strong. We shall examine the principle of this self-regulatory or self-destruct system in some detail in later chapters.

The bulk of the book, those parts which are not specifically amplifying the above two organizing concepts, focus on the analysis of social structure. Before you can do anything innovative, creative, or even sensible with regard to harnessing conflict in any organization, you must develop your analytical abilities. You must know the potential sources of conflict eruption and the conditions under which conflict flourishes or is sustained. The intelligent analysis of social networks of which one is an integral part is difficult under the best of circumstances. The major cause of the difficulty is our tendency to avoid, deny, or repress any facts or interpretations of facts that threaten our self-concept of being absolutely right.

In my management training workshops I encourage participants to think of this administrative stance as Sherlock Holmes management. To hell with who is right and who is wrong, which you cannot determine anyway, for all social systems are extremely complex interactive systems. The rewards from administration emerge by applying one's wits toward the unravelling of the intricacies of social interaction and the utilization of one's insights in the accomplishment of goals. As in chess, if one plays move by move, one never quite develops adequate skill to offer challenge to advanced beginners, so in management if one simply responds to situations, one is likely to develop the self-delusion of being a high-voltage, hard driving, brushfire fighter. And this self-delusion generally renders one both exhausted and out of touch with reality. Let us examine some repressive procedures that all bureaucracies drift into unless kept self-regulatory and constantly changing.

Repression

Although it is not essential, it is useful to identify the two opposite ends of the repression spectrum. On one end we have the general "law and order" zealots. They advocate the making of rules to legitimize the use of force in suppressing uncomfortable departures from the status quo. The threat of the use of force, in turn, is designed to deter persons from participating in such departures or protests for change in the future.

On the other end of the spectrum we find the repression that results from organizational senility or, more generally, from incompetence. Bureaucracies provide hiding places for the incompetent and the indifferent. They also become senile and irrelevant to contemporary needs. They are repressive because they dissuade persistent action for change at low levels of violence. The less violent and/or persistent protesters go away or are galvanized to more radical protest action.

Let us examine some bureaucratic procedures that make change at low levels of violence unlikely. Repressive bureaucracy, because it frustrates change agents, increases the likelihood of highly disruptive actions by dissenters. As we shall soon discuss in some detail, when peaceful dissent is ignored, protesters must create, so to speak, their own personal communication channel to the decision centers. Disruption and threat gain attention.

The Strategy of Nonaction

No-response is an act. It is a response, and in the first instance all dissent is ignored. People may listen to, cry at, sympathize with, consider, refer to, evaluate, or whatever, suggestions or appeals for change. In the first instance, however, such appeals are relegated to limbo pending more information, that information being the persistence of the change protoganists. If they go away or shut up then everything settles down. If they persist then alternate delay procedures are used to drain some of the dissenters' energies. We might call this the "marshmallow strategy." The function of administrators is to absorb the thrusts of dissenters. When the dissenters withdraw, the organization resumes its previous structural integrity without reform. The quality of an administrator then is determined by his ability to prevent at best, and absorb at worst, disruptive dissent. If one can ride out most storms, regardless of the apparent violence, the organization can ooze back to its original shape and form. Look at the university. The battles at Columbia, Berkeley, Wisconsin, Kent—all for different purposes—all now right back where they started; the changes are rather like a new coat of paint on an old boat—no real reform or important organizational change. Now again, it is totally irrelevant whether or not the nonattention to dissent is intentional or unintentional or whether it results from ignorance, lack of up-to-date information, or incompetence.

Inattention generates conflict; the motivation of the agents is irrelevant (see the section on violence in Chapter 2 for a discussion of the myth of intention).

Creeping Progress

Advanced forms of the nonaction response include administrative orbiting and due process strategies. Due process nonaction is the most sophisticated form. Generally the procedure involves establishing a recognized procedure for redressing grievances. The process should be complicated, risky, or costly, and slow. The examples of such due process systems are well known to us all. Legal action to compel a landlord to keep the letter, if not the spirit, of a rental contract is almost never considered. The efficiency of rent strikes to force change makes legal procedures for accomplishing the same change seem absurd by contrast. Appeals to the Income Tax bureaucracy is a perfect example of a system that encourages taxpayers to be dishonest at the outset. Grievance committees in companies or universities with employee or student representation again exemplify due process systems that dissuade dissent. For all due process systems are mandated to redress the grievances of persons or groups who are willing to expose their grievance to public scrutiny; to take the time to make the appeal; to accept the possibility of extension of the conflict beyond their particular grievance, which may be costly, risky, or embarrassing; and most important to accept the institution as an adjudicator.

Administrative orbiting is the more fundamental strategy of which the due process is a complex extension. Administrative orbiting means keeping appeals for change or redress always under consideration. Such procedures involve accepting appeals but not acting at all on them until the petitioners seek information regarding the disposition of the petition. Once pressured by the petitioners, the bureaucracy then submits the issue for consideration by a committee. The petition must be placed on the agenda and await its turn. Given less than satisfactory judgment the petitioners must determine bureaucratic channels for changing the initial judgment. Lost documents, vacationing principals, infrequently scheduled committee meetings, and lack of public information regarding the identity of persons with decision-making prerogatives, all ensure that petitions for change are delayed to an extent that all but the most diligent and committed pacifist is brought to the brink of mass murder.

Creeping progress and administrative orbiting are experiences that all managers have constantly. Petitions or requests that are addressed to bureaucratic superiors are ignored, forgotten, delayed, and kept under consideration but the burden for determining what progress the petitions for change have made through the bureaucratic morass is on the petitioner. If you do not put an idea in writing then your immediate superior frequently says "Oh yes, the issue that we discussed last Tuesday, I've been thinking about that, perhaps you had better drop me a note about it." After you drop him a note about the same issue, a further delay is encountered and when you again check on the disposition of your request you may get one of several responses such as: "What note?" "Oh yes, that seems like a good idea I'd like to think about it for a while," "I'm going to have a chat with the Executive Committee about your idea," "Let's get a group together to look at your idea in some detail," etc. In short, the principle of creeping progress is to force the petitioner to provide the impetus for moving the idea or proposal through the bureaucracy. As soon as the petitioner becomes less vigilant about the progress of the petition or forcing it through the bureaucratic channels then the progress of the petition comes to a silent halt.

Now administrative orbiting, creeping progress, due process, and similar bureaucratic delay tactics persist because, by and large, they work. Individuals who seek change are rendered powerless against such procedures unless they choose to dedicate their lives to persistent harassment of bureaucrats. What bureaucrats seem not to understand, however, is that such procedures make the possibility of highly violent protests likely indeed. Such procedures also encourage petitioners to seek the highest possible bureaucratic level for entering their petition. It has become part of the folklore that if you want anything—information, a good deal, change—"go to the top." Many protest agencies in the United States are publishing lists of the home addresses of corporation presidents, the assumption being that one cannot get satisfaction if one complains to the corporate departments established to deal with such issues. Students have occupied university presidents' offices to protest poor food or similar rather trivial issues. In short, such procedures designed to delay, block, or dissuade petitioners by draining their energy, resources, and patience result in increased pressure on upper-level administrators to handle increasingly trivial issues: an unmistakable indicator of senility, incompetence, or irrelevance of the administrative bureaucracy. It also indicates that the upper-level administrator may be unaware of the activities, or lack thereof, of subordinates.

The Strategy of Expansion

Organizations always drift toward complexity and senility. Even "well-intentioned" managers become repressive. They get lost in the overload of information. They become incompetent because the demands of their positions, and the skills required to be competent, change more rapidly than they can change. They are promoted to their level of incompetence according to the Peter Principle. They establish systems to deal with the imperatives of their positions and are caught in a total system of operations within the organization. They are in reality caught in the middle. Line officials in organizations set up in the traditional line-staff fashion are compelled to accept the concept of individual accountability. The concepts of participatory management and group accountability are so inconsistent with traditional hierarchical organizations that managers consider them heretical. To accommodate demands for keeping modern, they institute Machiavellian systems designed to give the illusion of participation.

And many people who have been involved in power sharing or group decision-making procedures by hierarchically oriented managers tend to reject such procedures as being a manipulative ruse, and to some extent they are correct. There have been many instances where participation, group decision making, power sharing, and the like have been used as a manipulative tool by managers who want to give the impression of being less bureaucratic than they really are; and there have been cases where such ruses have ended up in disaster. The usual form of the disaster is that a manager asks a group to make a decision about some issue, such as workloads, production levels, job responsibilities, etc., expecting the group to arrive at a decision (e.g., a production level) very similar to one that the manager feels is appropriate. If one can encourage subordinates to believe that they have participated in managerial decision. making, moreover, of course, one should enjoy the benefits of the increased satisfaction, cohesiveness, efficiency, etc., that participation is supposed to bring about. The disaster occurs frequently when the group perceives the procedure to be a ruse and comes up with a decidedly inappropriate decision (e.g., a hilariously low production norm).

Organizational complexity is both a cause and an effect of conflict. When the functions for which the organization was created become intolerably sluggish or inefficient, the bureaucracy's response is to expand administrative functions and personnel. That complexity, in turn, makes attempts to change basic features of the bureaucracy all the more difficult, for complexity is a response by the bureaucracy to protect itself; to protect the fundamental model on which the organization is implicitly based.

Nowhere is the process of bureaucratic expansion more clearly observed than in universities. Radical departures from traditional functions of the university are accommodated by the creation of "experimental colleges," "experimental courses," "black studies courses," "institutes," and the like. These appendages serve two functions. First, they engage the energies of those who press for changes in the university. These people are provided with their little spheres of influence, which can in turn become rigid and unresponsive. Second, the basic organizational and operational concepts of the university remain unchanged and are further protected from attack—at least from those who can be engaged in the appendage. Increased organizational complexity, then, is an inevitable defensive response of bureaucracies to threats to the basic fiber of the institution.

Now, "disciplined expansion" also protects bureaucracies. If a department in an institution becomes unacceptably inefficient, for whatever reason, the response is to divide the responsibilities of that department and add personnel. Administrators who cannot cope with their responsibilities get assistants. Functions that expand to levels beyond the capability of incumbent administrators are divided and redistributed to additional administrators. The basic assumptions on which the bureaucracy is based are never examined.

Secrecy and Sanctuary

The ratio of brain to brawn becomes increasingly and, I may add, ever menacingly small as organizations grow older. Power becomes highly concentrated in a few people (bureaucratization), with the result that change becomes a difficult and, for the change agents, a highly costly endeavor. Part of the problem of bureaucracies then is that decision makers become more isolated from the people they are supposed to represent. Low-violence protest goes unnoticed. Much energy is expended to maintain or expand the decision maker's sphere of influence (empire building), to amass greater power. To protect present positions, bureaucrats are careful to maintain secrecy regarding features of their operation that may elicit complaint or criticism. In short, they wrap themselves in a cloak of secrecy, publicizing only those activities that enhance or at least do not endanger their positions. With many hiding places available, bureaucrats slowly atrophy and become dangerously incompetent and unresponsive to changes in their organizations and to changes in society.

Now, the effect of organizational structures that feature secrecy and sanctuary is that not only are the people prevented from influencing bureaucrats at low levels of violence, but upper level bureaucrats, likewise, have to spend enormous amounts of time and energy trying to keep tabs on the people for whom they are responsible (i.e., subordinate bureaucrats). Secrecy, then, makes all bureaucratic systems, the consensorial, the democratic, the autocratic, or whatever, subject to only one method of reform: war. In a war, the object is not to change the opposition but to eliminate it. Coups and exposés become the system for bringing about change in most organizations, for in most organizations the disclosures of a bureaucrat's operations or an institute's operations is the burden and, therefore, the privilege of that bureaucrat or institute. Information about activities both up and down the organizational hierarchy is sifted, screened, censored, modified, and "sweetened" by the disclosing bureaucrat. The potential influence of both upper-level bureaucrats and constituencies is therefore seriously restricted simply because of ignorance. Change occurs in such situations at high levels of violence. Protests must be highly disruptive to gain attention, that is, to make bureaucrats admit that they have some decision-making prerogatives. And it is only when upper-level administrators find themselves in difficult situations, moreover, that they discover the subordinate screwups. Such discoveries generally take place only after things have gone too far out of hand. Information regarding the activities of bureaucrats, their assigned projects, and their responsibilities should be easily available to constituents. More important, upper-level bureaucrats must have accurate and timely information about the activities of the people for whom they are responsible. When you ask the Chief Honcho "what's going on?" he should not have to reply "I will certainly find out."

All organizations, of course, develop the procedure of maintaining secrecy so that they can make preemptive moves. Governments that wish to turn an undeveloped seacoast into a deep water port simply start the project. Citizens are caught offguard and unorganized, so that by the time a meaningful protest is launched, the project is at a point of no return. Perhaps the protest group can reduce the size of the project but preventing the project is out of the question. Defense departments start wars that take years to stop. Industrial corporations expand first and respond to society later. The list is endless, and alas, we all have been fatigued by witnessing such procedures.

Law and Order

Of course, the most obvious form of bureaucratic suppression is law and order, the suppression of protest by the use of force. For bureaucracies, say the State, to perpetuate the law and order myth, people must be led to believe that the State is a conflict manager, mediating conflicts that develop between the will of the Haves and the imperatives of various Have-Not groups. The government, then, is seen as the agent of control and regulation. The belief in law and order, or negative peace as it has been called, depends on the acceptance of the fallacy of collective security and the belief that the good of the State reflects the common good or the general purpose even though at the expense of some individual freedom. "*Recht ist was dem Staat nützt*" (whatever serves the State is right) was the Third Reich's straightforward extension of the collective security fallacy.

Now, to maintain the status quo, bureaucrats appeal to the principle of collective security. No matter how serious the disparities, problems, or needs of any group, a certain level of order is in the best interest of everyone. Even the most deprived person is better off when order prevails instead of physical violence. Government violence then is seen as temporary and legitimate for maintaining some degree of order, and a major challenge to government is perceived to be the control of violence. The force of the majority can be directed toward restricting the disruptive moves of an "unreasonable" minority. The fallacy of this position, based on the aggressor–defender model of conflict to be discussed shortly, is that the aggressor must be identified.

Society establishes control agents to provide collective security. Threats to that security are repressed and the threateners are identified as aggressors. The problem, of course, is that the cause of the disruption, the conditions that have given rise to conflict, are ignored. The focus of attention is on the act of protest, not the issues.

For a bureaucracy to be perceived as a conflict manager, it must be able to attribute blame for disruption. To legitimize the use of force, the disruption must be identified as unreasonable or illegitimate. To maintain power, bureaucracies attempt to maintain the status quo. They attempt to persuade their constituencies that pressure for change results from sick, criminal, irresponsible, or selfish minorities. To the extent that bureaucracies are able to legitimize the use of force against disruptors of the status quo, they can issue a threat to potential disruptors. Deterrence, in this instance, takes the form of a promise to harm disruptors if they engage in behaviors defined as criminal.

Generally, stigmatization of change agents takes three forms: first, labeling such people as sick; second, labeling them as criminals; or third, labeling them as not responsible (i.e., not capable of appropriate behavior because of some deficit of personality, intelligence, moral fiber, and the like). As is described in a later section, the conspiracy theory, or rather myth, perpetrated by control agencies maintains that a few troublemakers stir up trouble in groups of otherwise contented or at least resigned people. The central people, always a minority, are labeled for two reasons. First, to attempt to dissuade people from supporting or sympathizing with the disruptors; for if the leaders are criminal, crazy, or stupid, then why should one care to associate with them? Second, if these people are criminal, crazy, or stupid, then, of course, control agents must intervene to both protect society as well as to protect such people from themselves.

It is important to stigmatize the leaders, for that makes legitimate the suspension of basic freedoms. Criminals are incarcerated and acts of violence against them are never quite so bad as similar acts against people not defined as criminals. Insane people, people whose life styles, thoughts, or language are inconsistent or incompatible with the rest of society's, find that they have no rights. Society encourages locking them up to keep them from bothering people. People who are in some way deficit, low IQ and the like, have to be helped along whether they like it or not. Many of our laws and certainly a large number of the procedures used by control agencies are tolerated because people have been led to believe that control agents are protecting society collectively by suspending the civil liberties of persons who cannot help themselves.

We have "no-knock" legislation that permits the search of private property and one's person on "reasonable" suspicion of possession of drugs. We have conspiracy legislation permitting prosecution of those accused of crossing state lines for the purpose of inciting riots. Apparently serious professionals have suggested that school children be obliged to submit to psychiatric assessment for the purpose of identifying those who are potentially violent. And those potentially violent children would be psychopharmacologically treated. We have electronic surveillance being used by control agencies (to say nothing of the criminal break-ins at Watergate and at Daniel Ellsberg's psychiatrist's office). Informers and infiltrators are used to such an extent that more than half the membership of some deviant groups have been said to be federal agents. Police hardware is expanding at an extremely rapid rate and police tactics frequently involve exaggerating threat to justify the use of overwhelming force to suppress protest. Control agents precipitate violence to maintain society's sympathy for their peace-keeping efforts and to justify the use of high levels of violence to deter further disruptions. The circle is thus complete. Nonresponsive bureaucracies force change agents to be disruptive. The leadership or salient people in the protest are stigmatized. The population is polarized into protestors and others. The threat is exaggerated, justifying large-scale suppressive moves by control agents, which encourages larger scale violent protest. The prevention of wide-scale violence is justification for surveillance, control, infiltration, secrecy, and the violation of civil freedoms by control agencies. Such activities encourage a widening of the appeal of protest groups and an increased reliance on violent disruption as the influence method of choice. This in turn leads to larger and more violent control agencies. In all, this is a most inefficient method for accommodating change in any societal unit.

The law and order or the control ethos is easier to recognize when we look at some of society's absurdities than when we try to analyze it within the context of an organization. Within an organization the control ethos is usually cloaked in the concept of the integrity or well-being of the corporation or firm, which is always based on the concept of collective security. Although the actual procedures take a variety of different forms, once one gets used to identifying the basic concept of control based on collective security, spotting instances of it becomes quite easy indeed. A few workable examples: an organization coming under attack from an outside regulatory agency, such as when a parent corporation is considering shutting down a subsidiary because of a decreasing market; a university department coming under attack from student or government groups because of poor teaching, poor course offerings, inability to market (i.e., get jobs for) the students they are graduating, budgetary misappropriation, etc. Under such circumstances when an individual within the organization puts pressure on the bureaucracy to make changes, the bureaucracy frequently attempts to eliminate the disrupter on the basis of collective security. That is, an appeal can be made that in times of crisis, people whose actions can be defined as potentially weakening to the organization should be eliminated simply so that the organization can survive. The usual Pollyannic addendum is that if we stick together and ride out the storm we can always clean our own house. Because organizations are always in some period of crises, disruptors are always faced with the collective security ethos.

Incidentally, although we will be discussing this in some detail later on, it is interesting to note that most people within organizations who have been wiped out because of the collective security ethos have generally made their appeals for change through standard bureaucratic channels and generally have exercised care in keeping their protest activities confined to people or groups directly involved. The reason this is generally their undoing is that they are trying to generate change within the context of a forum they do not control. If we examine the strategy of successful protesters, in contrast, we find they tend to expand the process to larger forums that are beyond the control of the bureaucrats directly involved. For example, major shakeups in companies or major protests of students and professors in universities that make the newspapers more generally are resolved in a manner that does not involve firing or removal of the personnel involved. We shall examine this concept of expanding the forum of debate in later sections.

Trivial Success

The late Saul Alinsky, the organizer, stressed that groups should organize on many issues and must elect their own spokesman. This is important to any group organized for power, to prevent trivial success from either destroying the group entirely or allowing the group to fall into the control of the Haves against whom the group is fighting. Nothing destroys a group quite so fast as success. Groups organized around a single issue, such as stopping an expressway, find it difficult in the first instance to build a large dedicated group. People have different priorities regarding issues they consider important. More important, winning minor concessions from the Haves removes the function of the group for many sympathizers.

Now let us look at what a bureaucracy can do to a group that is beginning to gain some potential for disruption. The first thing an Establishment will attempt to do is to pick the leadership of the protest group. The Establishment picks members of the potential power group and brings them into the bureaucracy. Minor concessions are given to these selected leaders and they are represented as people with influence in the bureaucracy. The people whom the Establishment selects for leaders, of course, are the more conservative, wound-down people who have found means for coping with the system as it stands. For example, ministers, professionals, entrepreneurs, landlords, etc., are generally selected by Establishments to represent the protest community. Elected leaders, however, generally owe their first allegiance to the group that brought them to a position of power and prominence.

Minor concessions made early in a growing conflict can defuse a protest group. Generally this takes the form of recognition of the "merit" of the issue with the attendant formation of an advisory group to the Establishment's decision makers. Delays tend to defuse protest movements. People get tired and bored. They perceive discussions as a successful result of protest so that they can all go home and get on with their day-to-day activities.

Trivial success strategies are a most universal method for attempting to slow down or defuse change agents. The most trivial of trivial successes and the one most commonly used, of course, is chitchat. Bureaucrats faced with a persistent group of subordinates who are pushing for change, who have an adequate power base to prevent an immediate dismissal, and who cannot be defused or slowed down by administrative orbiting tactics are frequently led to believe that the bureaucratic superior recognizes the merit of the subordinate's proposal. However, the proposal must be examined in detail. A committee, of course, is the answer and the larger the better, including as many washed out and frightened middle-level housekeeping bureaucrats as possible. Such committees are characterized by two features: (a) they have no real mandate other than to take on the additional work of looking at someone else's ideas and (b) they have no administrative authority and are advisory in function. Such committees provide delaying functions and when the inevitable calls for further information are made by the committee, the subordinates petitioning for change are likely to be entangled in an exhaustive overload of extra work. The subordinates may consider this to be evidence of success in that the upper levels of the bureaucracy are setting the wheels in motion to consider the proposals. If the proposals for reform had appealed to many subordinates or were the joint effort of many subordinates, the formulation of the committee to entertain the proposals might well be received by many as adequate indication of success and therefore they would go back to their business as usual. That such committees can be counted on to delay, wash out, and totally emasculate any potent idea or proposal for reform, of course, is well known and well documented and an experience that we have all had too often.

Social Intervention and Action

The first thing a radical activist can tell you is that persuasion does not work. The government has spent a fortune on propaganda programs designed to stop people from smoking, stop drunken driving, encourage integration and "brotherhood," discourage drug use, and so on, without so much as causing a ripple on the water. People are changed when the social structure they find themselves in is changed. They change when such changes are seen as important to their well-being, that is, when such change will affect their ability to get what they want. All action-oriented people with social concerns argue that to change society and redress some of its ills, action and not words is required.

Now, bureaucracies understand intervention for social change. Well-intentioned bureaucrats advocate and often are able to institute change programs. Advocates of strong government have argued that such programs can only be introduced when a government can force its introduction. People have been led to believe, moreover, that a good person at the helm of a powerful government can redress the social ills of the nation in a few short years, at worst, or months at best.

Although we shall discuss at length some of the problems associated with the drift toward a reliance on centralization of power, it is appropriate at this point to mention a few of the obvious difficulties. Centralization of planning gives rise to centralization of power, which in turn gives rise to reduced freedom, and hence increases the likelihood of violent conflict. As the recent Nobel prize winner in Economics, Hayek (1944) stated in his early book *The Road to Serfdom*, centralized planning, however idealistic, inevitably leads to loss of freedom. Similarly, Papandreou (1970) points out:

> The progressive political forces in the United States supported the growth of the federal government at the expense of the States—in order to enable it to enact legislation favorable to social progress and racial equality—only to discover that in its spectacular growth it evaded popular control, and became increasingly a power house directed by little understood forces [p. 12].

A second problem with government-initiated programs of social research and social welfare is that the powerful define what is problematic. Not only do the powerful define what problems deserve attention in society, but they also attempt to force their own interpretation of the problem on the action programs. They decide which projects should be funded and which should not. In short, by funding trivial research or projects designed to indoctrinate recipients of the program's benefits into the "mainstream of society," they can divert resources from change programs to those which maintain the status quo.

Although the concept of violence is discussed in detail in Chapter 2, it is useful to point out at this point that any social intervention is to some extent violent. It is interference in the day-to-day activities of people. It restricts their freedom. It violates their right to privacy. We all tend to feel that it is okay to force the other guy to do what we think is correct. People we are helping should accept our evaluation of their situation and be cooperative. Let us never forget that all action directed at altering society is violent, even though by many standards the level of such violence may be trivial. Good intentions, or appeals to any constituency or body of regulations, do not alter the fact that intervention is violent.

Now, it should be perfectly clear that any time proposals for change are initiated from the top, one must expect that upper-level bureaucrats are defining the nature of the problem and they can, to a very great extent, determine the outcome. The usual procedure when a company or a department is in trouble is to seek the services of some dynamic person, usually outside the department or institution in question, and mandate that person with the responsibility of setting things straight. It should be recognized that before bringing in this person, upper levels of the bureaucracy have assured themselves that the outside person's and their own perception of the problem are consistent. I do not mean to imply that this procedure may not be suitable nor the most efficient procedure to follow. The only point I wish to make is that such intervention, even if it is consistent with our own assessment of the situation, must restrict freedom of personal liberty of people involved in the situation and therefore suits the definition of a violent act.

The Pathological System: The Establishment

"Oh, it's lonely at the top," a painfully true line from a Randy Neuman song, provides us with a point of departure. Chief Honchos can, with very little trouble at all, rapidly become the most isolated and hence most ignorant people in the organization. Top-level managers receive their information from subordinates. Time is so scarce that even sifted summaries and highly abstracted briefings receive only superficial attention. Chance encounters with people in the organization are minimized and channels for divergent ideas, criticism, insight, or just plain bitching are closed. Hence, simple lack of time coupled with reliance on a few subordinates to keep one informed can rapidly lead to involutional stupidity, which in effect severs sections of the cortex from the rest of the organizational body. The brain/brawn ratio then, is frequently kept unacceptably low simply because the brain, if you will, has little veridical information about the brawn.

Senior managers are also kept ignorant when their egos or their carelessness lead them to build and sustain pathological systems. A pathological organization is one that creates its own senility by creating its own *raison d'être*. Subordinates respond to praise, attention, and encouragement. When top-level managers discriminatively reward agreement, subordinates rapidly learn to say what the boss wants (or needs) to hear. Administrative mistakes, blunders, oversights, or plain disasters are never carefully scrutinized and evaluated in such systems. Redefined as necessary risk, inevitable, but alas, nonpredictable market fluctuations, courageous management, decision-making imperatives, or someone else's fault, the manager does not learn from his own behavior. Hence, inappropriate decisions or actions have a high probability of being repeated.

It should be noted that some administrative superiors reward criticism which can, if not kept in check, lead to long drawn out meetings regarding the most trivial of issues. High-level administrators, then, must constantly evaluate the type of information they receive. They must create systems that allow sufficient static to prevent the establishment of a feedback system in which the senior administrators receive what others think they "want" to know or should know.

Advanced forms of institutional pathology usually involve four easily recognized processes. Each of these procedures involves the creation of problems that become real and hence either justify the organization's present state or provide a reason for its very existence.

The Insight Error

Processes one derives from the mistaken view that if a little of something does not work then a lot will. Parents who punish children for an act frequently believe that transgressions reflect the need for ever greater levels of punishment. Therapists of any sort who have unsuccessfully treated virtually any type of disorder frequently fall into the trap of believing that failure indicates that further treatments are necessary. Products or services that have long histories of being marginal profit or loss activities for a company are frequently maintained in the belief that more sales effort, production economies, money for advertising or development, etc., etc., can make the situation profitable when, in fact, demand is limited or management is too hopeless to compete with success. Process one then refers to situations in which judgment is rendered faulty because of marriage to a belief, hope, or theory. If something we want to or have to believe in does not work, we are tempted to conclude that the cause of failure resides not in the process but in the object being treated or the environment in which the activity is taking place; and in some cases we conclude that we have not persisted long enough in the activity which may eventually turn out as we have hoped. Process one then is a type of scientific myopia, which is the inability to deal with contradictive evidence. Hence, one requirement for smart administration is to construct one's system so that you not only cannot escape negative evidence but, more importantly, that you receive this information from the beginning.

Incorrect Attribution of Causality

The most common form of system pathology, and the most difficult to control, is that of the incorrect attribution of causality. Similar to scapegoating, this process involves attributing success or failure to a person when in fact the principal cause resides in the organizational structure. Failures are attributed to persons with limited capabilities but one never asks how the hell they got into the organization in the first place if they have such deficits. Many organizations hire administrators who can tolerate an upper-level of management that is hopelessly inefficient or senile. Others hire persons who are cowardly or so concrete minded that they can be counted on to never have an idea. Serious conflicts in organizations are attributed to personality clashes or particular people who are abrasive. In short, the cause of any difficulty or success is attributed to people. The result of this is that the organization—its structure, its systems, its policies, its objectives—escapes serious scrutiny.

In a pathological system, then, one finds that reality becomes severely distorted. People become concerned with things that either do not exist or that they have generated. Corrective action is frequently rendered hopeless in such systems, for fiction becomes reality.

The Chief Honcho Syndrome

One difficulty that every savvy administrator recognizes is the tendency for subordinates to support the top person's position rather than his ideas. People assume that the top person must know best or that person would not be on the top. Hence, they do not critically evaluate the superior's proposals. This is a far more subtle, and I may add, a far more serious problem than the "yes man" problem. Yes men are easily recognized and can be ignored unless needed. The Chief Honcho syndrome results from confidence or habituation of people to trust the judgment of superiors.

Yes men agree with the boss because they want the praise and rewards that may accompany such support or they may be so insecure that they never announce themselves for criticism by stating personal opinions or ideas. The Chief Honcho syndrome, in contrast, derives from a belief that the boss knows best—otherwise he would not be the boss.

In its extreme form, the superior's proposals may simply escape scrutiny; in more subtle forms, a person feels that if the superior's proposal is as good as any he has in mind, why not support the boss? The problem, of course, is that the superior may not have his proposals evaluated. He may wish critical examination of an idea but receive support of his position not his idea.

The Self-Fulfilling Prophecy

Pathological process number four involves the creation of false realities. One of the clearest examples of the process can be found in pathological treatment systems. For example, a school that has as its primary function the treatment of children with learning disabilities can very easily become pathological by focusing on the deficits of a child rather than on the child's skills. Children who are not aware of a poorly learned skill are made aware of this deficit, with the obvious result that a real problem develops. The school's treatment team then focuses its attention on curing a problem they have created. More generally, children made to feel insecure develop social and intellectual problem areas, so that focusing the child's attention on a deficit in one area can, by eroding self-confidence, create problems in other areas also. Hence, the treatment staff is very busy indeed, caring for all of the screwed-up kids it generates. Now, such systems are difficult to change because some problems are real in the sense that the child had them before he came into the system. Pathology develops when the system starts to become a perpetual motion machine, generating false realities.

Mental hospitals are frequently pathological institutions in that one has to "get crazy" to get out. Patients are rewarded when they "recognize" their problem (i.e., confess to a deficit), which in turn rewards the therapist, who can cure the patient. The patient, then, finds that the road to freedom involves acknowledging and accepting a label attached to his behavior, discussing that behavior, professing new insight, all the while remaining obedient to the system. A patient's claims of being of sound mind, displaying independent behavior, or dissent are all interpreted by institutional staff as evidence of resistance or more generally as definitive evidence that the person is so sick he does not even recognize it.

A most enlightening study of such pathological systems was reported by Rosenhan (1973). Eight sane people (pseudopatients) including three psychologists, a pediatrician, a housewife, a painter, a psychiatrist, and a graduate student sought admission to 12 different hospitals. The pseudopatients reported hearing unfamiliar voices which, although often unclear, seemed to be saying such things as "hollow" and "empty." Beyond falsifying names, occupations, and employment, the pseudopatients presented their life histories to hospital officials as they had actually occurred. On admission to the psychiatric ward, the pseudopatients ceased simulating any symptoms of abnormality. Although about 30% of the real patients in the ward voiced suspicions about the pseudopatients with such statements as, "You're not crazy. You're a journalist or a professor (referring to the continual notetaking by the pseudopatients). You're checking up on the hospital," not a single hospital staff member detected that the pseudopatients were sane. The usual diagnosis was schizophrenic and the discharge diagnosis was schizophrenia in remission.

It is instructive to consider how information was ignored or modified by hospital staff so that it was not inconsistent with their belief that the pseudopatients were mentally disturbed:

A clear example of such translation is found in the case of a pseudopatient who had had a close relationship with his mother but was rather remote from his father during his early childhood. During adolescence and beyond, however, his father became a close friend, while his relationship with his mother cooled. His present relationship with his wife was characteristically close and warm. Apart from occasional angry exchanges, friction was minimal. The children had rarely been spanked. Surely there is nothing especially pathological about such a history. Indeed, many readers may see a similar pattern in their own experiences, with no markedly deleterious consequences. Observe, however, how such a history was translated in the psychopathological context, this from the case summary prepared after the patient was discharged.

This white 30-year-old male . . . manifests a long history of considerable ambivalence in close relationships, which begins in early childhood. A warm relationship with his mother cools during his adolescence. A distant relationship to his father is described as becoming very intense. Affective stability is absent. His attempts to control emotionality with his wife and children are punctuated by angry outbursts and, in the case of the children, spankings. And while he says that he has several good friends, one senses considerable ambivalence embedded in those relationships also . . . [Rosenhan, 1973, p. 253].

The facts of the case were unintentionally distorted by the staff to achieve consistency with a popular theory of the dynamics of a schizophrenic reaction.

The hospital staffs' reaction to patient-initiated contact is also interesting to note. Pseudopatients asked relevant questions in a courteous manner, an example of one such interchange is reported by Rosenhan (1973) as follows:

PSEUDOPATIENT: "Pardon me, Dr. X. Could you tell me when I am eligible for grounds privileges?"

PHYSICIAN: "Good morning, Dave. How are you today?" (moves off without waiting for a response) [p. 255].

Lest we make the error of misattribution of malfeasance or stupidity, we should also note Rosenhan's (1973) statement regarding the pseudopatients' evaluation of hospital staff to whom they were exposed:

It could be a mistake, and a very unfortunate one, to consider that what happened to us derived from malice or stupidity on the part of the staff. Quite the contrary, our overwhelming impression of them was of people who really cared, who were committed and who were uncommonly intelligent. Where they failed, as they sometimes did painfully, it would be more accurate to attribute those failures to the environment in which they, too, found themselves than to personal callousness. Their perception and behavior were controlled by the situation, rather than being motivated by a malicious disposition [p. 257].

Mirror Images and Self-Fulfilling Prophecies

It seems perfectly obvious to say that if we are aggressive or competitive or rude or nasty to somebody or some group that we should expect them to be rude, nasty, competitive, or aggressive in return. However, what if we believe the whole world to be made up of highly competitive, aggressive, or ruthless people? Could it be, that if we felt this way about other individuals, we might tend to act defensively in any social interaction? We might then act rudely, behave aggressively or highly competitively in an attempt not to be exploited or disadvantaged by others. The obvious result of such behavior would be that the other people in the situation, after experiencing our agonistic behavior and attitudes, would become agonistic in return, defensively. We have a tremendous amount of evidence to indicate that one very serious cause of conflict in bargaining situations is that of nonveridical perception of the other person or group in the situation. In 1961 Bronfenbrenner reported, as might be expected, that a mirror image phenomenon was operating in Soviet–American relations. Bronfenbrenner recorded many conversations with Russian people in the Soviet Union. He came to the conclusion that both the American and the Russian people had a mirror image of one another. This reciprocal perception consisted of serious distortions by both the American and the Russian people of the realities on the other side. Several studies have indicated that identical actions, attributed to either the United States or the Soviet Union, result in quite different evaluations by American college students. Identical actions are evaluated unfavorably if attributed to the Soviet Union but favorably or less unfavorably if attributed to the United States.

Eckhardt and White (1967) examined the mirror image hypothesis in the speeches of Kennedy and Khrushchev. The results support the mirror image notion in that the values expressed by both Kennedy and Khrushchev were found to be positively correlated with each other. Both leaders invoked such values as peace, national freedom, and sovereignty in their speeches but expressed sentiments that the opposing nation is an enemy of these values. Both Kennedy and Khrushchev, moreover, in spite of their expressed general devotion to peace, often expressed willingness to use force to preserve these values.

There is nothing terribly surprising in this. We have had a lot of experience, although we sometimes hate to admit it, of categorizing people or groups of people inappropriately. That is, if there is something that we do not like about somebody or a group, or if they are in direct competition with us over scarce resources, we tend to find it difficult to discover anything positive about the other person or group. However, what is more important and I think more distressing, is that if we have a general view of other people as being aggressive, competitive, deceitful, dishonest, or manipulatory, then any time we are in a situation of potential conflict we are likely to act in an aggressive, competitive, or threatening manner. Our acting in this threatening manner may force the opposition, whatever his initial inclinations, to adopt a defensive posture in bargaining situations. When we see the other person acting defensively after a short period of time in the bargaining situation, we have confirmed our hypothesis that the other fellow cannot be trusted, and thus we have been the victim of a self-fulfilling prophecy in that we have created the untrustworthy person that we have expected to find. There has been a fair amount of recent research addressed to this very problem. Kelley and Stahelski (1970), analyzing the behavior of persons in conflict simulation situations, present evidence to support their notion that there are two basic types of strategic orientations. There are those whose initial predisposition is that of cooperativeness, or those persons who seek out information about the opposition and as far as possible attempt to initiate a cooperative settlement to any potential conflict situation. These individuals (the cooperators) tend to see the world as a heterogeneous mix of individuals, some of whom are highly competitive, others of whom are highly cooperative, with many people in between. The major problem facing cooperators is that of determining just what kind of person the opponent is. Should the opponent be competitive, aggressive, deceitful, untrusting, and so on, then the cooperator adopts a defensive stance and behaves competitively or threateningly in order to defend himself.

Competitors, in contrast, are those individuals who have a unilateral or homogeneous view of the world. That is, these individuals feel that in any situation of potential conflict everyone acts competitively or aggressively or threateningly and no one can be trusted. Now, if we examine any interaction between two individuals or two groups of individuals in any conflict situation, the unhappy conclusion is obvious. If two cooperators have the happy good fortune to be placed together in a potential conflict situation, they each attempt to elicit information about the other person, determine that the other is potentially a cooperator, and both make cooperative gestures in an attempt to bring about a cooperative settlement. If two competitors are put together, both act competitively with the result that a cooperative settlement is made more difficult to obtain. A most unhappy pairing is that of a cooperator and a competitor, for in this situation, competitors, making the assumption that all other people in the world are agonistically oriented, start behaving competitively. This in turn elicits competitive behavior on the part of our cooperator in order to defend himself, with the result that the competitor has fulfilled his prophecy of the world, the unfortunate byproduct of which is the preclusion of a cooperative settlement.

The research findings also seem to indicate that cooperators are fully aware of the fact that they are influenced by the competitor and recognize the fact that their aggressive behavior or threatening behavior is defensive in nature. Competitors, however, seem to be unaware of the fact that they have influenced the other party to the conflict. The authors further suggest that competitors do not learn that their perception of the world is nonveridical because they assume that everybody is competitive or aggressive in situations of potential conflict. When the situation is not one of potential conflict, that is, when there is nothing of particular value at stake or when resources are not restricted, or when some other property of the situation forces people to be cooperative, then, of course, any cooperativeness or lack of aggressiveness they perceive in other individuals is attributed to the situation and not the person. This results in the maintenance of their nonveridical perception of people being highly competitive in any potential conflict situation.

The implications of this are rather disturbing. If persons in policy-making positions of our organizational units, be they nations, corporations, social organizations, or what have you, expect others to be untrustworthy, the implications seem all too clear. If these persons expect competition or deceitful manipulation or aggression, then they adopt a defensive stance and presumably advocate deterrence as a control mechanism. That is, they make preparations for war and expect war; they initiate policies that restrict the options of persons or groups they feel to be potentially disruptive. To the extent that they have punitive options available, they are in a state of readiness to use those options.

Because the structure of any organization is an important determinant of behavior of people in that organization, when people get a clear signal that the situation is arranged to handle competition or aggression, people may just act

2

Parameters of Power and Conflict

I have been talking about circumstances that should come as absolutely no surprise to any manager. Many of the problems of organizations are well known to us all. We now come to the guts of this book. We are going to be talking in some detail about power, conflict, and violence. We are going to be talking about all three because they are inextricably related. People who wield power, as all managers do, are going to be involved in conflicts and frequently serious ones. Conflicts that are not resolved early in the game, which implies an understanding of the basic properties of conflict, erupt into violence. Again the orientation is that of the Sherlock Holmes management style. As Sherlock Holmes once said to Watson: "No, I do not yet have a theory but I have a firm grasp on the facts." We are going to focus our attention now on the basic principles involved in conflict, violence, power, and strategy.

DIMENSIONS OF CONFLICT

For the purposes of defining the scope of a conflict situation we shall assume that every conflict consists of two initially distinct groups. The principal parties to the conflict we shall designate as the *protagonists*. The group that is cognizant of the altercation between the protagonists shall be referred to as the *audience*. The location of the dispute, which includes not only physical location but also the nature of the audience, we shall designate as the *forum* of the conflict.

Disputes end either when a power balance has been reached or when one side has exhausted its arsenal of tactics appropriate to any particular *avenue* of confrontation. In a university blowup, for example, students may seek a vulnerable spot in the institution, such as the computer center, to force a direct confrontation. Seizing the computing facilities provides the dissenting group with a potent threat of heavy destruction because major disruption and costly destruction of property can be accomplished in a very short period of time. The administration is then faced with the problem of defusing an explosive situation and the dissenting group is setting the requirements for the defusing process. Should the administration attempt to use force, the group holding the computer center could destroy several million dollars worth of facilities in a few minutes.

Now, the avenue of the conflict is that of seizing an expensive facility, which may or may not be jointly valued. The challenging group has a repertoire of tactics appropriate to this situation and the dispute is terminated on redistribution of power or on exhaustion of the repertoire of alternatives. Taking the last situation first, once the students destroy the computer the game has ended. It has ended because of exhaustion of capability, not because the conflict has been resolved—an unsatisfactory and unstable state of affairs.

In the first situation, the administration may provide the necessary assurances to equalize the power to increase the protestors' likelihood of obtaining a satisfactory outcome during bargaining sessions that commence on the surrendering of the computer facilities. This usually takes the form of changing the forum of the dispute, or, more precisely, changing the relationship between the audience and the protagonists. For example, if the dispute was over the firing of a new professor whom the students wanted retained by the university, an offer by the administration to turn the resolution of the dispute over to a group of persons and abide by their decision would constitute a change in the forum of the conflict. The nature of the audience is, of course, the principal concern of the protagonists. The administration's offer to submit the dispute to binding arbitration by a group of Deans and senior professors in the university would be received as a hilarious joke by the protesting students. Comparably foolish forums could also be suggested by the protestors.

It should also be noted that either protagonist yielding on an issue during the initial confrontation constitutes a power redistribution. Resolution of the dispute may therefore be analyzed along several dimensions. It may be analyzed in terms of the degree of power redistribution, the forum of the reconciliation, the avenue of the strategic assault, and the extent of the exhaustion of tactics or weapons given any particular avenue of assault. Strategic analyses examine the various combinations of avenues, forums, and the method of deployment of one's capabilities in a conflict situation. We shall delay the discussion of strategy until a later section.

There are two factors that must be considered when determining strategy: first, the size of the audience and, second, the initial or potential sympathy of the audience to the conflict. The audience to a conflict can be hundreds of times as large as the combatant group. The potential power available to either protagonist if he can galvanize the audience is enormous. Protagonists are therefore interested in limiting conflict by containing it within forums they either control or that at least are not sympathetic to the opposition. The weaker or losing protagonist, in contrast, wants to widen the scope of the conflict in the hope of marshalling greater might. In other words, the protagonist who controls the forum of the conflict determines the outcome, as Schattschneider points out. To the extent that the initially stronger protagonist can limit the scope (i.e., size and sympathies of the audience) of a dispute, the stronger side wins. As the scope widens, the size of the audience increases such that the potential force of the audience, if swung behind one protagonist, can alter the initial power relationship overwhelmingly. The outcome then depends on what the audience does.

Disputes, then, can frequently be analyzed in terms of the strategies used by protagonists to widen or limit the scope of the conflict. The powerful want to limit the scope and isolate the conflict. The weak want to widen the scope by "going public" for by doing so they can gain enormous leverage on the initially stronger party.

Nader's Raiders offer an example. During the summer of 1969 and 1970 groups of college and postgraduate students joined with Ralph Nader to investigate some governmental departments. Nader reports that the fear and defensiveness caused by his students requesting information and interviews for the purposes of examining the agency was incredible. That fear is understandable. Students committed to doing something worthwhile by uncovering inefficiency or incompetence or indifference or dishonesty can be troublesome enough to the Establishment in any of its forms. Such young people have the enormous drive, energy, and singleness of purpose to lay siege to and outlast all but the strongest of defensive barriers. Couple this enormous drive with Nader's access to mass media and powerful audiences and one immediately recognizes why barricaded bureaucracies and arrogant industries must experience fear when faced with such enormously powerful adversaries. It is, however, the threat to allow conflict to expand to very much larger forums with extraordinarily larger audiences that generates the fear.

A group of uniquely bright and concerned students working within a local context (i.e., a restrained and controlled forum of conflict), such as local antipollution groups or students doing theses and projects, generates more than trivial concern only when the potential conflict is likely to be uncontainable.

The most important distinction to be made between different types of conflict is that of means versus ends. *Ends conflict* is the most straightforward and familiar type; in it the two parties attempt to gain access over the distribution rights to a commonly desired resource pool. As the name implies, ends conflict derives from the friction generated when two people or groups of people want something, the amount of which is to some extent limited. There are endless examples of ends conflict: nations desiring political and/or economic control over the same territory; labor and management conflict over distribution of profits; students' conflict with university administrations over the planning of programs or the changing of policies; the black man's attempt to free himself and get some of the material benefits of decadent middle-class society; two children fighting for more than half of the bed they were instructed to share; two bucks fighting for a doe; political groups vying for control of a constituency; two drivers trying to get through a one lane area at the same time.

The second major form of conflict is *means conflict*. Again as the name implies, means conflict refers to a situation in which the two parties to the conflict agree on the final outcome they both wish to accomplish but disagree as to the methods or means by which they might bring this state about. Teachers may agree that they wish to provide their students with the best education but disagree as to the best method to accomplish this. Travelers may agree on their destination but disagree on the route. Christians may agree on where they wish to go but disagree on exactly how to get there and how many others they should bring along.

It is generally believed that means conflict is less volatile and more readily resolved than ends conflict, although we have little evidence to suggest that this is so. The assumption is based on the fact that the direction of the conflict process is restricted. The probity of this assumption is severely limited when one considers the possibility that satisfying the albeit agreed on end may be perceived by both protagonists as being possible only if the opposition is eliminated. The fact that two nations may really want world peace but threaten world destruction to accomplish it exemplifies the point.

THE GAME OF CHICKEN

As a point of departure, consider the game of chicken. I offer this model because so many of the situations with which managers must deal develop into games of chicken. Frequently, conflicts that begin at low levels of rhetorical violence increase in threat and violence so that the principals to the conflict lose sight of the issues. Having lost sight of the issues they become concerned with such things as not backing down, not appearing weak, not giving in, courage, not being a chicken, and so forth. Once individuals perceive a situation in those terms, then the situation has become nonnegotiable. A negotiable situation in which there was some scope for cooperative settlement, some scope for compromise and reason, has become nonnegotiable—the focal issue is that of who is going to yield. It is always unfortunate when this occurs and it is important for us to recognize what the characteristics of such chicken-type confrontations are.

Consider the following example of one of the traditional games of chicken played with automobiles. The situation may take place on a summer evening. A large number of people are standing along a straight road. Two cars are at the opposite ends of the road pointed head on. The rules of this game are extremely simple. All one need do is hop in one of the automobiles and accelerate it at full speed toward the other automobile. Determining the winner of this game is extraordinarily simple. The winner is that person who does not turn his wheels. The loser, the chicken, as it were, is that individual who swerves. This simplest of games points out a number of very interesting considerations in simple nose-to-nose conflict situations. First, it is nonnegotiable. The only consideration, and the only thing at stake here, is that of courage. This is a simple game of courage. The only issue is who is going to yield. The situation is nonnegotiable because winning or courage or not yielding are symbolic payoffs and are not divisible. There can be but one winner, if winning is to have any value at all.

Another interesting feature of chicken-type games is that small material payoffs may preclude play. If one offered a prize of say $5 to the winner of the automobile game of chicken, both parties to the conflict could and probably would simply refuse to play. Only a fool would play such an extremely dangerous game for such a trivial payoff. Large material payoffs might well encourage play. However, the intriguing feature of such games is that when symbolic payoffs are stressed, with either no material payoff or one that is ignored, then the tendency to play is enhanced.

One of the major problems with games of this nature is that such games are nonnegotiable—compromise is precluded. This is particularly true of simple nose-to-nose games of chicken. Consider the situation of the two automobiles speeding toward one another and one of the individuals wants to compromise. What he would like to do is initiate a cooperative move (i.e., make a concession). He would like to turn his wheels slightly, enough for the other player to recognize the fact that he has turned his wheels. He would then like the other driver to reciprocate so that when they reach the center point of the road, one driver would be on the right side of the road, the other driver on the left side of the road and they could pass one another. Neither could be victimized by the derisive cry of chicken because both have agreed not to play the game. The problem with this kind of situation is that one cannot yield and still maintain control over the expectancies of the opposition. As soon as one person realizes the fact that the other player is starting to weaken, that is, starting to turn the wheels, it is a signal to the unyielding party to increase the pressure, by accelerating more rapidly. The problem in this kind of situation is that you cannot yield without totally capitulating because as soon as you make a concession the opposition expects that, given that you started to weaken, you have no option but to yield.

Now, one method for handling situations of this nature would be to introduce a mediator. First of all, a mediator could slow down the bargaining tempo, that is, the speed at which the game is played. Second, a mediator can communicate concessions while at the same time keeping control of the expectancies of the protagonists.

Expectancies are controlled by mediators because offers of concession are not irrevocable commitments. Any offer may have originated from either the

other player or the mediator. The other player may not be aware of the offer
(e.g., the mediator may simply be exploring or testing options) or may not be
committed to the offer even if accepted.

In short, mediators permit protagonists to make concessions without such
offers being interpreted as signals for total capitulation. One may yield without
yielding. Mediators, of course, serve many functions other than the control of
expectancies. In chicken-type confrontations, however, such control is often a
most important factor in defusing a highly dangerous conflict.

Paragames

Regrettably, any time one person chooses to define a situation that has a
negotiable structure in nonnegotiable terms, and any time one of the parties
wants to play chicken, one does not have the option to not play the game. Any
time you refuse to accept a challenge, and any time you refuse to become
engaged in such a game, you have lost. This is one of the unfortunate
characteristics of nonnegotiable games. In short, you cannot not play. This
feature of chicken games gives rise to the paragame structure. Paragames refer
to extensions of the main contest in which protagonists can determine willingness to play at low levels of danger, cost, and humiliation. Consider traditional
gentlemanly honor rituals. Engaged in an increasingly heated argument, one
man removes his glove, reminding his opponent both verbally and symbolically
(removal of the glove) that he will not abide rude references to his woman. At
this point the opponent may yield at a very low level of danger and humiliation,
by indicating that he regretted making any remarks which might have been
misinterpreted. However, should the opponent want to continue to play, he
would force the issue by making the other fellow, as well as everyone else in
the room, perfectly aware of the fact that he was being highly insulting. Glove
off, the next move is the symbolic slap. The slap, signaling willingness to play
at higher levels of violence and humiliation, is then acknowledged by yielding
or by responding with the appropriate signal indicating willingness to be
formally challenged to a duel. The signal may be a retaliatory slap, for
example, which leaves the insulted fellow in the position of yielding or
formally challenging his opponent to a duel. The ritual continues with salient
interchanges allowing either protagonist to yield until the final statement made
by the referee, which is a formal plea to settle in a less violent manner. If
silence is the response, the duel begins.

Chicken Strategies

Although we shall be considering strategies in some detail in a subsequent
section, it is appropriate to briefly comment on the major forms of chicken

game strategies. Winning games of this nature depends on one party's misrepresenting his payoff schedule to the other party. It is very important for a person to communicate to the opposition that one would rather be killed than yield. If one is persuasive in communicating this ordering, the opposition, if his ordering of payoff priorities is that yielding is more attractive than being killed, has, of course, lost the game. In short, it is important for one player to attempt to convince the other player that death is preferable to the derisive cry of chicken.

There is a variety of different factors that affect one's probability of success. First is that of history or tradition. If one player is an experienced veteran of chicken-type confrontations, has played the game with a variety of other individuals, and has never lost (i.e., has never yielded), then the credibility of his going the full distance is greatly enhanced. Persons with reputations for daring play derive a certain insulation from such reputation. Notorious players receive few challenges from others, and notorious players can win in the paragame more easily, given that they are known not to yield.

A second strategic procedure is referred to as the rationality of irrationality. If one can communicate to the opposition that one has lost contact with reality, the opposition has lost the game. If an individual appeared to be suicidal or in some way emotionally unstable or was known to be intoxicated or under the influence of drugs, then, of course, the person under such influence has won the game. The reason he has won the game is that the opposition cannot depend on that person to act in his own best self-interest. If one player is roaring drunk when he hops in his car the nondrunk person cannot depend on the drunk individual's saving his own life. Because in the game of chicken the payoff is bilateral, such that if one person gets killed they both get killed, the person who seems to have lost contact with reality enjoys a strategic advantage. The reason that irrationality may be a rational strategy results from the payoff structure associated with the game of chicken. In the game of chicken the payoffs associated with deadlock are bilateral (i.e., if one person receives the negative payoff associated with deadlock, both do). If there is a crash, the crash involves both individuals. Hence, the person demonstrating less concern frequently wins the game.

Uncertainty

As Schelling (1963) points out, for a game of chicken to be played at all there must be some degree of uncertainty. If we change the rules of the above described game slightly, so that each car advanced, let us say, 100 feet in turn, the game can continue up to the point at which one party must drive the final 100 feet, which results in the crash. Neither party would drive that final 100 feet nor would anyone expect them to. Any time a person can be placed in a situation in which they alone have the last clear chance to avoid disaster, then the game of chicken is not played. It is only when there is some degree of uncertainty that the game of chicken is ever played.

It is not my contention that most important conflicts are simple games of chicken. However, many conflict situations that start off at very low levels of violence turn into games that have a chicken-type format. People become concerned with yielding and not yielding so that many of the features of the simple games of chicken played by teenagers in their automobiles are also appropriate to larger conflict situations. It is indeed unfortunate that so many conflicts must get out of hand before people become concerned with trying to control them. Very frequently before anybody becomes concerned with controlling a conflict, the situation has gotten out of hand with high threat levels, high costs associated with deadlock, and to the point where the protagonists have become more concerned with not yielding than they are with the basic issues. We are going to talk about a variety of such situations and how they evolve from low-threat to high-threat situations.

THEORIES OF POWER

We now direct our attention to something everybody talks about but few people seem to agree on. Power is a very complex issue. We have many definitions and much disagreement. However, all managers talk about power. We recognize that all organizations or institutions are systems of power. We are all well aware of the fact that people attempt to increase their sphere of influence (empire build), which is an attempt to gain greater power. We also recognize the fact that controlled administration, be it at the corporation level or at the government level, is to a very great extent based on the concept of conflicting and balancing centers of power.

In the later sections of this book we discuss a system of self-regulation that is based on the concept of the development of powerful subgroups within the organization. It is comparable to what many people refer to as power sharing in organizations which, for the time being, we can equate to participation in group decision making. A thorough discussion of checks and balances, the concept of pluralism, and group decision making, however, is postponed until Chapter 3.

Our present task is to try to understand the concept of power as it may apply in any number of the many situations in which managers find themselves. We constantly use the term and recognize that as managers we are wielders of power. Hence it would be nice to have some sophisticated understanding of the concept. We shall examine a number of different theories of power, again all of which are relevant under certain circumstances, and then we shall draw some conclusions about those particular concepts of power that seem most relevant for the purposes of introducing change into organizations.

The behavioral sciences, and I suspect psychology in particular, are fixated on causality. In an attempt to make sense out of social behavior, attention has been focused on linear causal explanations, with the attendant deemphasis of the circular and reciprocal nature of all interpersonal situations. This fixation is most apparent in experimental research in which investigators focus their attention on the reaction of people to various things that are introduced, changed, or manipulated in the environment. Theory construction, frequently, following from the above fixation takes the form of abstracting those features of social events that are assumed essential for understanding, describing, and predicting social behavior. Such fixations lead to what Whitehead (cited by Proshansky, Ittelson and Rivlin, 1970) has termed the fallacy of misplaced concreteness. The problem, of course, is that we attribute greater prominence, reality, and importance to the abstracted features than they deserve. We ignore other important features of the social situation. It also leads to complete myopia with respect to the reciprocal and circular nature of social processes. A moment's reflection should convince one that all social processes are circular and reciprocal.

The literature on power reflects the error of misplaced concreteness. There is an untoward fixation on cause–effect explanations of power and social influence.

At the most fundamental level, Person A is said to have power over Person B to the extent that A can get B to do something that B would not do otherwise (Dahl, 1957). Others have defined power as potential influence: one person, the Source, is considered to have power if he can change a Target person's probable behavior. Formally, power is frequently defined as the change in the probability of an act (or if actually performed, the degree of compliance) following the intervention of a Source. Power, according to this view, resides in the Source by virtue of that person's greater resources, be they physical, monetary, informational, charismatic, or whatever. The Target enters the calculations only tangentially.

There have been many variations on this theme of power which is built around the concept of one person or group exercising control over the behavior of another person or group. Max Weber (1947), for example, introduced the concept of conflict or competition over scarce resources when he defined power as "the probability that one actor within a social relationship will be in a position to carry out his own will despite resistance." Karl Deutsch (1963), extending this concept somewhat, defined power more broadly than simply altering another person's or group's behavior by including also the capability to force one's own perception of the world on others. His definition is that power is the ability of an individual or group to act out successfully its character or to impose extrapolations or projections of its inner structure on its environment.

Others have defined power as the ability to encourage or force others to act in accordance with one's own wishes in order to bring to fruition one's personal goals or aspirations. Meyer Zald (1970) maintains the concept of deliberate or intentional control of another's behavior but calls attention to a different purpose of the exercise of that power. He defines power as the ability of a person or group, for whatever reason, to affect another person's or group's ability to achieve its own goals (personal or collective). In this definition, therefore, attention is focused not on the Source's attempting to satisfy his own goals but rather on Source's ability to get Target to satisfy Target's goals. Others have been more liberal in their definition of power, simply indicating that any interference with autonomy is power, differing only in terms of the sanctions that Source can bring to bear on Target for noncompliance. All of the above definitions of power see the locus (or cause) of power as residing in the one person, the Source, who generates some change in the Target.

It is, of course, recognized in the above view that a Source's power varies from one situation to another. The greater the number of different situations in which Source can exert influence over Target, the greater the scope of Source's power—and the more Targets that Source can influence the greater Source's dominion of power. Similarly, the cost to Source for exercising influence enters into the calculations. The greater the cost to Source to use power, either because of direct costs (e.g., loss of money) or indirect costs (e.g., reduced prestige), the less powerful the Source is considered to be.

It is also recognized that there are different bases of power (e.g., see Raven & Kruglinski, 1970). Informational influence refers to Source's ability to alter Target's understanding of a situation. A physician can influence one's behavior by pointing out contingencies of which one may have been unaware. A person may encourage us to select a different route because he provides us with information about attractive sights we do not wish to miss. The ability of Source to make special appeals to accepted authority structures (e.g., a higher ranking military officer, or a policeman to an automobile driver) or to mutually valued social structures (e.g., Source encouraging compliance to protect the integrity of a specific social unit, such as a family or a social club) likewise are recognizable sources of potential influence. The most straightforward bases of influence are those which permit the Source to make contingent promises or threats. Giving Target something of value, or terminating something unpleasant, or Source's ability to expose Target to something unpleasant or to deprive Target of present satisfactions, then, are obvious bases of potential influence.

Psychologists generally are given to claiming that power resides in the Source by virtue of that person's ability to marshal greater resources in the eventuality of a conflict. The theories have rather a "chief chicken in the barnyard" flavor about them. Most of the above theories, although not solely the product of psychologists or sociologists, are all based on the assumption that power resides in the Source. Research carried out by behavioral scientists usually reflects this initial bias by assuming that power resides in the Source. You will find in many laboratory or field experimental situations that the ability of Target to react to an influence or power attempt is severely limited for the purposes of experimental control. In laboratory situations, for example, experimental subjects defined as Targets may only be offered two or three potential courses of action when exposed to an influence attempt. They may, for example, be able to resist the attempt or to comply with the attempt either partially or totally. It is perfectly obvious that such experimental procedures lead to the maintenance of the myopia of linear causality. The entire experimental procedure is structured to examine the power that resides in the Source. Let us examine some alternative conceptions of power.

Schattschneider (1960) offers the notion that power resides in the audience or forum of the conflict. In a fight between two men, the physical might of the bystanders, almost always, is sufficient to easily subdue either combatant. In any dispute, the winner is likely to be that person who has or wins the support of the forum. Because one who controls the forum of debate determines the outcome, power results from the relative degree to which protagonists can control the scope or limits of the conflict. Protest that gains wide publicity, for example, changes the forum of the conflict and increases the potential force that various sectors of the public can bring to bear to resolve the situation.

As has been mentioned in other parts of this book, groups that are engaged in losing battles therefore attempt to expand the forum of debate. They attempt to take the issue to an audience that is not controlled by their opposition. They may go public, they may approach the newspapers, hold demonstrations, spread the conflict to other groups within the organization, etc. The basic purpose again is to take one's chances, so to speak, with groups (audiences) less under the control of the opposition. Power then can very well be defined as the ability to limit the scope of decision making in organizations. The power can be exercised in at least two ways: one, by limiting the nature of the decisions to only safe issues or two, as implied in Schattschneider's conception of power, the ability to limit all decision making to forums sympathetic to one's own point of view.

Chadwick (1971), in contrast, focuses attention on the Target. Every person is being pushed and pulled by society to develop predictable adaptive and nondisruptive life styles that support the status quo. Target's power is defined as one minus the ratio of the distance from his desired state divided by how far away from the pull of society he wants to be; i.e., Power = 1 − (Frustration/Alienation). Or as Bert Raven[1] so well summarized the equation: a powerful person is one who determines where the stream of society is pulling him and then swims like hell to reach a point that is against the current.

Gamson (1968) points out that discontent is a source of power at least to those individuals who can mobilize and use that discontent. If you recall the story of Snow White and the Seven Dwarfs, there were two people with positions of influence, Snow White and Grumpy. The conceptions of power offered by Chadwick and Gamson are based on the premise that groups in

[1]Personal communication.

which there is a high level of satisfaction have minimal potential for the development of conflicting power. Discontentment and dissatisfaction, however, are the breeding grounds for disruption by encouraging the mobilization of powerful protesting factions.

It is interesting to note that during the human relations phase of management, attention was focused on generating cohesive and contented work groups, the assumption being that satisfied workers were productive workers. That overly naïve conception of the relationship between productivity and satisfaction was proved to be inadequate when it was discovered that job satisfaction and productivity were not directly related. It was found for example, that very satisfied workers could be inefficient and nonproductive workers. However, the point that I wish to make is that there were some notable success experiences within the human relations tradition of focusing attention on the generation of satisfied, content, and "happy" work teams. The reason for that success may well have been the diffusing of potentially disruptive power groupings mobilized around discontentment.

The essential difference between Chadwick's position and Gamson's is that Gamson speaks of discontentment as a source of power or potential power if it can be mobilized, whereas Chadwick's is a radical call for action indicating that the way to generate power is to find out where society is going and then turn around and go in the opposite direction.

It is important to keep in mind that dissatisfaction is a potential power base only to the extent that the dissatisfied are committed or "locked in" to the social system in question. One rebels or protests to bring about change either by persuasion or force. Should one have the option to withdraw from a social system, then one's dissatisfaction may not contribute to a base of power to introduce change. As Chaim Potok (1970) points out in his book *The Promise,* "Turning one's back upon ideas or institutions is . . . not an act of rebellion but an act of disengagement. The old is considered dead" [p. 293].

The storm created by Reich's (1970) optimism with regard to the Consciousness III revolution again calls attention to the fact that concepts of power which ignore the Target by focusing only on Source to Target influences are likely to be quite wide of the mark. In Consciousness III, Reich describes a source of power that has been widely recognized but traditionally ignored by both power theorists and many policy makers: namely, power that derives from repudiation of values. If Target has limited need for, or value of, resources over which Source has control, Source has limited power. To offer an extreme example, if one does not value one's own life the threat of death is inadequate as a source of influence. Reich maintains that if Targets can avoid acquiring needs and wants that government and business force on society, then Sources are deprived of means of influence and control.

Now every manager recognizes this source of power. One has control of several subordinates only when subordinates share one's own values. If a subordinate comes to you and tells you what you can do with your job, you are powerless. Hence, your control over the subordinate, that is, your base of power, resides in the subordinate's acceptance of a value system consistent with your own and his valuing or aspiring to obtain rewards or privileges over which you have control.

The argument can be made, then, that the locus of power resides in the Target rather than the Source. For a Source to have means of influence, Target must want or need those things over which Source is perceived by the Target to have control. I think the argument has equal probity for analyzing power relationships in gerentocracies, meritocracies, and democracies as well as for relationships that derive from military or monetary asymmetries.

Our discussion of the eruption of conflict will focus on the wants and needs of people in any societal unit. People want status or wealth or personal freedom over which others have control. Conflict erupts over attempts by people with little access to valued resources to gain a greater share of those resources. It is true, of course, that the Haves in our society are powerful only because the Have-Nots value the resources over which the Haves have distribution prerogatives. However, repudiation of values as a means of depriving Haves of their power, although correct in its assumption, is limited by reality. Few people identify personal freedom as the loss of everything of value. A popular song concludes that you are really free when you have nothing else to lose. Conversely stated, you are really free when there is nothing you want.

Our circle is complete. Wants create concern over the equitable distribution of resources capable of satisfying that want. Persons with control over distribution of certain resources gain power to the extent that they can create wants for those same resources. Conflict erupts when wants are made salient such that Haves hold and protect whereas Have-Nots get. We shall now turn our attention to a systematic analysis of this process.

RESOURCE POOLS

Society is the regulatory system that establishes priorities for the satisfaction of human needs or wants. To the extent that two incompatible needs occur simultaneously with the attendant attempts to satisfy them simultaneously, some system for determining and regulating priorities for need satisfaction is required. All of societies' laws, norms, and policies are derived from this basic conflict.

Needs or wants are incompatible to the extent that one person's satisfying his need necessitates nonsatisfaction or a loss of satisfaction to the second person. Totally incompatible need structures may be conceptualized as analogous to a two-handed poker game in which one player's winnings are the second player's losses. Need structures, of course, may be only partially incompatible. Two people may share a desire for background music but may have incompatible wants with respect to type of music or the desired volume level.

Wants and needs may also be incompatible because of the size of the resource pool (i.e., that which has the property of satisfying needs and wants). If the resource pool is limited in size or duration such that only one person's need can be fully satisfied, then two identical needs are rendered incompatible because both cannot be satisfied. Incompatibility of need or want structure then is not, in the first instance at least, an all or none situation. Rather, incompatibility of need between persons or groups describes a dimension that proceeds from total incompatibility to total concordance. In the latter, one person's satisfying his need results in the second person's simultaneous need satisfaction. Uncomplicated sexual intercourse where both parties to the act are concerned only with personal need satisfaction provides a workable example of need complementation. To the extent that persons in the happy position of experiencing simultaneous and complimentary needs act selfishly, the potential for conflict eruption is slight. Hence, most of our discussions must be primarily concerned with incompatible needs, including incompatibility that derives both from reality and from misperceived reality.

If the resource pool is large enough or if the wants are not incompatible, of course, regulatory systems are never developed. Not too many years ago, no thought was given to regulatory systems for breathing and the consumption of oxygen. Now that it has become obvious that this resource pool is not necessarily inexhaustible, new regulatory systems and structures are emerging to control the use and distribution of this resource.

The resource pool refers to the object of conflict. It represents that which focuses the behaviors of parties who find themselves in conflict. The resource pool defines the need or want-satisfying state that people are attempting to attain and exploit. To the extent that other people are attempting to exploit the same resource pool at the same time, the potential for conflict is enhanced. The characteristics of such pools then determine the likelihood of conflict, the course of such conflicts, and the potential for settlement.

Defining a resource pool as that which has the property of need satisfaction calls attention to the fact that conflict is affected by two groups of interacting factors. First, the value or importance of a resource pool derives from human needs or wants. Status has no value if not desired by people within a societal unit; food increases in value as hunger increases, and so on. In part, therefore, it can be said that people create their own objects and conditions of value by developing or allowing society to develop wants for these objects and conditions. Some needs, of course, are basic to the sustenance of life. They are typically modified by society's influence but nevertheless, should conditions of deprivation ensue, the biological necessity for need satisfaction becomes paramount.

Second, need satisfaction is dependent on the characteristics of the pool itself. One potato chip cannot satiate three starving people. An organization with hierarchical administrative structures cannot satiate status needs for all its members: hence, such organizational structures foster drive for advancement. Two people with one record player cannot listen to different records at the same time, whereas a beautiful pastoral scene may be enjoyed by anyone who notices.

The extent to which the properties of the resource pool interact with the need structure of protagonists then should be obvious. Hunger determines the value and importance of a cache of food. In the present section we shall examine those structural properties of resource pools that are importantly related to conflict analysis. If one can identify the object of conflict and understand the characteristics of such pools one may frequently anticipate the potential for conflict eruption and the course a conflict will follow should it erupt.

Resource pool analysis is not easy. Moreover, it is precisely because people have naïve notions about their own ability to analyze what people are fighting about that conflicts are made so resistant to analysis and to reduction, resolution, or management. Much of the misconception of the simplistic nature of conflict has come from the fact that popularized ethology has become fashionable. The full understanding of two elk bucks fighting over a female during rutting sessions may be satisfying and important, but any generalization to the human scene is foolhardy if not absurd.

Resource pools determine the nature of the conflict. Conflict is a structural phenomenon precisely because it is determined by the structural properties of the pool.

Tangible versus Intangible Pools

Any time someone continues an activity to avoid or prevent embarrassment, shame, pity, or similar humiliation, the resource pool or payoff is intangible. Similarly, praise, victory, and admiration are positive intangible payoffs. Such payoffs cannot be shared nor divided and thus tend to generate highly volatile conflicts because payoff is all or none.

Tangible payoffs, in contrast, are usually divisible or shareable. When a conflict develops over money, for example, the altercation can be resolved or reduced by altering the divison of the money.

The distinction of primary importance is that conflicts which develop over intangible payoffs are nonnegotiable. One cannot share victory with the loser if victory is to have any importance or meaning. If one engages another to demonstrate one's resolve or courage, anything short of victory may be unacceptable.

It often happens that protagonists redefine tangible payoff structures in intangible terms. Whenever one feels that when dividing the tangible payoff (e.g., money) one must "beat" the other fellow by getting more than he does, one has converted a tangible and therefore negotiable payoff structure to an intangible, nonnegotiable one as there can be but one winner.

There are many examples of nonnegotiable games—the clearest examples being such simple games of courage as chicken, described earlier. It is important to realize, however, that the structure of the conflict may maximize the protagonists' concern over intangible payoffs. The game of chicken again is just such a game, for one is materially better off yielding when the opponent is exploitative.

Heads of state have an unhappy tendency to define negotiable situations in nonnegotiable terms. There again, are many examples, my favorite being Rusk's (the Secretary of State during Kennedy's Cuban Missile Crisis) statement to the White House correspondent for ABC "Remember John, when you report this [the crisis] that eyeball to eyeball they [the Soviet Union] blinked first."

I like to refer to the tendency to define negotiable conflict situations in nonnegotiable terms as the gun-fighter's syndrome. So many persons in salient positions in universities, business, and government enflame the violence by defining conflict situations in simple yielding or not yielding terms. Many universities have exploded because some arrogant ass refuses to "yield to student demands," the very wording of the statement indicating total incompetence. Any time administrators feel they must demonstrate strength or resolve, it is likely that the conflict is in the intangible payoff range and likely out of control.

Size of the Pool

The size of the resource pool is also quite important. Conflicts usually do not occur over resource pools of abundance. Take the most straightforward example of two men obtaining their water from the same watering hole. If plenty of water remained, after both men had all the water they cared for, conflict over this specific resource pool would be unlikely. If, however, the size of the pool were continually reduced until the amount became insufficient, conflict might be expected. The very size of the pool then determines conflict and we usually define conflict in terms of distribution of "scarce" resources.

Now scarcity of a resource is not a sufficient condition for conflict. To borrow a concept from Kenneth Boulding (1963), two (or more) people utilizing the same depletable resource pool are in *competition* when the pool becomes inadequate to satisfy both people. The two parties are in *conflict* to the extent that they become aware of one another and the inconsistency between their wants or needs. Conflict, then, develops when protagonists perceive others to be desirous of satisfying needs or wants that are or may become to some degree incompatible with personal need satisfaction.

Divisibility

Some payoffs, although tangible, are not easily divided. The payoff may consist, for example, of one highly attractive and one much less attractive prize. Two people trying to cooperate to win the presidency and vice presidency of a group are likely to experience difficulty in deciding who shall be president unless some pre-existing rights, rules, options or moves determine the division. In payoff division card games, such as high–low varieties of poker, the two winners divide the pot evenly or to the lowest value chip (i.e., if the lowest value chip is 5¢, the pot is divided down to the last remaining 5¢ chip). The distribution of the odd 5¢ chip is highly ritualized to eliminate conflict, such as always going to the high-hand holder.

Depletability and Replenishability

Of all the concepts that we are going to discuss within the context of resource pools and, later, in terms of organizational power, the concept of resource pool depletability is without question the most important. Because we in the managerial and behavioral sciences have become fixated on the concept of linear mathematical and logical models, we have become completely and utterly confused about what makes organizations tick. We have accepted many of the models and methodologies in the management and administrative sciences that are appropriate to the physical and physiological sciences. In social science, it is entirely possible to have a situation in which two plus two makes five—for the human being is not a rock. Physical things can be understood in terms of physical laws and concepts. The concepts of intransitivity, transgeneration, and the like are appropriate because of the very high level of consistency that cause–effect relationships have within the physical world.

The social sciences do not lend themselves to the same sort of analysis. The explanatory principles and methodologies appropriate to the physical sciences are not at all appropriate to the social sciences. In the physical sciences, many parameters are additive. If I start piling rocks in my boat, which will sink, let us say, once I reach the combined weight of 300 pounds, it does not really matter how I load the stones. The critical variable is that the boat will sink once I exceed 300 pounds. If I put in a rock weighing 150 pounds, then one of 50 pounds, then one of 110 pounds, the effect is going to be precisely the same as when I load the rocks in the reverse order.

By way of comparison, if we want to encourage a child to go to the store on two different occasions by offering a 5¢ and a $5 inducement, it certainly makes a difference whether we order our inducements $5 and then 5¢ or 5¢ and then $5.

Man is to a very great extent unpredictable. If we observe his natural behavior on a day-to-day basis we find that he does a large number of things by habit and routine, such that our ability to predict his behavior is quite good. However, every once in a while he does something that is completely unpredictable, although perhaps not unexplainable. The person who normally sits quietly on a bus reading his newspaper on the way to work may suddenly get angry and swear because he recalled something that he had forgotten. Although we can explain such behavior on the basis of shifts in attention, interfering stimuli, and so forth, our ability to predict a person's behavior or group's behavior is based solely on our ability to either control or in some way assess the probability of interfering events.

Now this rather long introduction to the concept of replenishment and depletability of resource pools is to call attention to the fact that we cannot use the outdated simplistic mathematical notions applicable to the physical sciences of several decades ago for our understanding of the concept of resource pool in conflict analysis. Some very highly valued resources are nondepletable. Some grow so that they would satisfy the mathematical equation that one plus one is two, and one plus two is four, and two plus two is twelve, and so on. I do not mean to imply that it is not understandable, nor that we cannot eventually develop logical if not mathematical concepts that not only explain but allow us to predict with some margin of success. The reason for focusing on this particular aspect is to call attention to the fact that our conceptualizing social events in organizations in terms of the inappropriate concepts derived from the physical and natural sciences give rise to gross errors in interpretation. With respect to the depletability of some resource pools there are some things that, strictly speaking, cost nothing at all to give because the resource pool is nondepletable. Knowledge is certainly such a nondepletable resource pool in that my giving facts to someone else simply increases the size of the resource pool. I lose nothing by giving my knowledge to another person. Love is a similar sort of resource pool in that giving love may well generate more love than one started with. As Charles Hampden-Turner (1971) reminds us Romeo said to Juliet: "The more I give to you the more I have."

Power in organizations may well be the same sort of nondepletable resource pool. There is some reason to believe that sharing power in organizations by involving subordinates in legitimate decision-making situations increases the total amount of power available to the organization. This is Tannenbaum's (1968) notion that rather than conceive of power as a fixed pool in which the more you give away the less you have, it may be more appropriate to perceive power as an expandable resource pool in which the sharing of it generates a larger overall pie. Hence, by giving power away one retains more than one started with. There are, of course, limits to this concept of the ever-expanding resource pool of power and I am not for a moment suggesting that people simply delegate all of their power and responsibility. We shall have a great deal to say about the overlapping decision center system, participatory management, and power sharing in general, in later sections. The point that I wish to make here is that very frequently our hydraulic and simplistic notions about such resource pools as power and knowledge not only limits our ability to fully analyze conflict in appropriate ways but also frequently focuses our attention on completely inappropriate aspects of organizational dynamics. This, of course, in turn gives rise to inappropriate managerial styles, attempts to concentrate power, secrecy, guardedness, and so on.

Although we can argue that there are many resource pools which are not only nondepletable but also capable of unlimited growth if freely shared, one must also recognize that most people do not freely offer these things or allow people to have access to these resource pools. People do not freely share knowledge. They do not freely share facts. They do not freely share love. They do not freely share power or decision-making prerogatives. The reason they are not sharing these things can reflect several conditions. It may reflect that they have a distorted perception of what the resource is. They may see power, for example, as only a depletable resource in that the more they give away the less they have. They may perceive love as a manipulative resource in that one makes oneself vulnerable to another person when expressing love. However, I think it is more generally true that people do not freely give these things to others because the distribution is dictated by multimotive systems as opposed to unimotive systems. That is, people do not give away knowledge because they like using the knowledge for some other purpose. People do not give away love because they are conceptualizing love as a Machiavellian tool. We will now turn our attention to an analysis of multimotive resource pools.

Multimotive Pools

In two-handed poker, resource pool distribution (the pot) is almost always unimotively determined. Structured by economic concerns, the two players' behavior is directed toward obtaining as much of each other's money as possible. If a father is playing penny ante poker with his young son, however, he may well wish to lose a number of hands on purpose. The latter game therefore reflects a multimotive system.

The critical aspects, then, of analyzing a conflict situation are not only to determine the social–emotional or material–structural characteristics of the resource pool, but also to determine what motives each protagonist is attempting to satisfy. The reason people resist giving, say, knowledge to others is because they are satisfying some motive system other than the ubiquitously flagrant academic lie of "knowledge for knowledge's sake." Knowledge and love become valuable as tools of social control when they are made scarce but are desired by those who have limited supplies.

Information can gain value if distribution is restricted provided those without the knowledge share the same value system as those possessing the knowledge.

Because the information itself cannot be depleted by free distribution to others, persons resisting free distribution must be doing so to satisfy other motives related to the knowledge resource pool. For example, some facts can be sold and therefore must be jealously guarded to maximize the economic return for their restricted distribution. Other facts can be used as powerful weapons of social control such as knowledge of a person's personal life (e.g., blackmail).

Resource Pool Interdependence

Love, in contrast, exemplifies a resource pool that, although probably nondepletable in the strict sense, may be costly to distribute because it makes one vulnerable. To love someone publicly immediately limits one's repertoire of behavioral responses to the loved person. Therefore, the loved person can manipulate the lover by making excessive demands or by forcing the lover into a situation in which the most logical response is precluded because of the special emotional relationship.

Pacifism as a conflict strategy is similar to love in that it drastically restricts one's options for dealing with the other party to the conflict. Nonbelligerence again costs nothing to give as one does not have less when one is peaceful to a particular person. It becomes costly to give only when the giving affects some other resource pool, such as one's own emotional or material security. Likewise, as the police captain who ordered peaceful demonstrators arrested when Chicago Mayor Daley's neighbors became violent during a civil rights march stated:

> . . . it was easier to arrest the marchers for being disorderly because they were peaceful; whereas he did not want to arrest Daley's neighbors for disorderly conduct because they were disorderly and might fight. So the only way to maintain peace was to lock up those who were peaceful [Royko, 1971, p. 145].

It should be perfectly clear, then, the problem with conflict analysis is that we can never make the assumption that the two parties to a conflict are dealing with the same resource pools or that they have the same scale of values. If one person shares knowledge, the second may eagerly take it, not because he wants knowledge but because he wants something else related to that knowledge. He may want to gain social leverage over someone; he may want the information to store for future games of academic chicken in which, if successful, he can gain praise or admiration or retaliation for past embarrassing defeats. Likewise, pacifism may be a high priority resource pool for one party to the conflict but not shared by the second party.

Some resource pools are therefore costly to share because giving some away reduces the amount one retains. In this group we have such resources as money, status, and various forms of social power. Other resource pools are costly to share because by sharing one makes oneself strategically vulnerable with respect to another resource pool that one highly values and that is depletable. Such resources as knowledge, love, and emotional security are examples.

Indigenous versus Exogenous Sources

Still other resource pools require reciprocity for either party to enjoy any of the pool. That is, to gain access to the desired resource pool both protagonists must coordinate their efforts because maximum access to the pool is not individually accomplishable. Usually resource pools that require reciprocity are indigenous to the group, whereas most of the other resource pools are exogenous to the group. A secret is a good example of a resource pool that is indigenous to two persons and can be enjoyed only if both parties maintain the secrecy.

Indigenous resource pools may be thought of as bargaining situations that have a familial component. For example, management–labor disputes are familial in that the generation of profit requires the contribution of both parties. Conflicts that develop over the distribution of the profits are structured by the fact that one must keep one's adversary not too unhappy—otherwise one reduces the size of the resource pool that both parties value. One certainly does not want to eliminate the opposition in such disputes because by doing so one eliminates the resource pool.

Not all indigenous resource pools are familial in the sense that one must protect the other party. A secret, for example, is maintained if one eliminates the other person. Challenge, profit, sex, status, etc., in contrast, require that both protagonists ensure the continued participation of each other.

One further structural dimension is important to our understanding of resource pools. The structural property refers to the nature of the maintenance of the pool. When we think of conflict we usually think of a struggle over the distribution of a restricted amount of something of value. Two children fighting over the distribution of three pieces of candy is probably the traditional image of such conflicts. One attacks one's opponent and if he can be eliminated one gets more.

Resource pools that have the property of maintenance, renewal, or repetition, however, are most likely to be importantly related to the existence of the group. Conflicts that develop over access to such perpetual resource pools are likely to be limited by the constraint of needing the opponent to maintain the availability of the valuable resource so that something exists to be divided. Such conflicts are less likely to be volatile and less likely to lead to bilaterally destructive acts.

Unimotive and Unidimensional Pools

A unimotive resource pool is one that can satisfy many simultaneous needs provided the needs are consistent. A host can satisfy all his guests' wants for music with a single stereo system by playing Bach, given that the guests derive satisfaction from the particular selections.

Unidimensional pools, however, can satisfy any number of persons having the same need structure provided they do not desire satisfaction simultaneously. A group (audience) can listen to only one person's argument at a time, a one-lane bridge can provide passage in only one direction at a time, etc.

Overlapping Need Structure

The potential for conflict eruption, then, is influenced by the degree of disparity or incompatibility between need and want states of proximate parties; the degree of preference (strength of the need or want) for particular satisfactions that proximate parties have; the characteristics of the resource pool that dictate the degree and latency of need satisfaction; the degree of simultaneity of the needs or wants; and the availability of alternative sources of need satisfaction. Should two people seek need satisfaction simultaneously, the extent of the incompatibility of the overlapping needs derives from the structural characteristics of the resource pool.

The above distinctions and classifications are, of course, arbitrary and it should be recognized that all conflicts reflect a complex combination of different perceptions of resource pools and multimotive need structures. Conflict analysis requires that one attempt to untangle the different motives and perceptions, for if one can identify the resource pool one can go a long way toward anticipating the potential for conflict, as well as the possible avenues for conflict resolution.

Resource pools appropriate to specific situationally determined need satisfaction also, of course, typically require appeal to several of the above classification categories for definition. A status conflict in a specific organization, for example, may prove to be indigenous (i.e., status requires group acknowledgment—no group, no status) and nonnegotiable (i.e., a "winner take all" form of conflict) because it is nondivisible and intangible. The conflict may have limited longevity, however, because of low status need levels of protagonists or the availability of alternative need satisfaction opportunities.

THE PLAYERS AND THE SPECTATORS

I think it might bear repeating that if one could stand away from our planet and analyze it impassionately one would be compelled to conclude it must be the lunatic colony for the galaxy, if not the universe. We have poverty and physical pain, and illiteracy and slavery, and the equivalent of over 15,000 tons of TNT for every living human being. That we must change this would seem so obvious that commenting on that fact should bore even the most profound dullard. Regrettably, those who support the maintenance of the status quo, the conservatives, include some bright and eloquent people.

The important players in this game include conservatives, liberals, radicals, utopians, fascists, and the inactives. It should be noted that the most abused of the above labels is that of liberal. People who call themselves liberals are frequently conservatives clever enough to give the Have-Not people enough to keep them from sharing fully and equally in that which society could offer. Similarly, inactive and comfortable people, who identify with the liberal and at times the radical rhetoric, label themselves as liberals whereas their inactivity de facto helps maintain the status quo. These people also, if threatened with loss of privilege, are likely to be galvanized toward identification with the conservative position. For our purposes of analyzing political philosophies, we shall be considering the bona fide liberal political philosophy of disciplined change. We must keep in mind, however, that what a person does and not what he says defines his political philosophy.

Philosophies of Conflict

Prior to discussing the players we should discuss different conceptions of conflict that are related to the different organizational philosophies. At the one extreme we have the medical model of conflict. This position views conflict as a cancerous growth within an otherwise healthy society. The cancerous growth must be excised, otherwise the total society (or other organizational unit) will be destroyed. Conflict, like cancer according to this view, is caused and may be controlled by prevention, prophylaxis, causal or symptomatic treatment, or chronic removal. If conflict is bad then one must direct efforts toward getting rid of it or at least suppressing and controlling it. Racial conflicts within a society, according to this view, could be approached by racially restricted immigration, apartheid, fully regulated slavery, completely controlled protectorate states (e.g., Indian reservations), the use of overwhelming punishment by the powerful group for even trivial transgressions of norms, annihilation of a group, as well as specific treatment of the minority group's needs. The critical aspect of the medical analogy is not that conflict is a societal disease which should be attacked but rather that society is basically good and healthy and would purr along contentedly if the pockets of cancerous disruption could be removed.

On the other side of the dimension we have the friction model of conflict. In this view conflict is the inevitable by-product of social interaction. Like a motor, when a society is purring along, friction that generates heat is inevitable. Now the important difference between this model and the medical model is that the latter views conflict as evidence of illness in society, whereas in the former conflict is indicative of a healthy society. Society should be moving and changing, which both necessitates as well as gives rise to conflict and turbulence. A turbulent society is healthy and good, for it provides for the accommodation of change. Again, like a motor, if stalled and not moving anywhere, society will be free of conflict.

Conservatism

The medical model or concept of conflict is at the heart of the conservative philosophy. The way society or any organizational unit works today is, according to the conservatives, the best model of the way things should be tomorrow. Society is basically okay if we can just treat the surface irritations before they spread. I do not mean to imply that conservatism is necessarily an optimistic political philosophy. Many conservatives feel the cancer has metastasized and society is doomed unless massive surgery is attempted. Others are optimistic about the overwhelming power of the Haves and consider the Chicagos, Detroits, and Wisconsins irritations, it is true, but rather like a gnat bite on a rhinoceros' behind.

Radicalism

On the other side of the dimension we have radicalism and the difference between the radical and the conservative philosophy is indeed marked. For the radical, society can be sick or healthy and, far from being a sign of illness or malfunctioning, turbulence is a sign of health. Conservatives value quiescence and disciplined change whereas the radical's value system is the exact opposite. Turbulence and unstructured change are good and healthy and desirable and, I may add, fun. The only way to keep society going in the direction of freedom and equality is to keep it turbulent. Conflict generates change, it keeps energies mobilized, it structures debate, it makes issues more salient, it polarizes opposing forces. To the radical, quiescence is a sign of impending sickness or stagnation and one should deliberately jab at society if for no other reason than for the hell of it.

For the radical, revolution is a personal therapy. The purpose of revolution is not only to create a better society than today's but also to fulfill oneself. Turbulence creates change and is healthy and a sign of a properly functioning society. Because the goal of radicalism is turbulence, then the issue over which one jabs at society is not of principal importance. Radicals can accomplish their goal by affiliating themselves with anyone's fight provided, of course, the issue is ideologically important to a large group of people.

Many radical writers have advocated attaching oneself to others' issues once their potential for creating turbulence has been established. Others have argued that you must "do your own thing" as you must have ideological and/or emotional sympathy with the issue. Black radicals' rejection of white attachment to their fight is an example.

Again, within the radical group we have people who differ with respect to their optimism, tactics, motivations, etc. Some radicals feel that society is basically satisfactory but is badly in need of small, regulated, and restricted attacks on specific institutions or inequalities. Others feel that our society is both sick and weird and must be completely destroyed to be rebuilt.

Radicals also differ on the extent of the turbulence they consider necessary to introduce change and the extent to which they see using violence to accomplish it. Many people with radical orientations are very concerned lest conflict over an issue get out of hand, leading to insensate acts of violence and destruction. They advocate regulated confrontation conflicts that are highly organized to provide the control necessary to prevent the creation of a monster. Other revolutionary radicals feel that if a protest group evolves into a violent monster so much the better.

The conservative and radical philosophies then are directly related to the different perceptions each group has of conflict, the medical model of health being associated with conservatism, the turbulence or friction model being associated with radicalism.

Liberalism

The above are, of course, extreme positions. Many people are, in the true sense, liberal in that they consider turbulence necessary for and indicative of a changing state of society. They are concerned with the means used to accomplish the change and expect a reduction of turbulence once the change is accomplished.

Liberalism is identified with the view that society can and should be changed in a disciplined manner. Contented with the essential characteristics of the societal unit, refinements are made in accordance with due process systems. Legitimate organizational procedures are developed for the purpose of accommodating change and redressing inequalities. Liberalism, then, is a belief in the integrity and viability of legal or normative structures for regulating resource distribution. Properly designed administrative structures preclude the need for turbulent confrontations. Should serious conflict erupt, the liberal encourages an analysis to determine whether the claims are legitimate and whether the conflict has developed because of inflexible or sluggish procedures. The caveat in the liberal model of the world is that turbulence, being rather like body temperature, has normal ranges. Departures from these ranges indicate difficulty in the societal unit. Turbulence then is associated with change and inordinate levels of turbulence are indicative of either inefficient due process systems or unreasonable protestors. The caveat then is the necessity for attribution of blame or responsibility. The blame attribution leads liberals into peculiar positions, such as viewing the cause of black ghetto riots as the "revolution of rising expectancies." The causal chain includes the rising awareness of black people of what society has to offer (presumably from TV), followed by the frustration of desires to obtain society's goods and benefit, which leads in turn to anger, aggression, etc. Liberals are likely to feel that change takes time and petitioners for change are unreasonable, and therefore accountable for unacceptable turbulence, when they expect too rapid a change.

Utopianism

Although the different views of the nature of societal conflict and turbulence aid us in understanding basic differences in political philosophies, a second dimension defining views of the nature of the idyllic societal unit must be considered. This is the dimension of utopianism. Basically, any time we find that a person feels a perfect organizational unit or societal state can be identified and imposed or developed we are dealing with a utopian. The opposite to this position is the evolutionary philosophy of a constantly changing society and style of life — which has no terminal state. Utopians believe that they know (or can identify) a near idyllic societal state and differ with respect to how this state should be instituted.

Some feel it should be imposed, others feel it should be forced to evolve, whereas others feel we are in it. Utopians and fascists therefore are frequently very similar philosophically. Persons with an evolutionary philosophy, in contrast, feel that society must always be in a state of change. There can be no terminal societal state. They differ again with respect to their feelings about the change. Is change itself good or must it be guided and regulated? Should one move slowly or rapidly, and should one deliberately slow down change or speed it up?

One could argue that some utopians fall into the reactionary category. The reactionary holds an extreme conservative view, and desires to return to the past. Previous less advanced or complicated conditions of society serve, for the reactionary, as ideal or at least preferable models of the way things should be tomorrow. The reactionary can, of course, support extremist positions advocating violent destruction of present social institutions to bring about a return to previous conditions. There are therefore interesting similarities between the extreme opposite positions on the political philosophy dimension.

When we consider all the various dimensions on which political or organizational philosophies can be based, it is easy to see why communication is extremely difficult if not impossible. To talk about the good life when one person values turbulence whereas the other fellow values quiescence is sufficient to give each person the notion that the other is of unsound mind. When concerned people who agree that society is badly screwed up ask "After the revolution what?" or state that they refuse to tear anything down without some plan or design for what is to be constructed in its place, meaningful communication with a revolutionary activist is precluded.

One thing is clear. Conflict is inevitable given the many inconsistent value systems in society. There is no question about the fact that the social science of conflict management is the science of the future.

The Silent Majority

Of course, in terms of numbers the largest group are the socially deceased. These are people who are inactive and without philosophical leanings of any conviction. They contribute mass or bulk to all of society's units, which makes for a sluggish and unresponsive society.

Forces concerned with the maintenance of the status quo gain considerable advantage from the inactive population. Their bulk creates tremendous inertia and cushioning. Efforts to change things then must have sufficient endurance to overcome the societal inertia. Even if some turbulence is generated, moreover, the great bulk of society is likely to ooze back into the areas of conflict with the result that order is restored but without any real change.

The uncommitted group derive their inactivity from many sources. They may be comfortable and secure and may have never felt threatened. Neither have they felt anything more than polite concern for the socially deprived people or modest regrets about the war. There are inactive people who attribute their apathy to perceived powerlessness or long years of deprivation. Nonpeople who parrot the views and imitate the activities of others either to gain acceptance into social groups or to conceal ignorance, also contribute to society's bulk. The "copouts" who have repudiated society's values and simply create or become part of a sanctuary group, connections with society severed as much as possible, can also be considered part of the silent majority.

Inactivity, therefore, may derive from ignorance, stupidity, docility, and cowardliness as well as either general complacency and satisfaction with the way society is moving or disgust and displeasure with it.

Estimates as to the size of the inactive or unconcerned group are hard to make. Black radicals estimate that at least 75% of blacks remain uncommitted and do not participate in active protest. Such organizers as the late Saul Alinsky estimated that if one could get 3% of the people in a community committed, one could launch a successful power protest. The number of unthinking and unconcerned people in large business organizations runs in the order of 85% by the most optimistic estimates, with comparable numbers of university administrators and professors contributing to society's bulk.

THEORIES OF CONFLICT

On Scientific Theory

Scientific theory serves the function of economizing mental effort. A good theory permits one to understand many different complex events by logically developing a basic principle (the deductive process). The fewer the number of basic principles the better the theory. Scientific theory differs from other forms of knowledge development in that it is not expected to provide a pictorial account of an event. A good theory of conflict, for example, would not permit us to predict or reconstruct the number of people killed, the extent or type of damage, the strategic moves of the protagonists, or any of the other details provided by a film or other descriptive account of the confrontation. A good theory, however, by analyzing the social structure surrounding the event, would allow us to predict (or understand) the likelihood of spiraling violence, the tendency for it to end by settlement rather than by exhaustion of one side's capabilities, the speed of the conflict, and, most important, where uncontrollable conflict is likely to occur. It may also give us some clues as to when the conflict is getting out of control and likely to spiral rapidly to insensate acts of violence unless someone intervenes. We might even learn how to turn arms races into peace races.

Regrettably we do not have a good theory of conflict. We have some pretty sharp strategies and a few good peacemakers but our overall understanding of the basic principles of conflict is pretty thin. We are still rather confused about the difference among various forms of threat and counterthreat. Our understanding of the distinction between offensive and defensive strategies is also far from complete.

We do have, however, a few hints about what factors are important for a robust theory of conflict. Likewise, although our attempts at theory construction are rather tenuous and anecdotal we are developing a discursive nomenclature that I am sure can, in the not too distant future, lead to the development of a theory of some power. To these primitive concepts we shall now direct our attention.

Assumptions Inherent in Theories

Most of our theories of conflict are quite inadequate as reflected in three basic problems. First is what Whitehead (cited by Proshansky *et al.*, 1970) refers to as the fallacy of misplaced concreteness. Societal conflict is extremely complex and involves a lot of circular and reciprocal feedback systems and loops. In conflict theory, and also in research in conflict, we are fixated on the notion of causality. That is, we attempt to isolate the Source, which we consider the active agent, whereas we consider the Target of an influence attempt as simply a reactive agent, one that does not have any influence over Source. We use such terms as "active" and "passive" agent and we in fact define power in terms of perceived change in probability of the occurrence of an event following the intervention of an agent.

The second problem with both our theories of conflict and some of the related conflict research is that there is an implicit acceptance of the medical model of conflict. The medical model, again, assumes that conflict is a cancerous growth within a societal unit and that conflict is the sign of an ill societal unit and must be excised, controlled, regulated, resolved, or managed. The sign of a healthy societal unit is one that is quiescent, one that is stable—that is, in distinction to what is called a realistic or friction view of conflict, which maintains that conflict is evidence of health because it is in fact inevitable in any societal unit that is moving. It is the inevitable by-product of social interaction and social processes. The analogy is drawn between conflict in a societal unit and heat from friction in a motor. Friction or heat is inevitable in any moving engine and the only time you have one without frictional heat is when it is not running or going anywhere. This analogy is applied to social units; that is, a society that is stagnant, dying, senile, and not going anywhere is one that is quiescent, one that is without conflict, and one that is stable. A sign of health is a turbulent society. This also reminds one of Emil Durkheim's (1949) statement that crime is inevitable in any society and is the evidence of a healthy society.

The third problem is that none of our theories deal in any meaningful way with conflict eruption. That is, they are all theories that apply to ongoing conflict. They offer no assistance in the analysis of the initial phases of conflict but deal with conflicts that are recognized, which means, of course, that such theories are focused on the terminal phases of conflicts. The initial causes of conflict are usually described with platitudinal statements, such as "conflict arises from deprivation" or "it arises from greed or envy."

Let us examine a couple of theories that I think elucidate some of the assumptions, particularly the assumption of the medical model of conflict. They also indicate, I think, that a large number of our theories develop from implicit notions about how we deal with conflict. That is, the theory follows the notion of how to deal with conflict rather than the other way around. The following conflict theories are representative but not exhaustive.

Agressor–Defender Model

The first theory of conflict is a formalization of the agressor–defender model. As the name of it implies, conflict in this theory is assumed to occur when somebody desires to gain access to something that somebody else considers to be his own. It is a static model; it says nothing about how the disparity has occurred or what conditions surround the disparity. As a static model, it leads to moralizing, in particular the attribution of blame. One must attribute blame in order to take action. It also implies that the way to deal with such conflicts is to punish the aggressor. That is, it leads to deterrence mentality. If one can make aggression, as it is defined within the context of this model, extremely costly and painful to the disrupter, then such disruption should be deterred. Of course, this opens up all of the problems associated with deterrence mentality.

Spiral Theory

The second theory I should like to consider is the spiral theory. That is, the theory based on the spiral model of conflict. A reactive model as opposed to a static model, it makes the assumption that conflict increases in magnitude and becomes more severe because each protagonist is reacting to threats and counterthreats of the opposition. Each person is attempting to outbid the other in rhetorical, material, and/or physical violence. We shall examine the bidding spiral in detail in a subsequent section.

The spiral model helps us understand ongoing conflict, where it is likely to lead, and some of the problems associated with conflict growth. However, if we attempt to go in the other direction, that is, to understand where conflict came from, we have the problem of infinite regression.

The spiral model assumes that there are at least two ways of dealing with conflict. First, if conflict is in fact reactive, then the way to reduce or resolve conflict is to not react. That is, if you do not react then the opposition has nothing to react to, nothing to counterbid, and the conflict is reduced. The second notion derives from the strategy of rapid escalation. If conflict is spiraling, and one can assume that the opposition is not going to escalate up to insane acts of destruction, one can attempt to seize control of the situation by rapidly escalating, that is, making extremely large jumps in the threat–counterthreat bidding process, such that any counterthreat puts the opposition over his level of tolerance for the conflict.

Administrative Theory

The third model we should consider is based on structural change. There are several variations of the administrative model. One in particular that I think is of interest assumes that when conflict develops in any societal unit, persons obtain positions of prominence because they are dealing with a situation threatening to the group or societal unit. After the threat or conflict is resolved or starts to reduce or dissipate, then these individuals perpetuate the threat, fear, and conflict in order to retain their leadership position. The popular examples used, of course, are business executives and the military. Business executives who gain a reputation of being efficient, successful, brushfire fighters frequently perpetuate the fear of brushfires for the purpose of retaining their leadership position. The military, prior to, during, and following the Second World War is an interesting example. During the Second World War the military achieved a position of prominence in the United States. Following the end of the Second World War, the fear, threats, and the conflict were perpetuated by the military to retain a position of prominence and power.

Conflict that derives from organizational structures or procedures can, according to many theorists, be managed by changing the organization, and a new trend in the field of organizational behavior is that of organizational development. "Organizational development" refers to the process of gradually introducing change designed to move the organization along some preselected path. If centralization of power and poor vertical communication seem to be the problem in a company, for example, the change agents (e.g., company specialists, hired consultants) may gradually introduce modified procedures designed to remove barriers to upward flow of information and may distribute areas of responsibility more widely in the organization. Such procedures are unending processes in actuality, for given the exploding changes in all our technologies and all our social norms, companies must constantly be accommodating change to ward off senility and to harness conflict. Conflict, again, serves a very useful function in any societal unit provided we can harness and manage it.

The caveat in the structural change model of conflict and conflict resolution is that one may simply be creating a different elite. Presumably to deal with organizational structure conflict, persons are needed who can diagnose the problem, can work out the intricate details of the planned change, have the skill necessary to implement the changes, and have the empirical skills needed to assess the changes and to provide the feedback information necessary to alter the changes as required. In effect, one may be simply creating another position of prominence and concentrated power unless some intelligent checks and balances are built into the initial organizational power structure.

Again the three theories discussed represent only a sampling of theories that have basically different assumptions, and the sampling is far from exhaustive. It does point out, however, that the criticisms mentioned earlier apply to all three of the theories, which are theoretically quite different. The theories deal only with ongoing conflict. They do not deal with conflict eruption and there is an implicit acceptance of the medical model of conflict with the attendant fixation on causes.

I think the essential details that one requires in a theory of conflict is an understanding of what are the conditions that give rise to it. About the most that is said about conflict eruption in any of the above formulations is that some perceived disparities give rise to conflict, but that is not saying very much.

Instinctual Theory

For the sake of completeness, we should mention the instinctual theory of aggression.

There are a few concepts that are dangerous once introduced into the popular scientific folklore. One such concept is that of the relationship between racial phenotypes and racial genotypes. Once people consider the possibility that a relationship may exist between what a person looks like and what a person is, then, of course, concepts ranging from Pushy Jews to Musical Colored Folks emerge. When one considers what is important in this world of ours, notions such as the above are recognized as nonsensical trivia. That scientists spend any time at all studying such a relationship is so absurd it would be hilarious if not such a tragic waste of resources.

The concept of instinctual aggression is just such a dangerous concept. There are several variations of the instinctual aggression concept. A popular version maintains that man has retained his primitive territorial instincts, which force him to attack others whom he perceives as invading his territory. Many animals hold and defend territories against intruders. When an intruder is encountered the animal makes ferocious threatening gestures. Such territorial squabbles, however, almost never result in any blood being shed. Typically, the intruder backs off when threatened. Similarly, when animals have dominance encounters, the losing animal can withdraw or yield by displaying a recognized distress signal such as exposing a vulnerable part of the body. Once the distress display is signaled the victor allows the loser to withdraw from the area.

Why man kills other men whereas animals, for all their ferocious displays, seldom shed blood has given rise to several refinements of the instinctual aggression notion. Because animals can be made to kill or badly harm conspecifics if they are constrained within a limited pen area or if their environment is made severely stressful, persons have argued that man has become a killer because his environment has become stressful and constrained.

Others have argued that as man has developed weapons that kill at long range, he no longer receives the distress signals that limit the extent to which he harms his victim. There are several other interesting variations and refinements of the instinctual aggression concept that attempt to explain why or how man came to the position of being the only apparent misfit in nature.

The instinctual aggression concept, unfortunately, has become an opiate for the masses who feel uncomfortable with traditional religious concepts. The instinctual aggression doctrine has become for many a new doctrine of original sin which has received the mantle of scientific respectability. If man has such instincts then, of course, all the horrors that go on around us every day are understandable if not inevitable. If man's destructiveness can be limited, it may take the form of diverted or sublimated aggressive drives, such as vigorous sports, together with the development of powerful regulatory agents within our society.

The reason such notions are dangerous is that man grasps at them to make sense out of his life experiences. By doing so, he can enjoy the comfort of an original sin concept that has scientific respectability. More important, he may feel that such destructiveness and inhumanity is inevitable and controllable only by force. Hence, he supports the development of powerful defense establishments and arrogant intervention policies. Even more basic, he loses sight of the fact that conflict results directly from the structure of society.

Conflict, to be sure, is inevitable. It is the natural byproduct of social interaction just as heat is produced when physical objects rub against one another. However, when we are concerned with conflict, the focus of our attention is the social structure from which the conflict emerges. The extent to which man's violence results from genetics is of far less concern to us than the properties of the social structure that generated the conflict.

THE MYTH OF LEGITIMACY

It is perfectly clear that the bureaucracy of any societal unit can define its role as the agent of control or as a change agent. Change can be suppressed or retarded by any number of means, which we shall shortly discuss at some length, or change can be encouraged and accommodated.

We must always keep in mind that one cannot concern oneself with attempting to determine which belligerent in any conflict situation is right, or whose violent behavior has been legitimate. To seek to identify which side has used legitimate force and which side has aggressed does nothing but cloud the issue. Legitimacy, then, is like the attribution of intent. Conflict behavior springs from conflict of interests. Attending to the latter increases the chances for resolving disputes at low levels of violence. Attending to the former implies that one is dealing only with later stages of conflict situations. Again, one must deal with the social structure that gives rise to conflicting wants and needs.

For example, during the 1968 Democratic National Convention in Chicago, extreme levels of violence between the police and, among other groups, protesting youth was witnessed by large numbers of people. Although this episode was later defined as a "police riot"[2] it is interesting to examine the tangle one encounters as soon as one searches for legitimacy. We can ask when the riot started. Did it "start" when the riot police arrived or when the police outfitted special riot squads? Were the demonstrators "violent" and the police

[2]Given Watergate, the following comment written by Eldridge Cleaver in 1970 is interesting:

 Most people are eager to say that the pigs flipped out, or that they finally showed their true colors. I disagree, I believe that what happened in Chicago is a direct result of conspiracies hatched by the Republican Party and those who supported Nixon for

(Footnote 2 continued on p. 72)

conflict control agents? Was the police action justified to maintain order even though they "overacted"? Were the protestors' violent actions against illegitimate restraint and suppression justified? The questions, or rather interpretations, are endless when one's analysis is based on a biased definition of violence. Any analysis or theory based on such terms as "legitimate," "justifiable," or "abnormal" protest must be incorrect from the bottom to the top. Is plebeian violence against an illegitimate order justifiable? Is Establishment violence to maintain minimum order an example of justifiable force? Or is such violence more justifiable than partisan violence designed to create disorder to facilitate change?

When one's analysis of conflict situations is clouded by attributions of causality (blame) to one of the protagonists or by judgments of legitimacy, one's time is likely to be wasted. It is troublesome when conflict analysts, both practitioners and theorists, fall into the same trap so frequently because their confusion not only wastes our time but, more seriously, exposes us to unacceptable menace and danger.

Because attempting to assess the extent of legitimacy of violent action entangles us, it is tempting to divide bureaucratic repression on the dimension of intent. However, like attempting to include intent in a definition of violence, attribution of intent in assessing legal violence is equally misleading and simply confuses an already confusing issue. Does it really matter whether or not an injustice results from or is maintained by incompetence, apathy, indifference, ignorance, or malevolent intent? We argue, on compassionate grounds, that bureaucratic violence is more deplorable when it results from malfeasance than when it results from "well-intentioned" but, alas, incorrect action. However, as Margaret Atwood (1972) points out in her novel *Surfacing*, "stupidity is the same as evil if you judge by the results [p. 29]." Concern focused on the intent of legal violence encourages bureaucrats to label war departments as departments of defense, invasions or attacks as protective insurgencies, keepers as correction officers, and so on. All violence is defensive. Violence protects property, people, and privilege. The analysis of violence, legal or partisan, theirs or ours, is rendered hopeless when we entangle ourselves in such concepts as intent, blame, or legitimacy.

President, working hand in hand with the racist, right-wing John Birchers who control the police departments in many important cities throughout the country. The Republicans knew that they had to move in a decisive manner or risk the Democrats' winning the election by a close margin. Nixon, having lost once on a cliff-hanger, was not taking any more chances. So someone dreamed up the greedy idea of shocking the American people into fear and hysteria and at the same time both wrecking the Democratic National Convention and firmly establishing in the minds of the American people the image of the Democrats as being responsible for the violence going down in Babylon. The situation was made to order for a pig setup. And it worked [p. 9].

TEMPORAL CONFUSION AND THE MYTH OF AGITATORS

One of the criticisms of both our theories of conflict as well as our conceptions of power is a fixation on causality. When we can identify two events, one of which has preceded the second, we tend to attribute causality to the first event. That is, we are prone to infer that the first event has caused or influenced the second. Our confusion about causality usually comes about because we analyze restricted time periods. That is, we take a time slice, so to speak, and attempt to analyze the process taking place within that time period.

Let us look at a few examples. Successful commodity speculators are usually characterized by an adherence to a loss limiting rule. If they purchase an option on a future at, say, $2.00 per unit, they may set their mandatory sell level at, say, $1.90 per unit. If the price of the future drops below $1.90, they sell immediately. In essence they do not permit themselves to hypothesize about temporal events—a selection is either correct or incorrect. Once the price hits $1.90, the selection is considered incorrect and should be disposed of. Unsuccessful future speculators, in contrast, are reluctant to acknowledge that they have made a mistake. When the price goes down, they look for reasons to believe that the trend will reverse itself, thus verifying their initial good judgment. Successful speculators also tend to have a hard and fast profit-taking rule. Riding profit, for example, means that one adjusts sell levels as prices increase. As the price goes up from, say, $2.00 to $2.50 per unit, they may increase their mandatory sell levels by, say, 10¢ from $1.90 to $2.00, to $2.10, . . . to $2.40. The successful speculator, then, forces himself to ignore trends or causality after he has made a purchase. He imposes constraints on his alternatives to prevent erroneous causal analysis. His range of options in the above example are limited to a 10¢ drop in price, regardless of the overall price trend.

Another example is based on the misunderstanding of how one evaluates previous actions. Success or failure are poor indicators of the propriety or effectiveness of one's procedures. If a company is making a profit or if one's broker has fingered ten straight winners, it tells us almost nothing about the system, methods, or procedures of the company's management or about our stockbroker's acumen.

Success may be totally unrelated to the procedure we use to achieve success. It may have happened accidentally, it may have occurred because we fortunately have not done something, or it may have happened for reasons unrelated to our own behavior. The stockbroker error can be diagrammed as in Figure 1.

Let us assume that your broker is hot on oil stocks. Assume also that for who knows what reason the market trend for oils is increasing. Now regardless of when the broker says buy, if he can persuade you to hold the stock long enough, it increases in price even though there may be a temporary drop in price. After a few such successes we conclude that our broker is pretty sharp

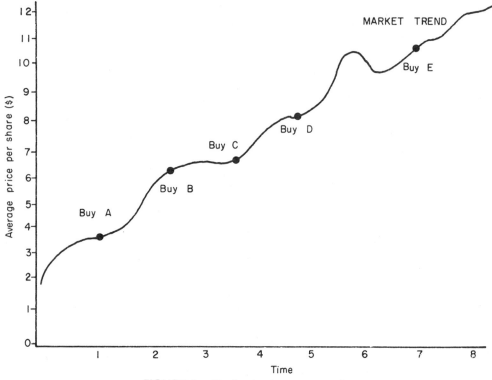

FIGURE 1.   Stock price increase over time.

indeed, having apparently developed an excellent forecasting system. The disaster that frequently follows this is known to many investors. In short, the causal fixation has led to an incorrect attribution of causality. Because our stockbroker's buy statement has preceded the rise in price we attribute skill to the broker.

Management typically makes exactly the same error. The classic statement, of course, is: "What we are doing must be right since we are making a profit." Success or goal attainment, then, is not an adequate indicator of the suitability, optimality, or effectiveness of procedures preceding that state.

The military has an unusual tendency to try to justify their procedures using the inappropriate attribution of cause. The purchase of weapon systems for the purpose of deterring a presumed enemy offers one of the more hilarious examples. Weapons developed for deterrent purposes must never be used. If they are used, of course, they have not deterred the opposition. If they are not used, then deterrence has been successful; hence, the original decision to develop and deploy the system must have been a correct one. Weapon purchases then must be justified on theoretical grounds. If you do not use them, then developing the capability has been a correct decision. If one does use them, then of course they have been needed and again purchase has been justified. This of course has all of the logical sophistication of any superstitious ritual from the stroking of a rabbit's foot to the offering of human sacrifices.

The myth of conflict instigation, being attributed to agitators, reflects this temporal fallacy. The propaganda spread by police agencies, federal police agencies in particular, attempts to lead the population to believe that a few troublemakers enter a situation, stir up discontent, and precipitate a conflict.

Now it is true that prior to and during highly visible conflicts, persons having activist reputations frequently have been involved. Usually one finds that a Rubin, a Brown, or an Alinsky has just given a talk or participated in a rally or a seminar. It is also true that conflict, like any other social action, has an identifiable leadership even if highly transitory. However, what does this mean? What does this tell us about conflict eruption?

People who hold the agitation model of conflict, conceptualize disruptions as a steep precipice. Agitators push well-meaning (and apparently sheeplike) people off the plateau of peace and quiescence into the trough of conflict and disruption. Conflict, however, as Schelling (1963) has pointed out, is more like a slippery slope. If allowed to continue, the opposing groups find themselves in a situation in which they slip into more and more serious conflict despite efforts to stop it. Consider the schematic diagram in Figure 2.

Conflict is a dimension that goes from trivial disruption to insensate acts of destruction. Low-level stages of the conflict having been ignored, disruption increases to the period of notice, at which time society's control agents (e.g., police, administrators, bosses) become aware of and keep an eye on the situation. If the conflict continues to the intolerable conflict range—the range at which the Establishment must react—the Establishment scans the brief history of its awareness of the conflict. Salient people or events are assumed to be casually related to the later intolerable range conflict. In the diagram below,

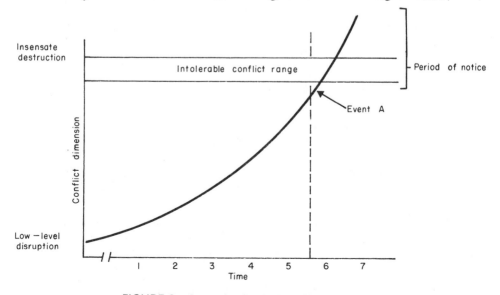

FIGURE 2.   Increasing level of conflict over time.

if Jerry Rubin was Event A and if he has given an invited talk at a university that has subsequently exploded, the attempt to find a cause for the conflict by searching backward from the intolerable range leads to an erroneous attribution of causality—namely, Rubin. Now it goes without saying that the presence of committed and active people should speed up or focus a social movement, be it a glass recycling campaign or a riot. It also goes without saying that leadership emerges in all social movements. The causal fallacy, the myth of conspiratorial agitation, is that of attributing control or causality to recognizable features of a conflict. Groups in conflict want leadership; protestors want to hear how the Alinskys brought some group to its knees; kids experiencing the exhilaration of active protest want to enhance their excitement and exhilaration by identifying with the Rubins; and activists want to go where the action is. The conflict itself, the protesting group, the issues, the unresponsive Establishment, the ideological appeal of the issues "cause" the appearance of the "agitators" and "leaders" as much as they "cause" the turbulence. To focus attention on the "outside agitators" or "local troublemakers" is rather like trying to blame the south pole magnet for pulling the north pole magnet across a table. It is logically absurd.

Now why do society's control agents propagate the agitator myth? The FBI, under Mr. Hoover, attributed many campus disruptions to a few agitators—usually Communists. Southern sheriffs in the early days of the civil rights protest attributed the turbulence to Northern "troublemakers." Northern politicians faced with ghetto riots similarly found other presumed agitators—always a small minority. Of course, it is a minority. If one finds ten active and concerned people in a hundred, one is sitting on a keg of dynamite.

Law and Order agents perpetuate the agitation myth for political purposes. First, it is simple and can be sold to a public who cannot understand why everyone cannot be nice and be satisfied with what they have. It justifies the development and use of police hardware. It supports the concentration of power and the development of restrictive laws and control and surveillance proce-dures. It makes laughable laws, which so flagrantly violate our constitutional rights, possible. In short, it is appropriate to the creation of a Law and Order elite.

Now in the broader context we are concerned with the data that adminis-trators have to evaluate the probity of courses of action that they are following. In short, the question is, "how do we know we are doing what we think we are doing?" The problem of evaluation is universal and it is particularly trouble-some for managers. Taking the common situation of a human disorder or ailment, we know that in a large number of cases such disorders simply go away if they are left alone. For the sake of argument, let us assume that we are dealing with a disorder that has a remission rate of 50%. That is, if we do absolutely nothing for or to the people, 50% of those people return to normal health. With that kind of natural remission rate it is easy to see how every well-meaning but, alas, uninformed therapist can stay in business and persuade an unwary population that the treatment procedures work.

Managers are in roughly the same sort of situation when they look at profit as their indicator of success. Using profit as a measure of success is a pervasive myth in society. The reason that profit is not a good indicator is because we do not know what is generating the profit and we can only make the assumption that what we are doing is in some way responsible. Companies may be making money because they are in a market in which it is impossible to lose money or because the other company's advertising is so offensive that they are getting a backlash of people buying their product simply because they do not want to buy the other fellow's product.

Sherlock Holmes management involves being very critical of simple-minded cause–effect explanations. In the area of conflict, for example, myopic administrators simply start with the explosive situation and look back in time to find the most salient preceding event. Managers whose departments are coming under scrutiny point to profit as an indicator of the merit of their procedures. Therapists, doctors, teachers, snake-oil salesmen, and TV repairmen, to say nothing of the marketers of hair growers, beauty creams, and muscle-building programs, can all follow the simple procedure of searching back through their files to pick up a few testimonials from contented people. The distressing part about the problem of temporal confusion and the errors of evaluation is that people may be convinced that their procedures are successful when they are not.

Returning to our therapist who has a 50% remission rate, the people he "cures," that is, the people who get better anyway, are those who remain in therapy through to conclusion. Individuals who are not "responding," that is, those whose symptoms or disorders do not naturally remit, do not see the therapy through to completion because they get frustrated and discouraged. Hence, at the end of the treatment the therapist has a long list of individuals who are prepared to swear and truly believe that the procedures being used on them are responsible for their improvement.

This form of confusion and mythology is extraordinarily difficult to counteract in any organization. The Sherlock Holmes administrator must be prepared to question everyone's source of data and be unrelentless in his search for adequate indicators. Most important, however, he must be prepared for individuals who are completely deluded about cause–effect relationships, people whose data or bases for their beliefs are logically unacceptable but are so caught up with magical thinking that they cannot impassionately assess the situation in which they have been involved.

A second part to this problem is that individuals very frequently are not capable of breaking a situation down into multiple causes and multiple effects. For example, there may be 15 or 20 things that a company is doing to make a product appealing. They may have done their market surveys appropriately, incorporated many features of design that are highly desirable, packaged the product so that it has a high degree of immediate appeal to customers, advertised it in the correct markets and with the correct appeals, etc. However, if the product is successful (i.e., a profit is made), the tendency is to accept all of the things that have occurred prior to the making of a profit as being correct or most suitable. The problem is an obvious one. We need indicators that are precise and flexible enough so that we can assess and modify any particular aspect of the procedures we are using to accomplish what we want to accomplish. The fact that we can place Event A before Event B does not imply causality. The fact that something desirable is happening does not imply that our activities brought it about, and reliance on such inappropriate indicators can only lure us into a smugness that blows up in our face once something goes wrong and we do not know why.

PREVIEW OF THE STRUCTURAL THEORY OF CONFLICT

Conflict is part of social interaction. It is inevitable. With respect to any particular resource pool there are individuals who have greater and lesser direct distribution prerogatives over that resource pool. That is, people at the top have direct access to it and people at the bottom gain access to the resources of the pool only through the high-status individuals. The Have-Nots are dependent on the Haves for access to the resource pool. The people with limited access to the resource pool are interested in turbulence. Only through turbulence in the society, in fact, can they increase their access to the resource pool. The Haves, however, are concerned with stability, the maintenance of the status quo, and quiescence, for by maintaining the status quo they retain their privileged control over the resource pool.

Now conflict, I think, erupts because of what happens to the dialogue between those with greater control and those with less control during the very early stages of perceived disparity. The individuals with less control attempt to petition the Haves for a greater share of the resource pool. Haves develop all sorts of procedures, particularly in organizational units, for dealing with these petitions, that is, for slowing them down. We have such processes as administrative orbiting; creeping progress; the development of grievance channels that do not lead anywhere; extreme organizational complexity that makes it very difficult for people to understand how to get into the organization, where to petition the organization, and how to keep track of what happens to their petition once it has entered the organization; and, of course, outright suppression.

Now, the critical aspect in analyzing conflict situations is analysis of the resource pools. There are some resource pools that are depletable, such as water or money. There are others that are nondepletable, such as knowledge;

for example, my giving away knowledge does not in any way reduce the amount that I have.

One important resource pool consideration is that of the overlapping need-structure system. Consider a situation in which an individual is alone in a room. He has, I think we can argue, a homeostatic relationship with his environment. If he is cold he puts on more clothing or turns up the thermostat. If he is warm he takes off clothing or turns down the heat. When he enters a room he turns on the lights and makes the light level and the configuration of the light consistent with the function that he is going to perform in that room. If he is going to read he has a certain configuration, if he wants to relax he has another configuration, if he wants to sleep, yet another one. He has configurations that are associated with relaxing environments, and others associated with working environments. With respect to sound or background music, for example, he comes in and he adjusts that level of music so that it is consistent with the function he is attempting to perform and to the extent that it succeeds or falls short of these limits then he adjusts the sound or light level or the heat level to what he considers to be optimal.

Now, consider a situation in which we have two people in the same room. We are now in a situation in which we have a social homeostatic system, which may, in fact, be a contradiction of terms. In this particular situation, let us assume that we have somebody who wants a high level of stimulation and somebody who wants a low level of stimulation. To what extent does this lend itself to bargaining? To what extent is it negotiable? Do you, in fact, get some middling level of heat or sound that is unacceptable to both parties? Or do you get one person satisfying his or her optimal level at the expense of the other individual and, if that is true, what factors determine who shall be satisfied? If you put strangers in the same room who, let us say, both like a low level of background music, does a situation of pluralistic ignorance develop in which either sets the level of background music above that which either would set it if they were alone in the room?

THE STRUCTURAL THEORY OF CONFLICT

Dynamics of Conflict

The basic truth, so to speak, of all theories of conflict is that there exists a restricted quantity of something of value that is coveted by some group of persons. The something of value, referred to as the resource pool, can be any tangible or intangible entity such as money, water, freedom, sexual objects, authority, responsibility, wine, bullfrogs, fishhooks, or victory. The only requirement is that the element be considered valuable by members of the group and that the amount be restricted. For two men in a life raft in the middle of the Atlantic, neither salt water nor air would constitute resource pools, whereas a gallon of fresh water or a single loaf of bread would certainly qualify.

The second principle is that with respect to any resource pool some person or persons has or gains greater distribution prerogatives over the pool than other persons who also want access to the same pool. Now, although it may seem as though we have taken a considerable and perhaps untenable logical jump by assuming that someone will gain greater access to the pool than others, we must remember that this inequality may develop as a result of virtually any normal difference between persons or groups. A stronger man can make greater claims to limited food supplies, patriarchs in societies in which they are respected have disciplinary prerogatives, administrators can limit your freedom because they can waste your time, the wealthy can make your needs or desires too expensive for you to satisfy, the brilliant can force the less intelligent to expend greater energy than they to acquire the same resource, and so on.

Will Durant (1954) in Volume One of his *Story of Civilization* describes this process of multiplying inequalities:

> As the life of a society becomes more complex, and the division of labor differentiates men into diverse occupations and trades, it becomes more and more unlikely that all these services will be equally valuable to the group; inevitably those whose greater ability enables them to perform the more vital functions will take more than their equal share of the rising wealth of the group. Every growing civilization is a scene of multiplying inequalities; the natural differences of human endowment unite with differences of opportunity to produce artificial differences of wealth and power; and where no laws or despots suppress these artificial inequalities they reach at last a bursting point where the poor have nothing to lose by violence, and the chaos of revolution levels men again into a community of destitution [p. 18].

The person or persons who have greater distribution prerogatives over the resource pool are referred to here as the Haves and the second group is referred to as the Have-Nots.

It should also be noted that the Have–Have-Not principle incorporates the assumption that all conflicts involve two and only two parties. Although we can think of many situations in which seemingly many separate groups fight over the same resource pool, history has pointed out that eventually coalitions and other alliances form between various groups so that effectively the conflict involves only two protagonists. Wars are our best example of the two-protagonist principle. Alliances, albeit at times temporary, form between the various warring nations. After termination of the conflict other alliances form, but for practical purposes during any period of time we care to examine, the conflict involves two parties.

It should also be noted that when analyzing a conflict we limit our analysis to one resource pool. In wars, as in other conflicts, the principle conflict may be between two alliances of nations. Within any particular alliance, internecine conflicts may occur over other, distinctly separate resource pools. The analysis of a complex conflict situation then requires that one correctly identify the single resource pool which is the focal point of the particular conflict in question. A large-scale conflict may involve many resource pools and therefore many separate conflicts. Keep in mind, however, that when we refer to Haves and Have-Nots we are referring to the distribution prerogatives over one and only one resource pool. Haves with respect to one pool may be Have-Nots with respect to some other resource pool.

From the above two principles we can now say a lot about what happens in conflict situations. As a point of departure, assume that with respect to a particular resource pool the group of protagonists is limited in size (Figure 3). Some persons within that group have greater control over the distribution of the resource pool. The group polarizes into Haves and Have-Nots because some individuals can contribute more to any alliance determined to inequitably distribute the pool than can those others within the group who have limited, if any, control over the pool. The polarization process continues, demarcating those with more from those with less control of prerogatives over the pool. The primary allegiance of all Haves, even those with limited privilege, is to the Have group. For only by allegiance to the Have group can the lesser Haves, so to speak, continue to enjoy their minor privilege.

As polarization continues, the distribution process for the resource pool becomes one in which the Haves' control becomes more complete, the exploitation of the resource pool by the Haves is direct and the Have-Not portion, if any, of the resource pool comes directly from the Haves as shown in Figure 3.

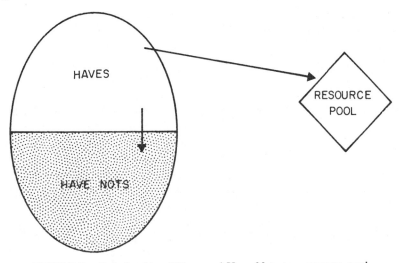

FIGURE 3.   Relationship of Have and Have-Nots to a resource pool.

Now, given the general Have–Have-Not structure many aspects of the conflict process become intuitively clear. Haves are committed to the status quo. They are concerned with stability and quiescence and have no interest in change, for change would or could deprive them of their special privileges. The Have-Nots, in contrast, have no interest in stability nor in the maintenance of the status quo, for only through instability and turbulence can they hope to enhance their control over the resource pool. The Haves are therefore concerned with surveillance and control (law and order), whereas the driving force from within the Have-Not group is directed toward activism, if not revolution.

Bureaucratization

Inequity or special privilege with respect to resource pool distribution creates bureaucratization. Systems must be established to maintain slow disciplined change, to maintain order to deal with undesirable disrupters, to deal with any attempts by Have-Nots to deprive Haves of their privilege by means such as theft or threat. Bureaucracies then are the protective buffers the Haves develop and maintain between themselves and the Have-Nots. They are effective to the extent that the Haves do, in fact, have firm control over the resource pool. Thereby, having control of distribution of the resource to the Have-Nots, the bureaucracies are accepted as legitimate adjudicating bodies.

The acceptance of the bureaucracy as legitimate is based on shared value systems between the Have and Have-Not groups. The feudal system depended on both groups accepting the rights and privilege of the land-owning aristocracy. University systems survive as they are because sufficiently large numbers of both groups within the institution share the value of societies granting special privileges to the duly initiated.

In the United States we have one of the poorest medical systems of any developed country in the world because for so long we have shared the notion of the "princely profession" and allowed questions of public welfare to be influenced by an organizationally senile and arrogant trade union. The examples of Have-Not groups legitimizing the social position of the Haves by identifying with the values of the Haves is, of course, endless.

The Have bureaucracy becomes most disquieted when it sees evidence of rejection or repudiation of the Haves' value systems. As we shall discuss shortly, Haves do legislate against values. The activist youth in our society, for example, are seen as a major threat to the Have establishment because they openly reject Have establishment values of special privilege within our society. The control procedures being used by the Establishment are such flagrant violations of our constitutional rights it is almost laughable.

Barriers to Change

A major function of the bureaucracy is to slow down, if not completely abort, any requests or appeals for change from the Have-Nots. The procedures or systems utilized by bureaucracies for maintenance of the status quo are numerous but share the function of either minimizing the frequency of appeals for change or by slowing and/or atrophying any appeals that do in fact enter the bureaucracy. When bureaucracies are kept complex and inefficient it becomes difficult to make a request or appeal, for one never can seem to find out where in the organization to insert the petition. The "It's not my job—see the guy down the hall" structure discourages a fair number of persons from making requests.

A second procedure used by Have bureaucracies is that of administrative orbiting. The basic procedure in administrative orbiting is that of accepting petitions for change but keeping them in a state of creeping progress until the energies of the petitioning group are drained. Losing a request within the bureaucracy is another method, but one that is usually not as effective as keeping the issues "under consideration" but at a pace too slow to pose any real threat of other than trivial changes. If well orchestrated, administrative orbiting can frequently drain the energies and resources of the petitioning group so that they simply go away.

Now, interpreted from the conflict position bureaucracies do not emerge and become complex and inefficient because such systems are dysfunctional; quite to the contrary, such cumbersomeness serves the purpose of protecting the privileged position of the Haves. Such institutions become senile and repressive when they have not been jibed, threatened, petitioned, and attacked to keep them active, if not turbulent. For the quiescence sought by all bureaucracies amounts to a perpetuation of the status quo, a perpetuation of early systems and definitions that, because they do not adjust to everyday changes, become completely inconsistent with, if not totally irrelevant to, present day society. It is the fear of most activists and revolutionaries, moreover, that should success be achieved with the establishment of a new or radically changed societal unit, any concentrated administrative function may become corrupted by the availability through conspiracy of special privilege or power.

The Eruption of Conflict

Given the Have–Have-Not system and bureaucratic buffering, Have-Not grievances must, to be in any real sense successful, operate outside of the organizational structure. To have some chance of success a petitioning group must (1) find an issue that has substantive if not ideological appeal to a potentially large constituency; (2) determine the extent of immediate and long-term support within the Have-Not group; (3) get the ear of the Establishment; (4) make delay costly to the Establishment; (5) monitor the change; (6) make departures from the Have-Not requests costly to the Establishment; (7) find new issues to keep the energies of the petitioners mobilized, for nothing more destroys a powerful protest group quite as much as success; (8) and make itself politically recognized as a bona fide representational group for a Have-Not constituency.

There is no question about the importance of the focal issue of the petitioning or protesting group. If ideologically important, the issue can markedly increase the potential size of the Have-Not activists who are to maintain long-term support of the petitioning. There may be issues that are so important that people not only march with signs but participate in guerilla attacks against property. An Establishment faced with such a potential early in the conflict may well find it expedient to accommodate.

Petitioning groups have a variety of methods for determining their bases of support. Marches, rallies, petitions, strikes, exemplar protests, and the like, all can serve the function of determining the potential size of the activist group. Community organizers, in contrast, tend to use individual contacts to both determine critical issues and get some feel for the potential size of their activists and their nonparticipative support. Most good community organizers make protest a grass roots, ground-swelling conflict that has great potential both in terms of size of the activist group and in terms of the repertoire of issues available to keep the organization mobilized. Amateur protestors tend to try to sell their issues to others and tend to rely on threats and noise as opposed to the mobilization of a dangerously large constituency and the strategic planning of the method for attacking the Establishment.

We shall concern ourselves presently with the threat—counterthreat conspiratorial model for spiraling conflict for it is, I believe, the basic form from which other special conflict processes can be derived. Following the above-mentioned steps in the protest procedure, the first issue is that of estimating the probability of success. If the dissenting group is large or the issue important enough to generate sustained and radical protest, then some uncertainty exists as to the potential success of any particular demand for change. One does not engage in sustained protest activities when the probability of success is zero. Similarly, one does not resist if defense is impossible. For conflicts to develop, then, the outcome after engagement of both parties must be uncertain.

After it is recognized that the Establishment is vulnerable, the Have-Not group must get the ear of the Have bureaucracy. Frequently, initial requests for change take place at very low levels of threat and are made through recognized due process channels. A student may take an issue to a Dean, an employee may petition his immediate superior, a welfare recipient may protest to a regional supervisor, a homeowner in an urban renewal disaster area may protest to the regional planning office, etc., etc. Such protests, although perhaps rhetorically aggressive from a conflict point of view, typically take place at very low levels of violence. To the extent that the Establishment delays or ignores such low threat level protests, the potential for increased threat increases. In order to get the ear of an indifferent bureaucracy one must move outside of recognized bureaucratic channels. To do so one must create, so to speak, one's own grievance channel. To get the ear of the Establishment, moreover, one frequently must wrap one's request for change in an envelope of threat. The threat opens the channel by getting attention. To the extent that Establishments ignore low-threat petitions for change, forcing petitioners to move outside bureaucratic channels with enhanced threats, the Establishments must recognize their contribution to starting a spiral of violence. The first threat gets an attentive reaction. We are now on the bottom step of the escalator of violence, to which we shall now turn our attention.

The Conflict Dimension

Conflict is a dimension. What few people seem to realize is that the same conflict that ends with highly destructive acts begins with quite peaceful requests or appeals for change. Highly violent destructive conflicts do not simply emerge out of society. Conflict is not self-generative. It must be born out of inequity and nurtured long and carefully before it has a fighting chance of developing into an event of prominence. The infant mortality rate of newborn conflicts is extremely large.

The confusion that prevails results from the fact that people only become aware of and consider terminal conflicts. Fully developed healthy conflicts that are violent and uncontrollable and likely to have a long and active maturity are the ones we read about. We also move away from them when we can because they are terribly frightening. Such terminal conflicts also draw much comment regarding strategies of control that should be or should have been used by protagonists with whom we identify or who represent us. For example, the FLQ crises in Quebec drew much comment about the appropriateness of the Federal government's response to the kidnappings and killings. The Black Panther Party's encounters with the police, the many student "uprisings," etc., all draw much comment about how the situation should be handled. The problem with analyzing terminal or mature state conflicts is that one cannot. Such conflicts are out of hand and moving at unnerving speed. There is no best response, only lucky breaks, when one has let a conflict get to such an uncontrollable state.

Conflict, then, is a dimension that goes from looks of disappointment at one end to mass murder at the other—again, remember, dealing with only one resource pool:

Early   Period of notice

---

reciprocal   The conflict dimension
recognition
of inequality

The FLQ crises, racial riots, ghetto riots, university explosions, etc. are all conflicts up in the shaded section of the above dimension. From a conflict analysis point of view they represent tiny cross sections of the total dynamic process, certainly too thin to be properly analyzed and certainly too thin or too late, I should say, to do much about. The conflict is out of hand. The time dimension related to the above conflict dimension should also be noted. From start to period of notice might be 20 years or even 100 years. The crises in Watts, Chicago, Detroit, Berkeley, Columbia, Kent, Dublin, Quebec, or wherever represent such a trivial time period within the total time dimension of the conflict that the answer to the "what should we do?" question is to do anything that may turn the head of the exploding violence, anything that may slow it down, anything that may lead to reversing the escalator of violence—and further violence should be the last, not the first, alternative considered. One hundred years of inequality cannot be resolved rapidly enough to stop an explosion. A bureaucracy that has become senile and rigid over a 10- or 20-year period and responds to a conflict that has been developing, festering, and gaining momentum over a 3- or 4-year period cannot hope to understand the conflict, much less deal with it.

I have been concentrating on the incompetence of the bureaucracy. I have done so because the senility, rigidity, and arrogance that develops in bureaucracies is the pivotal point of all sizeable conflicts. This concentration should not imply, however, that protesting or petitioning groups cannot be incompetent, immature, unreasonable, arrogant, or any other pejorative adjective one cares to imply. Protestors may be disruptive for the hell of it.

We have discussed the factors that give rise to the initial use of force or threat of force within the Have–Have-Not conspiratorial model of conflict. We have also discussed the time dimension of conflict and the fact that concentration on the terminal phases of conflict is myopic indeed. We shall now turn our attention to the details of the growth process of conflict.

The Conflict Growth Process

The terms *violence* and *escalator of violence* are to some extent misleading. It is true that threat elicits counterthreat and aggressive acts elicit retaliatory strikes. The terms are misleading to the extent that they lead us to concentrate on later stages of the conflict where the threat–counterthreat spiral is moving rapidly.

There are several concepts important to our understanding of conflict growth processes. First is the concept of bargaining. To bargain means that one makes a bid, or promises to act, under strictly defined circumstances. We promise to pay a barber to cut our hair when we sit in his chair. We promise to pay a contractor on satisfactory completion of the contract. We promise to hurt a child if the child disobeys. We promise to strike if an employer does not accede to a demand. We promise to retaliate if someone behaves in a manner we consider undesirable, and so on. Conflict processes are bid systems. In the opening rounds of a conflict, Have-Nots may appeal to the Haves' sense of guilt associated with the inequality. If the Haves deny the appeal or ignore it, the Have-Nots may counter with publicity. That is, they may tell others of the inequity hoping to bring the pressure of public scrutiny and disapproval on the Have group.

The opening rounds of threat bids in the conflict process are usually at very low levels of violence. However, if the conflict remains unresolved at that level, the bids of violence increase. Instead of threatening publicity, for example, the petitioning group may threaten mildly disruptive or disobedient acts. Work slowdowns, pickets, traffic blockades, sit-ins, organized nuisance complaints, etc. are all low violence level bids. The response to such threats is usually that of a retaliatory and more severe threat. Lost pay, arrest, suspension, restricted privilege, etc. are all retaliatory bids at a higher level of violence.

Now, the important aspect of the bidding system in a spiraling conflict is not the exact nature of the bids nor the specific strategies used by each protagonist. The critical point is that each counterbid by both parties to the conflict are ever greater levels of violence. The dynamic property of conflict spirals is that each succeeding promise to harm must be at a greater level than the opposition's preceding bid. To deter the opposition one must promise, and be perceived capable of delivering, a greater punishment than the opposition has promised. That is, the magnitude of the threat (or harm) must be ever-increasing over the immediately previous bid. The schematic diagram in Figure 4 shows the bid structure and the attendant temporal course the conflict takes. It depicts a conflict spiral with the time dimension fixed. Usually during conflict engagements, the bidding tempo increases. That is, the time between bids becomes increasingly shorter. With both time and bid size contributing to rapid escalation, therefore, conflict can literally explode.

As we move up the escalator of violence, each bid–counterbid unit is like a game of chicken in miniature. If one yields, the game is over, whereas if one can muster the resources to bid again one is still in the game. We are not concerned here with how one wins such encounters strategically or whether massive preliminary bids are more effective than a graduated game. The various strategies used in such encounters and their effects on conflict spirals are discussed in a subsequent section. For our purposes we are only concerned

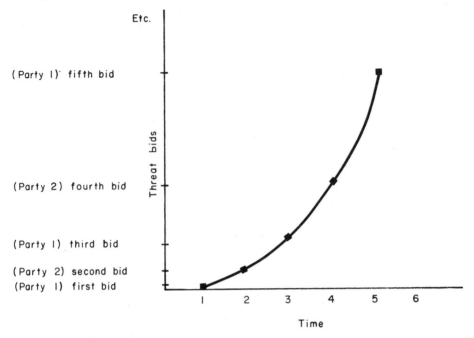

FIGURE 4.   Bidding process over time in conflict spiral.

with the fact that the attempt to win such encounters leads to increasingly larger bids of violence.

The second concept already discussed is the redefinition of the conflict structure from a negotiable situation to a nonnegotiable one. For a conflict to continue to the point of high levels of violence, both parties to the conflict must perceive the situation in win–loss terms. That is, both parties get themselves into the state of being more concerned with beating the opponent than they are about access to the original resource pool. In effect then both parties lose sight of what the conflict is or was all about. Rather than being concerned about the original resource pool, they become concerned with winning or at least not yielding. There can be only one winner, which makes such situations highly volatile and nonnegotiable. I may add as an aside that one of the major tasks of a mediator in such situations is that of correcting the perceptions of the protagonists, to get them away from win–loss definitions of the conflict and back to a clear perception of the original resource pool.

The third important factor in such conflicts is that of the tempo of bargaining. In the early stages of any conflict, the speed with which bids are made and countered is quite slow. As the threat increases, the pressure to respond rapidly both to prevent the execution of the threat or to minimize the costs associated with that threat as well as the pressure to escalate to seize the initiative is extraordinarily great. When the bidding tempo is great (fast) the probability of error is very great. Persons make mistakes when they do not have the luxury of time and when they cannot adequately explore alternatives. When one is responding to the other party's threat, the initiative lies with the other party. If you can rapidly escalate the conflict, the opposition is responding to you.

At high levels of threatened or actual violence, delay also implies defeat. One responds rapidly to a threat with a larger threat simply to demonstrate that one is still very much in the game and not at all close to the limits of one's resolve or capabilities.

In summary, threat–counterthreat spirals result from the increasing size of each additional threat, the redefinition of the conflict into a yield–nonyield format, and the increasing tempo of bidding. At the upper ends of a spiral the steps on the escalator are extremely large and the tempo of bidding is such that it gets out of hand, leading to insensate acts of violence despite the best efforts of persons on both sides of the conflict to stop it.

VIOLENCE LIMITERS

Punitive Capability

Not all conflicts blow up into insensate acts of violence. One is tempted to think that the violence of a conflict is directly related to the value or importance of the resource pool. A little reflection however, points out that the level of violence should be determined by factors such as the availability of weapons or the availability to in some way harm the opposition. The greater the available punitive options, the greater the tendency for persons or nations to use them.

Precision

The precision of one's weapons or options also affects the conflict process. For if one only has large-magnitude punishers available, each bid of the conflict is larger, with the result that higher levels of violence are reached more rapidly. Precise weapons or options permit each protagonist to keep each succeeding bid just slightly higher than each previous bid if they so wish. Imprecise power also has some related effects on the conflict process. Protagonists with only highly punitive weapons or options available may hesitate to use them except for serious threats or disruptions. Instead of reducing the likelihood of highly violent acts, imprecision may actually increase the likelihood. We shall discuss the effects of imprecise power more fully in the section on strategy.

Mechanical Limiters

The technological relationship between protagonists influences the conflict process in obvious ways. If the tempo or magnitude of bargaining is restrained because of the distance between protagonists then, of course, the speed of the spiral is limited, as is the upper level of potential violence.

Normative Thresholds

The most important conflict limiters for our purposes are those of social norms and traditions. The technological or mechanical limiters of the violence spiral are quite straightforward and obvious. The nonmechanical limiters to the violence process are not as obvious but are extremely important. A bargaining norm or tradition is an informal agreement or understanding between protagonists that establishes the ranges of generally permissible actions. The social understandings ritualize conflict and establish acceptable repertoires of potential action. In marital conflicts, for example, some couples may set the upper limit of violence at making the conflict public (i.e., screaming at each other); others may set it at first physical strike (i.e., the first person to hit the other loses); whereas still others may agree that anything short of drawing blood is acceptable conflict bidding.

One of the most clear-cut examples of bargaining tradition is that of the thermonuclear threshold in international conflict. The United States and the Soviet Union have a tradition of nonuse of thermonuclear devices in any of their ritualized skirmishes (e.g., Korea, Cuba, Vietnam). The social understanding is that bids of violence must be made with conventional weapons. Now, again, we are talking not about threat spirals in which both sides have threatened to use any weapon at their disposal but about violence spirals or the actual exchange of harm. In any conflict situation nations bid up to the limiter, at which time the conflict starts to decelerate. With limiters, conflicts usually are held in the lower ranges of violence relative to the total potential range.

One of the most important aspects of a violence limiter is that it must be placed high enough on the scale of violence to be effective. For example, thermonuclear weapons could be used in a conflict at technologically low levels of violence. Small yield weapons could be used only at sea or only for combat field artillery. They could be used only outside each protagonist nation's homeland, and so on. The problem with placing the thermonuclear threshold at a low level of conventional violence is that the threshold is readily crossed by nations in conflict with the result that the question is no longer one of use versus nonuse but of how large a device to use and with what frequency. Therefore, thresholds at low levels of violence do not operate as meaningful limiters. In Vietnam, for example, the United States' use of airborne gases, such as various riot control gases used in disruptions in the United States, has caused concern because it introduces chemical weaponry at a technologically very low level of violence. Once crossed, the threshold becomes not chemical versus nonchemical but rather which chemical to use.

Many conflict situations have no bargaining traditions either because the conflict is too new and the protagonists have not reached any understandings or because the conflict has taken on more serious proportions such that old violence thresholds have been crossed and new ones at higher levels of violence have not been established. University conflicts are an example in point. The conflicts are new and in some circumstances have crossed traditional under-standing of how such conflicts should proceed.

STRATEGY

Of all the areas of conflict, strategy is by far the most intriguing; for when people start talking about strategic maneuvers, they call to mind Strangelovean scenarios of people trying to outwit one another in games of skill where the costs associated with error are horribly great. It is true that a clever conflict analyst who is a competent strategist often makes the difference between victory or defeat for a group in conflict. A strategist must be able to analyze the conflict structure, the resource pool complex, the resources of both sides, the costs associated with various moves for both sides, and by all means make sure that he does not become involved in irrelevant conflicts. Given an understand-ing of the conflict structure the strategist must devise moves that have the maximum desired effect at the least cost and risk.

Strategies differ, of course, depending on what one wishes to accomplish. Offensive strategies differ from defensive ones. Sometimes it is important to lose small confrontations to increase the likelihood of winning large decisive fights. At times one wants to eliminate the opposition. At other times one wants to win but to also keep the other party from being beaten so badly that he withdraws permanently from the interaction.

The Deterrence Model

Deterrence follows from the assumption that one can prevent a person or group from behaving in a particular manner or can compel them to act in a desired manner by the issuance of threats. The threats in the deterrence model are contingent promises to do harm or to deprive the party one is attempting to influence. Powerful persons or groups tend to rely on deterrence systems. They also tend to develop the deterrence mentality, which identifies right with might, and they feel that conflicts are resolvable if they can only bring sufficient force to bear on the opposition.

Deterrence is a most common form of adversary engagement. Parties wish to avoid hostilities but threaten violence to attain one's desired ends. We threaten children with punishment if they disobey, nations threaten other nations with nuclear retaliation for transgressions, university administrators threaten students with expulsion if they do not leave an area, and so on—the list of examples of deterrence confrontations is endless.

Offensive Deterrence and Defense

Although we tend to think of deterrence as associated with defense, such as threatening punishment for anyone who disrupts the status quo, deterrence may also be used offensively. The distinction between offensive and defensive deterrence is that in the former one threatens the opposition with severe and unacceptable punishment if he defends or blocks one's exploiting the resource pool. Very powerful Haves typically use deterrence offensively because they can marshal a counterretaliatory strike against any Have-Not attack that is totally intolerable to the Have-Not group. In short the Haves can make Have-Not efforts to change the status quo extremely costly to the Have-Not group. One can argue that the latter is defensive in nature and not offensive. The distinction between offensive and defensive deterrent actions, then, is fuzzy at best. Whether one's actions are offensive or defensive depends pretty much on one's perception and definition of the system. Formally, whenever one is helping oneself to something the other fellow defines as his, under the protection of threatened punishment should the other fellow defend himself, then the offensive deterrence label is appropriate.

The distinction is somewhat easier to see when the thermonuclear balance of terror is used as the example. Nations build up their thermonuclear arsenals and delivery systems to use them as threats against other nations. Nations do not construct such devices because they want or expect to use them. Any time a threat must be executed it indicates that the threat has not been successful. Strikes that take place, the firing of employees, expulsion of students, the slapping of children, and ICBM's that head toward their targets are all unsuccessful threats. Nations hope to have their missiles sit on the ground but use the threat of their use as a deterrent. When a nation threatens to retaliate against the other nation's first strike then we tend to think of the threat as a defensive deterrent—i.e., deterring the other nation's first strike. When a nation has a second-strike capability exceeding that tolerable (in the technical sense of being able to absorb the strike) by the other nation and threatens to deliver that strike in counterretaliation should the attacked nation retaliate we are then dealing with offensive deterrence.

Bilateral Deterrence

The punishment need not be unilateral for it to be used offensively. Take, for example, a bank robber who threatens to detonate the five sticks of dynamite he is holding in his hand unless given some money. The robber is saying, in effect, "Give me what I want or I will blow us both up." It should also be noted that if the punishment is bilateral, the offensive party need not control it to use it offensively. To take an extreme example, assume that the bank manager had engaged Dulles as an advisor and therefore had completely wired the building with dynamite charges. The manager hopes to use the severe punishment as a deterrent by letting it be known that should anyone try to rob his bank he is going to detonate the charges. A robber may then walk into the bank and help himself to the money saying to the manager, "If you don't like it, blow us both up."

The bank robber is vulnerable, however, to a "moral victory" should the bank manager feel that the lives involved are of lesser importance than a principle. A few "Death Rather Than Dishonor" signs hung about the bank might give the bank robber reason to pause. The concept of the strategic rationality of irrationality is discussed later in this section.

Credibility

When one is using threat, the name of the game is credibility. How believable is the threat? What are the realistic odds of the threatener's executing the threatened punishment? The science of making one's threat appear more credible to the opposition holds fascination for everyone from the amateur chess player to the inner circles of governments. I shall be using the term "weapon" in its technical sense of available behaviors or actions that have a potential for harming or harassing the opposition. A protest march, a bullhorn, noncompliance, guerilla destructive raids, a rifle, a strike, and an ICBM are therefore all weapons.

Credibility of threat is affected by many factors, such as the properties of available weapons, the history of the conflict, the cost (to the user) associated with threat execution, and, of course, strategy. We shall now turn our attention to an examination of some of the structural and strategic factors that affect threat credibility.

The Weapons

Several books can be filled on the effects of the available punishers on the credibility of various types of threats that can be made to use those weapons. A nation may have a powerful first-strike force but vulnerable second-strike capabilities. Protestors may have a large constituency but only one opportunity to use it during, say, a convention. The authorities, for example, may threaten to arrest and detain all protestors for the duration of the convention. Unions can only hold full-blown strikes one at a time. University administrations cannot expel an entire student body. The list of restrictions on credibility inherent in the nature of the weapon itself is unlimited.

Defensive Vulnerability

Although one may be trying to make sense out of schizophrenic logic it is interesting to consider the reasons for various strategic maneuvers of contemporary thermonuclear chessmasters. While the thermonuclear delivery systems were developing it became obvious that the missiles would have to be used first, or not at all. That is, because they could be wiped out by one of the opposition's missiles, they could not be used as a retaliatory threat. The first nation to strike would "win" unless the attacked nation could get its missiles off the ground, so to speak. This situation leads to a highly unstable situation, one that encourages preemptive or "preventative" strikes and certainly leads to superalert stances. When one has to be overly concerned about being the first to attack or, at very worst an extremely close second, one keeps oneself in a high state of readiness and mobilization. This makes the opposition nervous, for the distinction between defensive and offensive moves in such circumstances is difficult to make.

Such considerations lead to weapon-protection measures, such as hiding them by keeping them mobile, or hardening them by putting them in subterranean silos. The weapon-protection considerations also lead to building ABM systems to protect the missiles rather than to protect the population. It is interesting to note that our administration attempted to soft sell the ABM network by claiming that it was only a limited umbrella over our defensive missiles. Fully protected defensive missiles become offensive deterrents and encourage the opposition to develop better penetration systems, and a new era in the arms race begins.

Punitive Precision and Escalation

Although weapon vulnerability is interesting and does have relevance in nonnuclear conflict, the effects of punitive precision are of far greater importance. Escalation as a strategy refers to the gradual increase in the threatened or actual punishment used by one side to impose its will on the opposition. The rule of the escalation game is to threaten punishment that is highly credible but just severe enough to force the opposition to yield. It is a measured response system in which the greater the number of separate steps one can distinguish on the escalator, the more control one can exercise over the conflict. Credibility in this case refers to the use of the immediately threatened punishment as well as one's resolve to go up as high as is necessary on the escalator of violence. Each step is like a miniature game of chicken and bidding in violence takes place in graduated precise steps.

Now, frequently one's weapons do not permit one to move slowly up the escalator of ritualized conflict. More frequently, however, one's strategic incompetence limits the precision of one's weapons. The problem with imprecise punitive power is that one is relatively helpless against a strategy of escalation if one relies on imprecise punishers. For example, irate mothers cooking important meals frequently tell children to stay out of the kitchen. Having been invited to play a game of chicken, the child harasses the mother until she issues a threat. If she says that she is going to deprive the child of his afternoon cookie if he enters the kitchen, she is very likely to execute the threat the first time the child crosses a territorial marker. Her threat then has high credibility and if precise, such as the deprivation of the child's dinnertime dessert, the territorial marker has some salience for the child.

However, if the mother is sufficiently irate to issue a massively punitive threat, such as that she is going to give the child's bicycle to the garbage man, then of course she is helpless against creeping infractions. For one does not use such punishment for say, one-quarter of a big toe across the threshold. And if one-quarter of a big toe is acceptable, what about one-half or, say, one whole toe? The problem, of course, is that if the threatened punishment is too great, each little infraction is too trivial to justify such massive punishment. The Eisenhower administration under Dulles acted like the irate mother by depending on nuclear weapons and a massive retaliation policy which, of course, was impotent against escalation.

Powerful persons who rely on massive punitive threats frequently find themselves being exploited. If one must rely on large punishers, the credibility of one's using such large punishers is low for small infractions of rules. The low credibility of threat execution invites further escalation and thus we find such persons caught in the functional equivalent of the "nuclear age dilemma," i.e., punishers that are too large for most of the opposition's disruptive actions.

A most serious aspect of this problem is that such imprecision may increase the probability of the use of the severe punishers. When only imprecise punishers are available, the powerful hesitate to use such weapons for minor disruptions. This hesitation then reduces the risk associated with minor infractions. Because the risk of punishment for each minor encroachment or disruption is reduced, disruption is encouraged. Now the problem is that the use of severe punishment is usually a threshold phenomenon in which three infractions or disruptive acts may go unpunished, whereas the fourth releases the full blow. We can often see this occurring with parents' treatment of children. Frequently, parents escalate the punishment they use with their children to the point at which severe slapping is used for every disciplinary action. The parent, not wishing to slap the child for trivial disruptive behaviors, lets three or four such acts accumulate and ends up beating the child for laughing too loudly when someone is sleeping in another room. The threshold notion, then, is that because the risk of threat execution is reduced on each individual occasion of disruption, the probability of continued infractions increases, which in turn increases the probability of the punishment being used. The situation is somewhat similar to playing a coin flipping game in which one loses as soon as one flips heads. Although on each flip the probability of hitting a head is .50, given an unbiased coin, the probability of flipping the coin four times in a row without getting a head is .50 × .50 × .50 × .50 = .0625, or about one time out of every 16 attempts.

One could argue that the nonuse of massive punishers for minor infractions reflects not a threshold phenomenon but a situation in which the powerful protagonist simply does not notice such trivial disruptions. When he does notice a disruptive behavior, the threat is immediately executed. For the purposes of analysis, however, it matters little, if at all, whether the powerful protagonist actually hesitates to use his power or whether he is perceived to be hesitant or perceived to be inattentive. In such cases the encouragement of disruption with the attendant increases in the total probability of threat execution is the same as when the powerful protagonist does in fact hesitate to execute threat.

To carry the analysis one step further, assume that a very powerful protagonist who has severe punitive capability chooses not to use such punishers, preferring to use some less belligerent method of persuasion. Should that person be peaceful and cooperative, the nonuse of the punisher may be perceived not as salubrious conciliatory behavior but as hesitancy to use the punisher motivated by that person's fear or guilt which, in turn, encourages escalated infractions or exploitative attempts.

The use of threats of severe punishment as a deterrent may increase the probability of hostilities in still a further way. If one threatens you with harm should you scratch your nose, you would certainly feel that this was an arrogant restriction of your personal freedom. You may have absolutely no interest in scratching your nose but feel compelled to do so simply to demonstrate that your freedom has not or cannot be restricted. Naive use of deterrent threat, therefore, can markedly increase the probability of a disruptive or undesirable action by the opposition even though in the first instance the opposition has had no intention of acting in that particular manner.

Punitive Relativity

There are a few considerations regarding the relationship between each protagonist's punitive capability that it becomes necessary to discuss; for the nature of the power relationship can importantly alter the nature of the conflict process and markedly alter strategic considerations.

Coincident punishment. Coincident punishment refers to the Doomsday machine type of conflict process. The game of chicken described earlier, in which deadlock leads to a headon collision, is also a case in point. Essentially, the coincident punishment–conflict process involves a situation in which, if threat is executed by either party to the conflict, both parties, the threatened and the threatener, are harmed.

Independent punishment.   The above situation contrasts with independent punishment situations. In these, each side can execute its own punitive capability which, although perhaps costly to them, is punitively independent. For example, if two angry men in a barroom each have a stick of dynamite that they threaten to detonate if the other fellow does not leave the bar, the punishment is obviously coincident. If either man detonates his dynamite both men are killed. Contrasted with the above is a situation in which both men have revolvers, each threatening to fire his revolver to kill the other man. Although in the latter situation firing one's own revolver probably results in return fire, punishment is not coincident.

Punitive balance.   In arms races, each side is attempting to either attain greater punitive capability than the opposition, or at worst to have a sufficient punitive capability to deter the more powerful protagonist from utilizing his advantage. Punitive balance, then, refers to the relationship between both sides' *potential* punitive capability. One side because of greater wealth may be able to produce weapons more rapidly given the outbreak of hostilities. Even though both sides presently have about equal weapon arsenals, therefore, one side has greater punitive capability because of greater resources, such as more money, more people, etc.

Power balance, however, is a complex concept, because the severity of one's weapons depends to a very great extent on the absorption capability of the opposition. If two men have long sticks of equal size and weight we may be tempted to talk about arms balances, punitive comparability, and so on. We are less likely to be so naïve when we hear that one man weighs 87 pounds, whereas the other protagonist weighs 230 pounds.

Two businessmen may get into a price war, accepting exactly the same loss on every item sold. We tend to think that the wealthier businessman must win. However, what if the poorer fellow said to the wealthier, "I know in the long haul you will defeat me but if you don't compromise I promise to go to the limit of my resources and make the price of victory extremely costly indeed."

The Strategy of Conflict

Within reasonable limits the cutting edge in any conflict is the clever strategic use of one's capabilities. Protagonists who have traditionally had superior power and resources fall into the trap of the deterrence mentality. This mentality makes them so much more vulnerable because they are predictable. Conflicts, then, are not won or lost because of simple differences in punitive capabilities. Instead, clever strategy makes the difference, and to some of the important concepts in conflict strategy we shall now turn our attention.

In conflict situations one frequently threatens to do something that objectively is foolish or costly. One threatens strikes when salaries are to be lost; or more extreme, nations threaten other nations with weapons that in the final analysis lead to total mutual annihilation or certainly the destruction of both nations' economic and societal structures. When punishment is coincident the credibility of one's threat is seriously weakened. How can one's threat be made credible when at no time during the conflict is it ever in the interest of the threatener to execute that threat? Again taking an extreme example, if a nation has a doomsday weapon and threatens to use it unless the second nation ceases serious aggressive moves, at no time during that interchange is it ever advantageous to execute the doomsday weapon.

The problem in chicken-type confrontations, then, in which protagonists have severe punitive capabilities that are either bilateral or coincidental, is how to make an essentially incredible threat credible. Factors other than probability of coincident or retaliatory punishment affect threat credibility. For example, unequal punitive costs can affect the believability of one's threat. Two drivers trying to get through a one-lane passage frequently engage in the threat tactic of driving, usually slowly, on a collision course until one fellow stops his car, allowing the winner to go through first. In such a situation we frequently think that the driver with the newest most expensive car will yield first because his costs associated with threat execution are great. A fellow with a $25 junkyard special, however, is usually thought to have a decided advantage given he can execute threat of minor collision at little or no cost to himself. As Schelling (1963) states, however, the threat to smash an old car with an expensive new one is effective to the extent that it is believable. The threat to engage a markedly wealthier business competitor in a price war, or the threat to use large-yield nuclears against another nation, similarly involves making incredible threats credible.

Escalation

Escalation is the procedure of increasing the size of one's threats and/or punishments if the opposition replies to one's earlier acts of threat and force with noncompliance or counterthreats. Although the opposition may counter one's threats with counterthreats, the essential aspect of the escalating strategy is that of gradually increasing one's own threats and acts of force until the opposition complies with one's demands.

Escalation as a strategy can enhance the credibility of one's using highly destructive capabilities. The enhancement can occur in several ways. First, small conflicts have a tendency to spiral out of control, and few people can spot the critical point at which each side starts to lose control. One's willingness to engage others in low-level hostilities, with gradual increments in threat and violence, is therefore itself a deterrent to the opposition because of the risk of the limited conflict's exploding into a high-level conflict, forcing the use of high-violence weapons.

Second, escalation can affect credibility of the use of high-violence weapons by providing a conflict history in which the size of the bids and the ante are normatively established. For example, in an auction, if one finds oneself in conflict with one other bidder for a particular item, one may allow, say, four rounds of $1 bids and then jump the bids to, say, $3. The previous rounds of bidding established the background for evaluating escalated bids.

One also can increase the ante, so to speak, by increasing the size of one's bids. In the auction example, increased bid size increases the price of victory. In the automobile situation one can increase the ante by increasing one's speed. At higher speeds one is not dealing with scratched fenders but with rather serious damage to the automobile and perhaps personal bodily injury.

Sometimes one can also increase bidding tempo in escalating conflicts. In auctions for example, one can establish one's upper limit for an item to, say, $50. Once bidding starts at, say, $2 a bid one can simply keep one's hand held up such that counterbids occur without delay. Should the bidding continue to the $50 one drops one's hand following the preconflict strategy. Without pauses or preplanning the opposition must make all strategy decisions during his retaliatory period. One's own threat credibility is also not affected by one's own delays in such high-tempo conflicts.

Escalation strategies then are methods for establishing credibility at lower levels of threat and violence. By making the threats graduated, the credibility of immediate retaliation or counterbid is higher than if one threatens with more serious harmful acts. The potential that one may use highly potent punishers is also increased because one moves toward their use in smaller steps, each of which individually is highly credible. Escalation also can enhance credibility by providing a forum for demonstrating one's resolve. The small businessman can demonstrate his resolve to go to the limit of his resources even though if forced to do so he will lose. Threatening to go to the limit can be demonstrated by taking escalatory moves that can make the price of victory unacceptable to the wealthier businessman.

History

Although some terrifying risks have been accepted to establish reputation, it is true that one's behavior and performance during previous conflicts can be a source of strength. Future credibility can be established by demonstrations of one's willingness to go the distance. In the game of chicken, for example, the protagonist who wins enjoys a certain protection in the sense that he receives fewer challenges to play. The more daring his performance, moreover, or alternatively, the better the reputation of the player he beats, the more credible become his threats to accept enormous risks.

Within the context of a single conflict, history again is important. In long-standing conflict, one protagonist's frequent yielding leads to an expectancy of his yielding. The first person to make a concession in a dangerous situation may find that he has lost the conflict for within the albeit brief history, he has demonstrated lack of resolve of escalating to more serious levels of violence. In long-standing conflict situations one also finds that exemplary blows may affect credibility. One might, for example, use a weapon to demonstrate one's willingness to escalate the conflict to that level or to demonstrate the importance of the issue. Strangelovean strategists have therefore suggested that in serious international conflicts it may be advantageous to enhance the credibility of the nuclear deterrent by using one in an exemplary fashion. One could argue that the testing of thermonuclears by the United States and the Soviet Union, for all the flap about requiring the detonations to collect information, were nothing more than exemplary blows demonstrating, first, that one had workable weapons and, second, that one was reckless enough to expose parts of the world to high-megaton explosions and therefore might actually use such devices on other nations.

Other exemplary blows include "accidental" detonations, combat zones only, such international areas as oceans, in remote areas of countries within the opposition's sphere of influence, etc.

Lunacy

Within the context of conflict history or tradition, there are several different specific strategies one can follow that increase the credibility of one's threat. If it can be demonstrated to the opposition that one shares none of his common values, then one enjoys a strategic advantage. If protesting students can demonstrate that they do not share university officials' reverence for degrees or nondestructiveness to open buildings, then the administrators have fewer means of coercion. If a racing car driver can demonstrate that he does not value his own life, he enjoys an advantage over other drivers who share the value of survival. When others do not share what we consider to be basic values, we consider them to be lunatics. A person with an impending psychosis, however, enjoys a very decided strategic advantage, for if one cannot depend upon the opposition to act in accordance with *his own* best self-interest, then one is exposed to enormous danger.

For example, in the automobile variety of the game of chicken, your being obviously dead drunk or having recently attempted suicide places the opposition in the most peculiar position of not knowing whether or not you are likely to try to save your own life. If you are not and he wants to save his own, then he has lost the game.

If one wants the landlord to install new electrical wiring, one wants to do it oneself in a hopelessly dangerous substandard fashion, which one calls to the landlord's attention by, say, blowing a main fuse. The rationality of seeming a lunatic cannot be overemphasized. Not only does one enjoy a strategic advantage accruing from forcing the opposition to assume responsibility for protecting not only himself but you also (for again, if you destroy yourself you destroy him), but one also enjoys lessened risk of retaliation. Lunatics are not motivated by evil but act the way they do because they are out of touch with reality. One does not retaliate against crazy people.

Short Fuse

Related to lunacy is the short-fuse strategy. Like the trigger-happy gunman image, short-fuse behavior makes others tread very gently for fear of sudden and extremely rapid escalation of the conflict to a totally unacceptable level. For example, if one expects to have a long, hard bargaining session with a business associate, one wants to arrange for a prenegotiation dinner at which it is agreed to discuss no business—just a friendly dinner before the hard bargaining begins. During the dinner one wants to orchestrate a trivial disagreement with, say, the bartender, such as the league standing of a sports team. As soon as the bartender says he thinks you're wrong, you violently overturn the dinner table while admonishing the bartender not to disagree. If one were also armed at such an occasion, the short-fuse strategy would be particularly effective. Availability of weapons, of course, drastically affects the potential of such strategies as lunacy and the short fuse.

The short-fuse strategy, often mistaken as a personality characteristic, is very frequently used in emotionally or normatively bonded situations such as in marriages and business partnerships. By establishing the fact that he can never gauge your potential reaction in even the most trivial of conflicts where at times, without any advance warning, you may explode, the other party must be extremely careful. If he is not careful, a trivial conflict may trigger extremes of rhetorical or physical violence. As in the case with the lunatic strategy, the more reckless one is with his weapons, be they verbal abuse or machine guns, or the more indifferent one is to such interchange, the greater is one's strategic advantage. The shorter the fuse for highly abusive or violent conflict behaviors, moreover, the greater the advantage, provided one is never predictable. That is, at times one explodes on trivial issues, whereas on some other decidedly more important issue one slowly escalates the conflict. During the slow escalation, the opposition is constantly faced with the possibility of violent increase in the conflict for each trivial prolongation or delay of his not yielding.

Readiness

The simple availability of weapons obviously affects the probity of any threat one makes. If one discovers that one is dealing with an armed lunatic, even trivial threats, such as "I'm going to be angry at you," are not to be ignored. The important aspects of readiness are that it increases the probability of escalated violence, and mobilization to bring oneself to the full alert or readiness state is a signal to the opposition. Mobilization signals that the issue is important and that one expects escalated violence. The opposition, if not already mobilized, replies by preparing his weapons for immediate use. The initial reciprocal mobilization establishes reciprocal expectation, which increases the chance of increased violence.

A high state of readiness, or full alert as it is called, is also used as a strategy to increase the effectiveness of one's demands. At high levels of readiness, the natural delay in responding is shortened to the point at which the probability of accidental but nonetheless highly violent interchange is increased. For example, if one had a disagreement with one's neighbor over the neighbor's dogs' indiscretions on one's lawn, holding rifles trained at one another's heads while discussing the problem might well lead to accidental use of the weapons. In such high-alert situations, one must either preemptively use one's own weapons should hostilities be likely, or at worst retaliate with the least possible delay. Because in situations in which preemptive or preventative attacks offer the attacker a very marked advantage, each protagonist cannot but help assume that the other party also recognizes the advantage. The preparation for hostilities then may escalate to the point of readiness in which the attacker enjoys a marked advantage. Such states are extremely dangerous because they are unstable (i.e., no effective deterrent to the attacker) and thus complete the cycle of preparation leading to use.

In theory at least, we can reverse the readiness spiral. A number of procedures for reversing arms-readiness spirals have been suggested. Basically, one simply takes weapons out of readiness. The problem is that you must make the opposition fully aware of what you are doing. The first reduction must be small so as not to expose the opposition to an inevitable advantage for attack. After accepting a reasonable risk by reducing your readiness, which has been preannounced to the opposition, one waits for a reciprocal reduction. Should the opposition reciprocate you demobilize another weapon unit.

Bluffing

Bluffing is such a universal strategy in card games and military operations that little need be said about it. The only really critical aspect to bluffing in Have–Have-Not conflicts is that one bluffs to be caught. Threats are successful if never used, whereas a bluff is successful when the opposition, having previously called one's bluff, is lured into a highly costly defeat. In card games for example, one frequently bets on poor hands to prevent the opposition from determining one's strength from the size of one's bet. In protest moves it is often advantageous to stage emaciated attacks or demonstrations to lure the opposition into maintaining a defense that is decidedly inadequate for one's important move.

Contre-coup

Medically, a contre-coup is an injury to one part of an organ brought about by a blow on the opposite point. Strategically, the contre-coup is the weakening of a resistant opposition by striking at a vulnerable but critical point. The point may be vulnerable because it is essentially undefendable or because no one expects disruptive efforts to be directed toward that point.

Taking a straightforward example, consider a taxi company that has no black drivers and has been resistant to pressure to hire black drivers. I recall such a situation in Nova Scotia several years ago. Now one can attempt formal protests, picketing, or boycotting; however, from a strategic point of view all of the above actions are relatively impotent because the ratio of strength of the protestors relative to the company's clientele, needed to be at all effective, is unrealistically high. One must conservatively assume that the taxi company reflects community attitudes so that a boycott or picketing cannot seriously affect the company's business.

To be effective the protestors must disrupt the client's efforts to engage the taxi company's services, which almost always occurs by phone. A contre-coup in this situation would be to jam the company's telephones, especially during peak periods. Ten people calling the company consistently could effectively discourage clients and force them to use other taxi companies, at least until the siege is over.

Strategic planning is an exciting enterprise and not devoid of humor. Consider the following use of the "sit-in" procedure as a contre-coup. To jam up, so to speak, the administrative offices of a university, a group of determined students could hold the sit-in on all of the toilets in the vicinity of the administration building. The students' right to sit on a university toilet has never been questioned and if enough students exercise this right they can strike a blow at a most vulnerable point in the organization.

The contre-coup can also be developed around a bluffing strategy designed to lure the opposition into deploying his forces in the wrong place. To create an area of weakness, escalating attacks are launched against a particular target. The opposition builds up defenses to protect the target. One continues to launch increasingly more energetic attacks against the target, luring the opposition to relocate its resources to defend itself against an apparently eminent and severe offensive. One then attacks one of the weakened positions. Many will recognize this as the strategy General Giap used with great effectiveness in Vietnam.

Humor

No account of strategies would be complete without mention of humor. If one can make the opposition appear foolish and unworthy of serious attention, preferably in a public forum, then one can frequently demoralize a protesting group. The following is an example of such an attempt. The Principal of Hertford College, Oxford, replied to a list of students' ''nonnegotiable demands'' under threat of ''direct action'' as follows:

> We note your threat to take what you call ''direct action'' unless your demands are immediately met. We feel that it is only sporting to let you know that our governing body includes three experts in chemical warfare, two ex-commandos skilled with dynamite and torturing prisoners, four qualified marksmen in both small arms and rifles, two ex-artillerymen, one holder of the Victoria Cross, four Karate experts, and a chaplain. The governing body has authorized me to tell you that we look forward with confidence to what you call a ''confrontation'' and I may say even with anticipation.[3]

Ridicule as a strategy in conflict situations is dangerous for it gives rise to anger and frustration, which may inflame the conflict. Furthermore, protestors may conclude that communication under such conditions is impossible and therefore turn to other, perhaps more destructive, forms of protest.

Uncertainty

To make threats credible one must place the burden of avoiding the punishment on the other party. One must in effect allow the threatened punishment to get sufficiently out of your own control that despite your best efforts to stop the violence you may not be successful. When one is keeping complete control over one's weapons, one can be intimidated. A nation's threat to use thermonuclear weapons in retaliation for a conventional force's attack becomes credible only if, given the attack, the weapons may go off despite the best efforts of either side to stop them.

To use an analogy, what one needs in any conflict engagement is a device that electronically rolls dice and, depending on the result, executes a threat. The device should be wired so that once set it cannot be defused. For instance, one may threaten to blow up the house if one's spouse makes another lousy martini. One may place a few sticks of dynamite in the cellar with the dice rolling device set to make a single roll and detonate the dynamite should a 7 be rolled. Once the martini is made, one tastes it and then decides whether or not to start the machine. Now the device is not yet perfect, of course, because one

---

[3] At the time of this printing some question remains as to the authenticity and authorship of the text reprinted above. Some have attributed the statement to Sir Maurice Bowra, the late Warden of Wadham College, Oxford. However, the Dean of Wadham College has recently informed me that it was the Principal of Hertford College, Oxford, who replied to petitioning students in terms similar to those set out in the statement reprinted above. Further, the librarian of Hertford College has pointed out that he believes the quote as reprinted above is somewhat embellished. However, for our purposes, as an example of the use of ridicule in conflict situations, the above note, although perhaps not the authentic text, is an excellent one indeed.

still has the last clear option to avoid the punishment. One can, of course, simply not push the button that starts the probabilistic punishment device. To make the device absolutely perfect one must put all of the burden of avoiding taking any chance of blowing up the house on the martini maker. To accomplish this one need only wire oneself up to a lie detector that automatically starts the dice rolling machine should the true answer be that the martini is lousy. Despite all forms of intimidation, personal regrets, promises, or second thoughts on one's own part, therefore, the probability of punishment remains unchanged.

Many of the same characteristics would be incorporated into a science fiction-type doomsday machine deterrent. Namely, to be most effective no one should be able to turn it off.

In most conflict situations one must find strategic substitutes for the dice rolling device and for the automatic engagement of the device. Many strategists use the normal unpredictability of the conflict process itself as the dice rolling aspect of deterrent threats, for many small brush war types of engagements explode into full scale wars; many minor protests have escalated into insensate acts of violence, etc. Conflict cannot be precisely limited, so that the threat to engage an adversary in limited conflict is in effect a threat to roll the dice.

A second procedure used to roll the dice, so to speak, is that of moving to a state of full alert. For as discussed previously, when one mobilizes one's forces, the risk of accidental execution of punishment goes up very markedly. Despite one's very best efforts to be careful, someone or something somewhere may make just one tiny mistake.

In crowd-type protests, such as demonstrations, the leaders cannot truly control everyone, so, if large enough, protests always involve the risk of rapidly escalating violence. The major threat such protest demonstrations or movements have is that of the unilateral action of smaller groups within the larger group. That is, smaller groups take action under their own initiative, which cannot be controlled by the initial organizers.

Guaranteed engagement can be rather difficult to orchestrate. It is essential, however, that the opposition be confronted with the threat and not be able to force one to make the last clear choice to avoid the threatened punishment. The stationing of United States troops around the Soviet Union was presumably an attempt to make the defense commitments of the United States to other nations credible. Assuming that any aggressive move by the Soviet Union would take the form of conventional force advancement, the engagement of the United States forces was certain. Therefore, the decision to enter the conflict would not be clearly with the United States.

Labor unions' desire to keep contracts of short duration is another form of unavoidable engagement. Every two years or so, therefore, the conflict process with threatened strikes, lockouts, etc., must be encountered.

In protest situations, marches, demonstrations, rallies, teach-ins, and so on can force engagement. In such areas as the antiwar movement, however, one must have large groups of persons with shared value systems. Further constrained by the fact that they are not recognized as legitimate advocates for any constituency, such protest groups must force engagement by violating a societal law, more, or norm. Socially disruptive behaviors force the engagement of society's control agencies. To the extent that such agencies cannot depend on commonly shared values, they must depend on suppressive violence. The open demonstration of repudiation of society's norms is a very great threat to the Establishment because of the risk of high levels of violence. We shall turn our attention now to an analysis of shared values and violence.

VIOLENCE

One of the most misunderstood concepts in social science is that of violence. The definitions we have are loaded with biases, as we shall shortly discuss. An understanding of what violence is and from where it erupts is central to good management, for the business of management is the harnessing of conflict, and violence and conflict are inextricably related. Management is the use of power, and violence is the exercise of power. It comes as no surprise to anyone, I hope, that the few powerful persons in any organizational unit, be it a church, a university, a corporation, a city, or a nation, tend to use their power to maintain the status quo—and frequently the status quo is exploitation and deprivation of the rights and equalities of large groups of less powerful persons.

The powerful have all manner of means of blocking, delaying, and frustrating the efforts of petitioners for change. They can impose confusing organizational procedures, close communication paths, marshal repressive agents, suspend due process, etc., to drain the energies and resources of all but the most patient nonviolent protestor. The powerful have greater access to and control over the means of protest than do the protestors. They have greater access to the public through the mass media, enjoy greater protection by police, and, of course, have far greater financial capability to wage conflicts of attrition.

What makes a slum? What makes a ghetto? Why do arrogant and socially irresponsible polluting industries survive so easily? I have been asking myself these questions for many years; and like most people I have been angry and sick and apathetic and anguished and have had most of the other emotional reactions one experiences when the realization of one's own moral weakness cannot be avoided. Such conditions survive and then flourish because we run away from them. Urban slums are areas that the more prosperous have abandoned. It is the departure of the relatively wealthier classes from an area that starts the blight.

We should, of course, inquire as to what precipitates the exodus of those who can afford to do so. Being a structuralist I again should like to see what the person is moving away from rather than what the person is attracted toward. Ghettos and slums start because people try to isolate other people. They move away from them.

Polluting industries arrogantly carry on their destruction of our environment because instead of saying "NO!" the more powerful local residents move away from the industry. The vacuum is then traditionally filled with persons either too poor to get away or dependent on the industry or both.

Real estate agents then carefully determine the ghetto movement, prevailing winds, and the like, to direct their wealthier clientele toward safe and attractive neighborhoods. In the sanctuary of neighborhoods protected by high property prices and taxes, as well as favorable prevailing winds, powerful members of our society generally sit on their asses and complain about the welfare costs.

I am, of course, not being very fair to many people who are truly concerned but feel helpless. It seems perfectly clear however, that one is not likely to fight as vigorously when one can avoid or block out the problem. To fight any social problem one must move right into it.

It is truly astounding how many people think of integrating as blacks moving into white neighborhoods. This conception is based on the implicit assumption that the black ghetto area breeds blacks, who if they are well motivated and accept other cultural values, may make something of themselves. They have completed at least high school and must be steadily gainfully employed before they can afford to pass into white neighborhoods. This conception leads to the concern of liberals in breaking down any discriminatory barrier to blacks entering white areas given they have the money and inclination to do so. Many blacks who in fact integrate into white areas are vulnerable to the accusation of abandoning less fortunate blacks and many in fact do.

Headway toward integration can be made only when the ebb of societal movement is reversed, that is, when the prosperous and the nonblack start reversing the abandonment movement and begin reclaiming slum areas for their own habitation. Like all major structural changes this reversal will take a long time to accomplish.

Industries and government facilities that are arrogant polluters survive for precisely the same reason that slum areas develop. The prosperous person who can afford more expensive shelter and can afford the transportation to get to it abandon the areas adjacent to the polluters. The abandoned areas are filled with the poor who cannot fight or will not fight and with persons dependent on the polluters for their livelihood.

The prosperous live away from the polluter and either do not care about what is happening or, when they realize that they are being adversely affected, are encouraged to force the polluter to make suitable adjustments to reduce the changes to them. It is indeed a sad commentary on humanity that we have known for a long time, for example, that the incidence of emphysema is several times as great in the population around certain heavy polluters. Similarly, as Brodeur (1974) points out, companies have consistently disregarded information about the dangers to which their employees have been exposed. Company physicians have lied to ailing workers regarding the nature of their work-related ailments. Medical experts on boards of both industry and government have biased their advice to the good of industry, and many Government officials do not give a damn. In 1974, the estimate was that about 100,000 workers in the US would die from occupational diseases. However, society started pressing for reforms not when industries started polluting but only after it was demonstrated that the pollution might seriously affect the lives of the prosperous.

Again, the prosperous make the structural error. They wonder why people live in pollution areas. Why would a person subject himself and his family to such unpleasant and unhealthy conditions? Clearly a person who does not move out is not a go-getter. Anyone who does not abandon the area, as the prosperous have, deserves to be there for one reason or another. From a structural point of view one should look at the emitters of the assaulting toxic substances, which includes everything from automobiles to steel foundries, and ask what has happened to the senses and soul of man to permit such destruction of the quality of life? What has happened to the senses and soul of man is that man has moved away from problems rather than toward them.

We also tend to wonder why people living near polluters do not become actively involved in protests against the offending industry. This hardly needs comment when one considers that many of these residents are dependent on the industry for employment. More importantly, the poor do not have the necessary relationship with authorities to permit successful protest at low levels of threat and violence. To protest, the weak in our society must rely on physical strength and disruptions. It requires considerable anger and frustration to overcome these obstacles to protest, and when they do occur, therefore, such protests tend to be characterized by violence. The authorities then engage their suppressive agents, the police, and protest necessitates violence.

If conflict is inevitable in any society, then we must conclude that violence is in the very nature of things. We must be extremely careful, however, that we do not fall into simplistic categorical notions of violence. Personal violence, like conflict to be sure, is a dimension that goes from acts of interference with a person's freedom to act, a restriction of power such as blocking his passage, to acts of mass murder. Violence against property similarly describes a dimension of low-power reduction, such as chalking obscenities on walls, to high-power reduction acts, such as blowing up a building.

We must also exercise some care about placing value judgments on violence. Although no social change or democracy can be existent in a violence-free society, we must not assume that violence and democracy are synonymous terms. Social mobility generates disorganization and disruption, which give rise to conflict, and violent behavior. To say that democracy requires violence may be closer to the truth than that a Utopian society is free from all violence. However, such statements are as naïve or rather as trivial as the question of instinctual aggression in man. The question of importance is not that of categorizing violence or of assessing its value. Surely what is important is to analyze violence and determine what we can or should tolerate or, conversely, how much we must use.

We must keep in mind however, as Dahl (1970) points out, that "Some of the most profound changes in the world take place in a quiet country like Denmark, where hardly anyone raises his voice and the rhetoric of revolution finds few admirers [p. 4]." Dahl also suggests that there may be an inverse relationship between the rate at which the word "revolution" is used in a given country and the rate of change in the distribution of power and privilege.

It is regrettable that, aside from a few socially deranged types who feel that physical violence is a necessary religious cleansing of one's soul, people abhor physical violence and yet find that it is a necessary reality of life. They feel they must defend themselves if attacked and must strike out if treated unfairly. They feel that nothing of any consequence ever gets done in society without violent acts or highly credible threats of such violence. A serious problem in society, I believe, is that persons have a simplistic notion of what violence is. They treat all disruptive acts as violent and respond in a simplistic fashion that inflames the spiral of violence. In the present section, then, we shall examine the components of violent behaviors and discuss some of the important dimensions.

In keeping with the original notion of power being the fundamental concept in social science, power again being defined as freedom to act in relation to some resource pool, violence is then the restriction of power. Violent behaviors are those which interfere with another person's freedom to act. One can perform violent acts against another's power, then, by acting against his person, his property, or his symbolic sources of power.

The restriction of a person's freedom to act can occur, of course, at the most trivial of levels. We restrict children's power by forcing them to drink their milk. We force people to stop doing something by getting angry. We force persons to spend time reading a particular book by making their life difficult without that knowledge. We affect people's lives by threatening to cut off their income or threatening their lives. Violence is a technical term that should not be used inappropriately. It refers not only to highly destructive acts against people or property, for such use of the term forces us to look at a behavior and decide on its magnitude or severity while totally ignoring the essential nature of the act. Violence is the restriction of another's freedom, no matter how trivially. The severity or extent of that restriction determines not whether the act was violent but rather the magnitude of the violence.

Shared Values and Violence

The control of violence necessitates the establishment and maintenance of shared societal values, for without such value systems one would need one law enforcement agent for every two people in society. If people did not share the high valuation of human life or personal property, law enforcement agents would have to be everywhere at all times.

We are, of course, seeming to witness a breakdown of the shared value of human life. The familial murder rate in cities, such as Detroit, has led many observers to comment on the apparent deterioration in society's value system. Once the taking of a human life was for most people an unthinkable act. Now however, killing seems to be a less unlikely terminal state for interpersonal conflicts.

Repudiation of shared values is a most effective form of violence. Obscenity, for example, is effective because it violates a society's expectancies of what should not be said in certain public situations. If one wants to do violence to a restaurant manager, for example, one need only sing "mother fucker" to the tune of the *Hallelujah* chorus of Handel's *Messiah* during his busy mealtime hours.

Society does legislate in the areas of values and taste. People are arrested for the public use of obscene words. Society has had and presently has laws regulating a person's sexual behavior and the types of personal experience he may indulge in. We have laws about the use of marijuana, the use of which is a crime without a victim. Society legislates in these areas because repudiation of shared norms deprives the powerful of methods of control. The use of marijuana has been associated with unusual dress, rejection of materialism, and repudiation of maintenance of special privilege groups in society. Laws prohibiting the use of such drugs or prohibiting atypical life styles frequently derive from efforts to control groups that reject normative life styles. Law enforcement agents react to such rejections of values with physical violence, which in turn elicits counterviolence, thus completing the cycle.

Society cannot legislate against styles of life with any effectiveness. Usually rejection of values involves symbolic violence as opposed to violence of a physical or economic nature.

Symbolic violence may be thought of as psychological violence. One's notions of how the nation's flag should be handled with reverence and respect is in no way affected by others' treatment of the flag. When one attempts to legislate against value systems, however, one is limiting the freedom of others to act.

Now, symbolic violence, of course, is used to invite a reply; for only with a reply from the repudiated group can the conflict take form, positions polarize, and the protesting groups mobilize their respective constituencies. Because we do not adequately understand the distinctions among various types of violence, we tend to respond to all forms in the same way. Physical violence is usually most immediately available and so has a very high probability of being the method of reply for all types of violent attacks, including symbolic.

I have initiated this discussion of violence with some statements about symbolic violence and physically violent replies to make clear the technical usage of the term "violence." One uses violence to restrict freedom to act. The extent of that restriction of power determines the magnitude of the violence. Burning the flag is a violent act, as is clubbing someone, burning a building, blocking a person's freedom to move, or in any way jeopardizing a person's economic, physical, or psychological freedom to act.

Basically three different types of violent behaviors can be clearly distinguished: symbolic, physical and economic (or property) violence. Each class of violent behaviors may be further classified according to the purposes or motives for the behaviors.

Symbolic Violence

Symbolic violence is designed to call attention to one's rejection of accepted value systems. One uses obscene language, burns people in effigy, burns the flag, displays unpopular symbols (e.g., the VNLF flag), tells people things they do not wish to hear (e.g., calling cops "pigs"), displays oneself in socially unacceptable ways (e.g., nudity), and so on, as acts of repudiation of societal systems. Such violence is always on the same dimension as rhetorical violence. One may harm a person by destroying his arguments in a reasonable manner, by calling him unpleasant names, such as stupid or uninteresting, or by communicating with him nonverbally by transgressing an important social norm. One may use another form of violence for symbolic purposes of course. The burning of ROTC buildings on college campuses is economic violence that is not for personal gain. Instead, it is an act of violence against government property for symbolic purposes.

Economic Violence

Violent acts that affect the property or economic resource of another person or group are called "economic violence." Economic violence is one of the most intriguing and complex forms of violence, for one can restrict a person's power not only by destroying his resources but also by forcing him to use his resources in a manner in which he would not normally choose to use them. For example, arms races can be used for the purposes of economic warfare. A very wealthy nation might slow down the progress of a less wealthy nation by engaging the latter in an expensive arms race. Threatened with superior force, the poorer nation attempts to build up its armaments. The wealthier nation keeps spending slightly more than the poorer nation, with the effect that the rich nation may be spending 15% of its GNP on arms, whereas the poorer nation may have to spend 50% to keep up.

This diversion of resources is a very powerful form of violence for wealthier groups to use against poorer ones. Wealthy businesses can slow down the development of competitors by engaging them in expensive price wars. People can force others to spend their time (an economic resource) reading certain material instead of engaging in other more desirable activities by exposing that person to continued threat (e.g., embarrassment) for noncompliance.

Economic violence then can take the form of acts of destruction against a person's resources, such as burning a building, or of forcing the person to divert his resources to be used in a disadvantageous fashion.

A most interesting example of a type of strategy that can be used in economic conflict is offered by Schelling (1967). Assume that two nations with nuclear capabilities jointly share the desire to avoid accidental nuclear war. If one can be sure of the adversary's desire to prevent accidental war, rendering his warning system less reliable may force him to divert resources from other military efforts into the warning system.

When considering economic violence, then, it is important to determine whether the act is for economic gain, such as a theft, or for symbolic purposes, such as the burning of an ROTC building. From the point of view of social psychological analysis of conflict, it is also important to distinguish between acts of violence against public property versus private property, for in our society, acts of violence against a man's personal property are considered acts of physical violence against his person. The treatment of physical and personal property violence by law enforcement agents is the same. Acts of economic violence against public property for symbolic purposes have always been considered less serious.

Civil disobedience and other nonphysically violent forms of protest may be classified as economic violence. The purpose of such acts of protest is not only to force the issue into public attention but to also force enormous diversions of economic resources by the local or federal government to maintain political control. The politicians' political constituencies simply do not tolerate severe social disruption and demand "law and order." If such socially disruptive protests are large enough, they exceed the capabilities of law enforcement officials to deal with them without resorting to high levels of physical violence. As the law enforcement agents increase their hardware of violence, a shift in protest tactics occur. Instead of depending on massive protests of either physical or nonphysical violence, which can be technologically controlled (i.e., gas, bombs, guns, riot forces), the Have-Not group switches to guerrilla tactics. However, we shall reserve the discussion of guerrilla tactics for the section on the tactics of protest.

For our present purposes, economic violence limits the opposition's freedom to act with respect to an exchangeable resource. His property, money, time, etc., are all economic resources. We can do economic violence by theft, destruction, diversion, or devaluation of the resource itself. Other forms of violence, say physical, can be used to serve economic motives. One can threaten to shoot a person if he does not use his economic resources in a manner in which he would not choose. We might use symbolic violence to lessen a person's ability to exploit his resource. On learning that one's neighbor is going to try to sell his house, one can do him economic violence by placing a large sign on *one's own* house stating Jesus Saves.

Physical Violence

We have reserved for too long the term violence for physical injury and marked destruction of personal property. This of course is convenient for the Haves in society. As discussed earlier, Have-Nots, to gain greater access to the resource pool, are frequently forced to threaten or do injury to an inattentive Establishment that is determined to maintain the status quo. To refer to Have-Not acts as violent when suppressive diversionary acts, such as administrative orbiting, are not considered violent seems a most convenient but nonetheless inappropriate use of the term.

Physical violence really requires little in the way of explanation. We are violent against the opposition's person whenever we threaten or actually restrict his freedom to act. "Off-limits" signs, blockades, physical abuse, arrest, murder, rape, involuntary detainment, etc., are all on the dimension of physical violence. Marriage is a physically violent association whenever the Have sees the relationship as a set of restrictions whereas the Have-Not had a partnership in mind.

To the extent that we recognize violence only when we see blood or hear explosions, we are being hopelessly myopic about conflict. Highly violent insensate acts develop out of very low levels of violence that incubate and then spiral. To the extent that we can recognize violence in its infancy, the better becomes our ability to deal with problems at a low level of threat and violence.

Why Violence?

Acknowledging that violence is a term which is not discriminatively applied to the protest actions of Have-Nots or limited to physical abuse of others, we can recognize that every act or episode of violence starts off nonviolently. We ask such stupid questions about why so-and-so or such and such group has become violent because we choose not to acknowledge our contribution to the inevitability of increased violence. Every severe conflict situation that involves terrifying levels of violence against persons and property is foreshadowed by expressed grievances which, whether legitimate or not, were not dealt with at low levels of violence. The Kerner (1968) commission reported that virtually every one of the 1967 ghetto riots was foreshadowed by an accumulation of unresolved grievances and widespread dissatisfaction among black peoples combined with the unwillingness or inability of local government to respond. University conflicts of serious proportions always have their beginnings in some dispute or protest that although they start at a low level of disruption escalate to the events we remember. The free speech areas, people's parks, student participation in decision making, specific student grievances, and so on always preceded disruptions of any consequence.

Instead of asking questions, therefore, the naïveté of which may further enflame conflict, we should direct our attention to understanding some of the specific features of protest situations that are related to increasing violence. We should also examine means for identifying and dealing with dissatisfaction that is likely to erupt into serious violence.

Protesting groups use whatever force they have at their disposal. The protest strategies should be effective, least costly to participants, and capable of sustaining active involvement. Have-Not groups usually have few resources for staging successful protests. They have restricted access to due process systems for redressing grievances. They have limited hardware. They have little experience with organizational skills needed for strategic planning, tactical operations, and keeping the protest group dynamic. They lack bargaining skills and have restrictive information about the reality of the options available to the Establishment for redressing grievances. They do have people.

When the major resource is people, several strategies suggest themselves. "Nonviolent" civil disobedience, for example, requires that people simply restrict the freedom of others by their presence. They might lie down in the streets, sit-in at lunch counters, fill shopping carts with frozen food to be abandoned in the market, and so on. Rent strikes and economic boycotts of stores use the economic pressure that large numbers of people, if organized, can bring to bear on specific individuals.

Similarly, marches are disruptive for they force the deployment of police and they call attention to grievances. Visitations, where large numbers of people descend on officials' offices, are used to call public attention to grievances, to force official statements of intended action, and to give the official some indication of the potential disruptive force the group can bring to bear if violence escalates.

Tactically, of course, the variety of "nonviolent" (read nonphysical) forms of protest is limited only by the ingenuity of the protesting group once committed to such a strategy. It is important to understand, however, why nonphysical force is chosen as a protest strategy. Therefore, before we can answer the question "why violence?" we must ask the question "why nonviolence?"

Why Nonviolence?

The simple answer is that nonphysical force is both effective and available to many protest groups. Lying down in the middle of a street to protest the involvement of the United States in Vietnam should call public attention to the protest. It should force the disrupted group to choose sides. They can lie down in the street, or do what they can to avoid the disrupters, or force their removal. The control agents are engaged. They must remove the protestors and take measures to prevent recurrences of the disruption. The protestors' disciplined nonuse of physical force is supposed to get the message across that the issue is a moral one. The appeal is to the public's and the Establishment's sense of justice and guilt. The protest is also designed to impress the opposition with the fact that the disruptive potential of sheer numbers of persons is more than they can cope with.

Why Nonviolence Leads to Violence

The use of low levels of physical violence as a successful form of protest requires leadership, a responsive opposition, and committed followers. To stage successful protests, the efforts and actions of the group must be coordinated. To keep the protest under control, that is, at a low level of violence, the opposition must respond and, hence, acknowledge the protest. Finally, as such protests depend on the size of the group, a large and committed group of persons is required.

Now, higher levels of violence are encouraged when the conditions for successful low-violence protest do not obtain. To take an extreme example, if a small number of people wish to seriously harrass a governmental unit, terrorism or guerilla attacks require far less leadership than protests at lower levels of violence. Terrorists need not even communicate with each other because they agree to take every opportunity to cause severe, but limited, destruction of persons' property or the social order. Similarly, guerilla groups need only attack and rapidly hide to similarly destroy confidence in the social order and the present authority. Communication between groups is unnecessary and leadership is required only insofar as a spokesman for the group is required. Given that the legitimate authorities wish to respond to the disrupters' demands they must have some means for dealing with them and some guarantees that the spokesman represents the entire network. During terrorist campaigns, therefore, the authorities find it most difficult to control the terrorists; finding and prosecuting one "cell" does not improve their chances for finding other cells because each cell may, in fact, be unaware of the identity of other cells or cell members.

Defense against terrorism and guerilla attacks, then, must take the form of infiltration, informers, or other reliable surveillance procedures. Conventional defense against such procedures simply does not work.

The appeal of higher levels of physical violence in the first instance, then, is that it requires less leadership, less discipline, and fewer people and has the intrigue that forceful action always provides. It assures a reactive opposition, takes less time, and is the only method for defeating the opposition as opposed to negotiating a settlement.

Protest movements do not simply dive into highly violent actions, however. The appealing, satisfying, and otherwise attractive properties of violent protest are not responsible for encouraging groups to commence a protest at a high level of violence. All disruptions are born of discontent. Again, the discontent may reflect inequity, deprivation, or conversely, simply greed or need for power. The legitimacy of the object of controversy is of less importance to us than the dynamic features of the conflict.

Low violence level protests gain momentum when they elicit a level of response from the opposition that is perceived to be inadequate by the protestors. In university power struggles, an unresponsive administration was characteristic of most institutions experiencing severe disturbances—the marsh-mallow effect. A thrust into the administration was found to leave no identifiable impact. The lack of response encourages increased violence. First, lack of attention or response gives rise to frustration—a motivational state that can all too easily be diverted to aggressive action. Second, no response can indicate either an inattentive administration or one that considers the threat potential too trivial to entertain. On both counts enhanced violence is encouraged—either to get the attention of the Have agents or to persuade everyone concerned, protestors as well as administrators, that the protestors are serious.

Violence increases as protest continues for two other reasons. First, the most seriously deprived in a societal unit (i.e., those who have the most to gain from change) are generally not the first to join protest movements. As a protest movement continues and has some record of success, severely deprived Have-Nots may be encouraged to join. If the group size grows the potential for violence grows.

Second, and I think most important, is the peculiar effect partial success has on protestors. One cannot defeat an opposition at any conceivable bargaining table. If a previously unresponsive opposition gives outward signs of weaken-ing; that is, where change or compromise is seen as resulting from the opposition's inability to defeat or suppress the protestors, then further violence may be encouraged to bring about total victory. Violence leads to attribution not only of blame but also of cause. Change resulting from a peaceful petition that is accommodated by a Have group is perceived as caused by the Have group. They did it. They allowed it to happen or brought it about. Change that results from recognized violence is perceived as caused by the violent group. Violence therefore gives a feeling of power and autonomy, and violence may therefore erupt even when genuine reform is imminent.

Who Becomes Involved

Now, visible conflicts do not just occur like lightning from a cloudless sky. The signs of developing social conflict that is likely to be more disruptive than the general level of ambient social friction we expect are easily recognizable to anyone who pays attention. Conflicts become serious because people who must become involved eventually are not attentive to the early signs of social disquiet. I have argued, however, that such visible conflicts cannot be attributed to the instigation of a few troublemakers, rabble rousers, agitators, or other, by implication, sick or deranged people. Conflict develops its own leadership. It attracts people who find social action personally therapeutic. It attracts people whose reputation as notorious disrupters necessitates their scurrying about the country finding causes with which they can become identified. It attracts leadership. It attracts those who are morally and ideologically committed to the issue. It attracts the bored, the crazy, the concerned, the angry, the brilliant, the stupid, and in short it is likely to attract virtually any type of person save for the apathetic, the despondent, and the hopeless.

The agitator theory frequently derives from a peculiar aspect of social conflicts. Persons who become involved during the early phases of a protest or social movement are usually not those people who are most seriously affected, in objective terms, by the outcome of such protests. Those who become involved early in such movements are generally people who are somewhere in the center of the Have–Have-Not dimension. Frequently, they will not enjoy immediate benefits from any change in the status quo. Misery itself is not a sufficient condition for active protest. Trotsky (1957), for example, stated that "privation is not enough to cause insurrection; if it were, the masses would always be in revolt." Others have commented that the Have-Not status of one does not ensure receptivity to social protest. Recent economic disruption or the awareness of some success of a protest are more likely to be associated with participation in reform protests. We find, for example, that blacks have been conspicuously underrepresented in many early protests. Draft exempt students spearheaded the draft protest movement. Student radicals who participated in university reform protests, as well as who provided the protest leadership, were found to be bright, middle-class students who had the most to gain from the maintenance of university systems. Middle-income people in any particular community are most likely to be receptive to new political movements. Pollution action groups are not comprised of people living next to arrogant industrial polluters or city dumps. Welfare rights organizations derive their thrust not from the most desperate recipient.

Now politicians or control agents who, forced to attend to a particular disruption, see white middle-class kids involved in a black cause or a welfare rights protest conclude that they are troublemakers. If they would go away, the small issues could be settled peacefully. After all "our people," "the common working man," "hardworking students," etc. are led into these disruptive activities by people who thrive on trouble. "It's a small minority." It simply does not make sense for a person to be so offended by another person's victimization or deprivation that he or she would *actively* participate in moves to redress that situation. A university professor's decision to refuse to partici- pate in an archaic and absurd teaching procedure is seen as motivated by a desire to be troublesome or to shirk responsibility because, after all, he has the most to lose and the least to gain by changes in the system.

Now it is not difficult to understand why the upper levels of the Establish- ment in any societal unit do not become meaningfully involved in attempts to redress inequities in their areas of influence. People with privilege like to keep it. People who are identified with institutions, who are presidents, directors, mayors, etc. feel that they are the institution. They formed it, they lived it, they made themselves in the image of the institution. To change it, they must change a part of themselves. People who are deprived, be they financially impoverished, socially ostracized, educationally restricted, or deprived of personal freedom, must be categorized. If they are to be helped, of course, it is going to require personal effort, personal loss of privilege, acknowledgement of unfair distribution of resources, and so on. If one does not help, of course, then one is either a nonperson—unconcerned about the welfare of others, or it is their own damn fault. The poor are poor because they are lazy or not too bright, or they "think poor." The attitude toward Have-Nots is universally that of paranoid superiority. They are Have-Nots because they have some basic deficit. They are not go-getters. Incidentally, it is interesting to find many "liberal" advocates of such social intervention policies as wars on poverty arguing that such and such a condition must be eliminated because of its adverse effects on society in general. Thus, the focus of concern is to remove features adversely affecting society rather than to help the people involved.

The lack of participation of the most deprived during early phases of a movement has been attributed to the hopelessness, fatalism, and despair that develops from long experience with deprivation. Taking poverty as an exam- ple, severely deprived persons develop single-minded concern about surviving. Their long experience with privation leads to apathy and lack of hope that any action, individual or collective, can meaningfully improve their circumstances.

They tend not to have much experience with such social organizations as unions, church organizations, community groups, etc., and so do not have the skills and techniques necessary for sustained collective action. In addition, such lack of exposure leaves the severely deprived with a feeling of unreality about social or political action. The relationship of such activities to their personal circumstances is unclear or unreal to them.

More importantly, I think, is the fact of perceived impact or effectiveness of movements on personal circumstances. Long-term deprivation can lead to an acceptance of one's status. Time goes on with the attendant going and coming of policies, speech makers, saviors, programs, etc., but things continue relatively unchanged and the traditional methods for coping with the world still remain the most reliable. To engage the chronic Have-Nots one must demonstrate a margin of success sufficient to revive hope. There must be sufficient progress to introduce uncertainty into the conflict situation. To the severely deprived the outcome of most any confrontation is certain—they are going to be no better off and possibly worse off than prior to the confrontation. As soon as the outcome becomes less certain, that is, as soon as there is some chance for gaining leverage sufficient to force a recognizable improvement, hope is renewed and receptiveness to the movement is enhanced.

Violence and Force

I must admit I find completely untenable the concept that violence is a product of passion and illegitimate use of injury and disruption, whereas force is the use of legitimate power deriving, say, from a government to subdue or suppress disruptive citizens. Violence requires the use of force. Whether or not one happens to identify with the side possessing greater might seems to me to be quite an untenable reason for deciding whether a group has been violent or has exercised legitimate power through force. Violence is the restriction of another's freedom to act. Should the other be a criminal, schizophrenic, radical, student, or women's liberationist seems quite irrelevant to our primary concern, which is the extent to which one side has reduced the other's freedom to act.

I have defined violence as any interpersonal act the effect of which is the restriction of another's freedom to act. There are problems with this definition, of course, but it does direct our attention away from egotistic definitions. The literature is replete with trivial if not absurd definitions of violence and the distinctions between violence, force, aggression, and so on. Violence is what others do; aggression is that class of behavior of others which affects our central values. Force, however, is coercion, the use of which has been legitimatized. The methods I must use to coerce or deter someone from disturbing me or my state of life are force. Societal authority uses force for the community good. In short we tend to apply the word "force" to define coercive methods used by oneself or by the Have group. The Have group in society possesses all forms of coercive influence. They have economic, legal, and informational forms of influence. They have control agents (e.g., police) and technological hardware. They have control and surveillance hardware. They can incarcerate, deter, waste time, ignore, fine, etc.

The Have-Not group, in contrast, has only one instrument of power and only one way to influence, as they have restricted access to due process forms of power. That form is disruptive violence, which is the most primitive form of influence. It is universal and the form of last resort. To label Have coercion as force and Have-Not coercion as violence or aggression does not seem parsimonious. Why not simply conclude that Have is right?

Control of the Control Agents

It is true, of course, that people in any societal unit are, in theory, supposed to delegate responsibility for carrying out the aims of the society to some small group. These people may be elected. With the mandate to carry out the communal will of the society, such groups develop control systems that are considered legitimate. The problem is that such control agencies develop autonomy insulated from regulation by the society they have been, in the first instance, developed to protect. Our military and police agencies are notorious examples.

The lack of control society has over such agencies is reaching science fiction proportions. In the first instance, such agencies are highly secretive. Everything more sensitive than ordering washroom paper towels is censored. The classification system in the military complex has the effect of preventing public scrutiny. It prevents the public from controlling its own control agency. You cannot stop things of which you are unaware.

A second feature of modern day force agencies is a decrease not only of outside society's control, but also of insider's control over the influence their own agencies are having on society. This second feature derives from the increasingly complex decision-making procedures being utilized by such agencies. The computer is the most salient but certainly not the only example. In complex agencies, such as the military, computer programs must be developed to control all of "our" highly automated machines of war. Computer programs and interlocking systems of extreme complexity are not built the way one may build a house. Quite the contrary, they represent the work of many people who patch together vast computer programs and computer hardware. They develop techniques to make a system work. The internal logic of the system becomes lost because it eventually outlives everyone who worked on it. It becomes too complex for one mind to hold together.

In such a system, one switches concerns. One becomes concerned with making the system work and keeping it working when new parts or programs are added. Concern for the basic principles guiding policy decisions is then lost, as is the ability of people to determine whether or not the internal logic of the computer program is still consistent with new avenues of activity. The machinery may determine what is problematic because the system can only handle one kind of problem or can deal with problems in only one way.

Violence and Intention

We frequently think of violence as any deliberate or intentional act directed against, as Gandhi said, the essence of man. That is, acts directed against a person's (or group's) physical or psychological being with the intent to do harm. The problem with the concept of intention is that it diverts one's attention from the features of social interaction that give rise to conflict. If I harm unintentionally, am I absolved from accountability? If I initiate a course of action or support an agency or group whose actions result in deprivation to some group, am I not responsible because I did not or chose not to consider the inevitable consequences of my actions? If I was one of the 20-odd people who watched Kitty Genovese murdered without even so much as telephoning the police, even though the incident lasted about 30 minutes, am I accountable? After all, I intended no harm.

The problem with the concept of intention is that it encourages attribution of blame for harm to the system, the victim, deranged people, etc. If I make a remark that threatens someone, must I have recognized my wish to harm the other person before I acknowledge that I have limited his freedom to act? When your remarks threaten someone (e.g., discussion that may lead to that person's humiliation), that person must restrict his repertoire of behaviors. He must attend to your behavior and adopt or search for some method of defense. He can withdraw, counterthreat, change the conversation, or decide to grin and bear it.

We have learned from ethologists that in dominance or territorial squabbles between animals, the loser admits defeat by offering a distress signal. This signal suppresses the victor's threatening behavior and the loser withdraws. Bloodshed is most rare. If the animals are placed in a small enclosed area, however, frequently fierce fighting continues with serious injury or death resulting. The reason the fighting continues, apparently, is that the loser has nowhere to withdraw.

On the human level, I think it is reasonable to say that society does not permit withdrawal. Losers are encouraged to not cry "uncle." They stay in the battle until they are beaten to the extent that they cannot fight. Beating up on losers certainly restricts the freedom to act of the eventual victors. After all, they could be doing something else. Is it the victor or the loser or society that is being violent? So much violence takes place after everyone has forgotten about intentions, initial or otherwise. For our purposes violence derives from conflict. Both are inevitable. Violence does not only refer to departures from tradition, the ordinary, or the expected. It does not only refer to recognized intentional acts. To not act can be as violent, despite all the compassion one cares to assume, as unabashedly deliberate attacks on another person.

3

The Distribution
of Power

We have concentrated so far on the factors that give rise to and maintain conflict. We have examined various definitions of power and conflict and have discussed a number of myths regarding who starts trouble and why. The implication throughout all of this discussion has been that our organizations and the attendant bureaucracies as well as the attendant control agencies must find methods for regulating conflict in the societal units for which they are responsible. I do not mean law and order!

After spending a number of years as a management consultant to government and industry, my experience has been that there are many concerned and well-intentioned administrators whose desire to institute reform, as well as their desire to keep themselves responsive to a changing society, have been thwarted by hopelessly archaic bureaucratic systems. They cannot delegate responsibility because the system encourages the incompetent to hide. They cannot institute radical changes because the organizational structure discourages true reform. Organizations reward rhetoric and sham procedures designed to give the illusion of reform. In my relationships with administrators I have attempted to point out that radical system changes are not only necessary but also possible to accomplish within one's sphere of influence. We shall examine a system for keeping organizations up to date and under control and shall comment on some proposals others have made for keeping bureaucracies responsive to changes in society. It is so easy to criticize bureaucracies for their arrogance, prostituted values, senility, irresponsibility, or what have you. Recommendations for system reform that facilitate change at low levels of violence are something else again. We have hundreds, if not thousands, of recent books on social change and social disruption. Millions of pages of journals and popular periodicals have been devoted to analysis of violence, social change, social intervention, social control, and the like. Most read like crank letters to *The New York Times*.

The proposals for bureaucratic changes are generally naïve, over-worked cliches, such as to open up a dialogue or to respond to miniriots with overwhelming police force. Still more engage in criticism of the fashionable problems of the day and many become highly regarded prophets of doom with absolutely no suggestions for how concerned people can bring about reform. We have had highly cogent analyses of many problems, such as the impossible bind police officers are in; our penal system, welfare system, and educational system; the institution of marriage; women's rights; etc., etc., but most fall into the trap of the great person myth. That is, the belief that if one can get to the decision makers and set them straight, persuade them of the unmistakable merit of reform, that they can in turn fix things up. Reform that does occur from such literary efforts seems to be limited to situations in which the Establishment's resource pools are threatened.

Bureaucracies pay attention to demands for reform when bureaucrats perceive that the protestors are not weak. Therefore, the weak, the poor, the black, the client, the student, the people locked into any arrogant system must make themselves strong and heard. Concerned bureaucrats may be able to facilitate change if they consider how reform does eventually occur and then design a system that makes the reform procedure more efficient.

Dictatorships are of course responsive. Coups force radical changes every so many years with attendant radical shifts in outlook of the totalitarian regime. The regime's rigidity forces the development of other groups that, sooner or later, capture power.

Political power in democratic situations obtains when voting blocks threaten a politician's future, or when protestors can generate such disruption that politicians in office are perceived to have lost control of the situation. Power produces change: the power of numbers, the power of publicity, the power of physical might, and the power that derives from any resource.

Have-Nots do have plebeian power. If their rights, needs, and wants are ignored, eruptions of increasing violence are inevitable. However, Establishments represent the interests of the Haves. In government, the interests of the wealthy are represented. University administrations represent the interests of the aged faculty and the system-supporting junior faculty. Industrial bureaucracies represent themselves and, secondarily, the major stockholders, and, as we well know, ignore society. The list is endless and well known to everyone. Bureaucracies are conservative agencies of retardation. They serve the function of protecting special interests. They become sluggish and senile and do not respond to society or their constituencies; instead, they are dragged along by, as Galbraith (1967) said, the imperatives of technology and organization.

A major problem of all organizations is that they become senile and irrelevant because most, if not all, have no provision for accommodating changes in society. Political parties differ chiefly not in terms of differences in leadership or platforms for improvement, but in terms of how far behind public concerns and inevitable social changes they follow. The managerial positions in all of our organizations do not lead, they do not guide, they do not steer. They do the necessary housekeeping duties required to protect their interests in an organization that is expanding in ways they can neither alter nor control.

The brain–brawn ratio in organizations makes Neanderthal man seem remarkedly astute and intelligent by comparison. The enormous destructive might of organizations, the exploding technology, the environmental destructive impact, the atrocities such progression has on the quality of human life, all are out of the control of the decision network. Airlines are deploying jumbo jets because technology has made them available. One man of limited information-processing capacity controls a 300- or 400-horsepower machine that consumes three or four times the fuel required to transport him, which results in all of the related problems associated with the energy crisis. His inability to control the device is obvious from the highway death and injury statistics. Again, the list of examples of man not being in control is endless.

Ralph Nader captured the essence of the problem well when he suggested that we should develop the legal concept of "corporate insanity." Organizations that are out of control and beyond the reach or influence of the society to which they must be accountable should be declared "insane" and their destructive or wasteful activities brought to a halt.

AUTHORITY

For our purposes we will simply use the term "organization" or "organizational" unit to connote any group of individuals assembled for the purpose of accomplishing a recognizable goal. Some organizations are characterized by hierarchical structuring. There are several types of hierarchy, of course, but two are of primary interest to us. The first is the involuntary hierarchy that represents an autocratic system in which one person is defined as the ruler and makes decisions for people over whom he rules. The second type, or more precisely the other side of the dimension, is the voluntary hierarchy, in which one person is given the authority to make decisions for the people for whom he is responsible. The cutting edge in one's assessment of hierarchies is based on the concept of authority.

Authority is the recognition of the right to restrict freedom to act. It is based on shared values within the societal unit. Police are mandated with the right to direct traffic. During a recognizable crisis, however, anyone can venture into the middle of a road and direct traffic. People will move their automobiles as directed by the person waving his hands. Such authority is based on the shared value of efficient traffic flow. I am willing to be directed, provided others accept the same authority, to preclude the necessity of my personally influencing every other driver in the traffic tieup. Collectively, all drivers are better off if each does not try to get through the tieup first. Taking turns, for example, means that accepting a minor delay by allowing others to precede oneself results in a generally better payoff with less general delay than does open competition for precedence.

Authority breaks down when it becomes irrelevant and compliance must be augmented with threat of force. Authority refers to the establishment of accepted rules and norms of protocol for limiting conflict. The rules must be in the common interest of the parties to conflict in a society and must be accepted. Rules and the authority that derives from them are transitory. That is, the rules themselves change as society changes. The trap conservatives fall into is the delusion that rules provide for stabilization and quiescence in a society. Rules, so conceived, are designed to maintain the status quo. The fallacy then, is the belief that authority generates the rules, which must be complied with by virtue of that authority. Authority, however, as a moment's reflection should indicate, derives from accepted rules designed to secure shared values. When values are not shared or rules are not commonly accepted, authority does not exist. Instead, powerful people generate rules and force compliance by means of promising punishment for violation. They have no authority and must develop powerful control agencies to force compliance. Noncompliance by groups not sharing the values on which the rules are based is defined as a crime.

Police forces are crumbling as responsible agents of authority in society because they have been burdened with enforcement of unenforceable laws. Rules (laws) have been created by governments responsive only to narrow interests which attempt to control life styles and values. Enforcement of such laws by police is rendered hopeless, and their authority similarly rendered trivial, when large portions of the population simply ignore the law and repudiate the values on which such laws are based. Had the rule formation process been sensitive to the population for whom the authority-creating procedure is supposed to protect, such laws would not have been developed. A rule, law, or norm etc., is a contract between groups. It must be in the common interest of the groups and based on shared values. The extent to which it is accepted by the groups comprising the societal unit defines the extent of the authority of that society's control agencies. Laws and rules regarding sexual behavior, censorship, gambling, prostitution, alcohol, drugs, hair length, dress, or what have you are more often than not legislation against life styles that threaten the positions of the Haves in society. They are unenforceable and lead to erosion of previously legitimate (i.e., accepted) authority. Police should chase bank robbers, find lost kids, and as far as possible regulate conflicts of interest by such actions as breaking up fights and directing traffic. In short, the police function is to regulate noncriminal conflict and to prevent crimes that have victims. Moral issues, crimes without victims, and the like give rise to unenforceable laws with the attendant blackmarketing and erosion of all law enforcement. Such laws, designed to control gambling, marijuana, drinking age, prostitution, and the like, represent the control efforts of one group over another.

The marijuana legislation offers an excellent example of laws that result in erosion of all authority. Polls have indicated that large numbers of college students use marijuana regularly and other evidence indicates that a substantial number of relatively young middle-class people are also fairly regular users. The punishment for possession of marijuana is as high as 20 years in some states. Science tells us that there is no physiological dependency associated with marijuana although psychological dependence may develop; some people can stop smoking tobacco, others cannot—a psychological dependence. Science also tells us that the primary effects of marijuana intoxication are a slight increase in heart rate, reddening of the eyes, and a slight disturbance in both memory and the performance of complex tasks.

Who would jeopardize hard-earned careers and risk going to jail to experience these? Nonsense. As Charles Tart (1972) comments, young people who hear scientists or physicians making such statements about marijuana intoxication simply sneer and have their antiscientific attitude reinforced. What is more, laws based on such obviously irrelevant data and lack of understanding are simply repudiated along with law enforcement agencies and society in general. I might add that such ignorance has been thought by many to be responsible for many soft drug users experimenting with, and becoming addicted to, the hard or physiologically addictive drugs. If government propaganda considers marijuana and heroin use to be similarly menacing to a person and both crimes, then perhaps the "authorities" are as ignorant about heroin as they are about marijuana.

Authority derives from rules based on shared values. To the extent that rule enforcement becomes a method for the one group to control the behavior of other persons expressing alternate life styles, authority becomes hopelessly eroded.

Anarchy

All of our discussions about systems or procedures bureaucracies can adopt to maintain a low level of violence and to accommodate change must be considered against the opposing view of anarchy. The logical extension of any administrative system is totalitarianism. Power becomes concentrated with the effect that people within the system have no means for self-determination. The system rolls along with administrators making way for it. The means available for concerned minorities to influence any societal unit's courses of action are limited to power confrontations. To enunciate the list of society's screwed-up priorities would be an insult to the reader. They are obvious and the feeling of powerlessness concerned people have when faced with due process change systems is ubiquitous.

Rather than concerning ourselves with procedures for making participative democracy more than a laughable phrase, we can argue that society should be rejected along with its guardians. The bureaucracy having one purpose, to control, regulate, and subordinate the individual to the general purpose at best and to specific interests at worst, should be repudiated. Stress should be placed on individual judgment; no decision-making hierarchy should be recognized. In short, one can argue that any form of societal government or administration is illegitimate for it subordinates the individual to the general purpose.

When compared with the atrocities of powerful government in any societal unit, be it a company, a university, a church, or a nation, anarchy has enormous appeal. And I am personally pleased that we have countercultures expressing anarchist life styles. My pragmatism forces me to conclude, however, that alternate methods are required, for apathy is not anarchy, and anarchists cannot boast a large constituency.

The systems of government and concentrated power must be made responsive to minority needs, plebeian needs, and human needs. Anarchy is a repudiation of values, certainly a source of power. Reich's Consciousness III revolution is based on just such a repudiation of values. Anarchists' desire to bring down the system makes them cotravelers, at least for part of the trip, with all revolutionary ideologists.

Nonparticipation, however, is a crime. If one disagrees with a system and, however pleasantly, refuses to participate, one encounters one's own control agencies *most* rapidly. Nonparticipation in unionized medicine, unionized undertaking, abstinence from drug-produced altered states of consciousness, compulsory education, compulsory racial and economic desegregation, etc., are all crimes. We get ourselves in a box because we lend support to our agencies of control when we identify with their activities. When they act to suppress activities we feel should be suppressed we again make the error of attribution. We feel that the agencies are acting as our agents carrying out our wishes. That Daley's battalions cracked not only hippie and yippie skulls but also those firmly attached to solid citizens should dissuade such optimistic trust in the authorities. A moment's reflection should reveal that drug repression legislation is highly beneficial to control agents and agencies. War is the business of, and is beneficial to, defense agencies. Regulation and control is the business of bureaucracy.

In short, we must realize that when the bureaucracy of any societal unit makes control or regulatory moves that we feel are appropriate, be it the introduction of safety equipment or pollution abatement devices, a new pension plan, the imposition of forced economic and racial integration, right to work rules, free clinics, free lunches, or whatever, any harmony between the bureaucracies' activities and our wishes should be considered as a pleasant coincidence. We must never make the error of assuming that the bureaucracy is, can be, or should be, a disinterested third party whose function is the regulation of conflict within the societal unit.

That we at times find our goals as managers or as individuals and the organization's goals to be consistent is, of course, fortunate. However, the bureaucracy serves the bureaucracy, satisfying the interests of concentrated power. That we may enjoy the benefits of specific bureaucratic activities is a pleasant coincidence but nonetheless a coincidence. If our goals change and thereby become inconsistent with organizational goals, we go; the organization does not change.

I believe it was Harry Truman who said that there were no statesmen, only good politicians. Whether he said it or not, I think that we do tend to be deluded into thinking that administrators whose actions seem consistent with our wishes are acting unselfishly or independently. The fact is that good politicians understand plebeian power and are able to harness it. That is, if a highly organized protest group can be encouraged to back (e.g., elect) a politician who makes specific promises to that group, both the politician and the protest group satisfy complementary wants. Is the politician a statesman? Politicians remain "good" politicians, responsive to partisan wants, as long as the partisans remain powerful.

I consider the perpetuation of the Statesmanship myth a repressive bureaucratic procedure because it encourages people to believe that if a great person can be placed in power things are going to be okay. For example, people or groups listen to bald-faced liars make promises, or are exposed to vulgar selling procedures, and then choose the "best" person. In organizations, the most energetic systems-supporting people are brought to power. Now the problem with the statesman myth is that it leads people to misdirect their energies. Politicians seek out powerful people and groups. To make decision makers responsive to partisan wants, the partisan group must become strong enough to influence decision making, regardless of the incumbent bureaucrat. The statesman myth helps keep people weak.

DEMOCRATIC TYRANNY

That democracy can be troublesome is captured in Indira Gandhi's statement, "What do you want me to do? I'm surrounded by a bunch of idiots. And democracy . . ." (Fallaci, 1975, p. 14).

There are conditions, however, under which democracy is rendered tyrannical. As a general rule we should respond to our gut feeling of disquiet, when high-ranking administrators throw open their arms and say "I wish to be democratic about this,'' with quiet observation of the violence of majority rule. You recall our earlier discussion of Schattschneider's (1960) concept that power resides in the forum of debate and accrues to that person who controls the forum. Similarly, in committee meetings, board meetings, staff meetings, etc., power refers to the ability to swing sentiment toward or against specific proposals.

However, should one find oneself in the minority, one's ability to persuade the majority is preempted by a call for the question, under conditions of majority rule. Whenever a clear majority sentiment exists, all procedures designed to increase the speed and efficiency of voting may be considered as forms of coercion that force minorities to either withdraw or to seek alternative means to represent their interests. Hence, there is nothing democratic about calling for a vote when a clear majority already exists.

The paramount function of the chair is to protect minority opinion. Stated alternatively, the control of the decision-making forum should not be preempted by majorities, status, patronage, sponsorship, or any other source of influence other than logical argument, which may take the form of data, statistical prediction, reasoned deduction, and so on. However, as we are talking about the real world we know that not only is there no sanctuary from halfwits, but even when everyone, including oneself, is alert, intelligent, motivated by genuine self-interest, and concerned about the impact of decisions, fiascos occur.

A danger signal, then, is when everyone seems to agree. Not that legitimate consensus does not exist; but when one finds little disagreement one should examine the sources of influence operating in the decision-making group. People may be agreeing with high-status people or may be so uninterested in the issues that they are aware only of the time and are acquiescing on all issues in the interest of terminating the meeting. They may be agreeing with friends, as Kurt Vonnegut's character Kilgore Trout points out:

> Ideas on Earth were badges of friendship or enmity. Their content did not matter. Friends agreed with friends in order to express friendship. Enemies disagreed with enemies in order to express enmity [Vonnegut, 1974, p. 28].

However, the people may not understand the issues or may be so intimidated by the complexity of the issues that they agree with anyone on anything. Furthermore, many people are really disturbed by conflict and disagreement and agree to almost any proposal to avoid or reduce such disagreement.

If you are in charge of a decision-making group then by all means harness conflict. Your function is to protect minority opinion, so keep it alive. Remember, conflict mobilizes energy, polarizes and clarifies issues, and most importantly, keeps everyone awake.

Consensus Rule

A special variation on the majority-rule procedure is management or decision making by consensus. The principle is that nothing happens unless everyone agrees. This procedure usually grows out of the "We are all one big happy family" myth which, of course, is a variation of the collective security myth discussed earlier. Consensus rule changes the size of the majority necessary to take action. It results in increased pressure on minorities, for if they are not easily won over on the issue itself then seductive appeals are made to be one of the gang and keep the happy family happy. If one chooses to hold out, moreover, then one is stigmatized and ostracized from the happy family with all that such exclusion can entail.

I am, of course, pointing out the dangers rather than the advantages of consensus rule. In small groups, consensus normally ensures more enthusiastic implementation of decisions and a greater feeling of member satisfaction with group activities. However, as Bertrand Russell commented, a foolish thing said by a million people is still a foolish thing, so an idiotic unanimous decision remains an idiotic decision. Consensus of opinion tells one absolutely nothing about the merit of the proposal.

PLURALISM

Before we get to the specifics of power sharing within an organization, I think it useful to look at the concept of pluralism in the broader context. Later in this chapter we shall be examining methods by which pluralism in society at large can be encouraged.

K. C. Davis stated that "we have learned that danger of tyranny or injustice lurks in unchecked power, not blended power" (cited by Kittrie, 1971). The Madisonian concept of pluralism envisioned the regulation or checking of power in the creation of multiple centers of power. Truman (1953) argues, for example, that the presence of multiple overlapping groups serves to reduce conflict by encouraging compromise. Multiple membership in such groups places each group in the position of risking a breach in its own group if it presses its own interests in a conflict to the fullest. The reason, of course, is that people who have membership in both groups form both the potential cleavage point as well as the potential source of discontent and disruption within each group. These people are therefore natural compromisers and mediators.

Basically, then, the concept of pluralism is based on the notion that multiple power centers balance each other. At times two or more centers combine to achieve an objective but because of inevitable diversity of interests and objectives such groupings are transitory and vulnerable to other power blocks formed to pursue their own interests. Bureaucracies, of course, are the antithesis of pluralistic organizations.

Pluralism is premised on the notion that the blending of the power of groups requires concordance of interests that occurs only temporarily and by coincidence. Natural and inevitable differences between groups encourage consistent regroupings and hence constantly shifting power. The effect of pluralism, then, is supposed to be the checking of power. It is obvious, I think, that the natural balancing of power in society is a myth. We shall examine a few methods that organizations can use to encourage pluralistic balancing in society at large as well as within the organization itself. Revolution or less dramatic disruption procedures discussed earlier, of course, have a power-balancing effect. When bureaucracies move toward power-balancing the initiative remains with the organization and development or change should occur at a reduced level of turbulence and disruption.

The bureaucracy, however, is an organizational structure in which power is concentrated in the hands of a few people, presumably experts. As Weber (1947) expressed it, strictly bureaucratic administrations optimize precision, speed, unambiguity, knowledge of the files, continuity, discretion, unity, strict subordination, reduction of friction, and a reduction of material and personnel costs. These features are optimized the more the bureaucracy is dehumanized. Many criticisms have been directed against the concept of bureaucratization of organizations. Mannheim (1941), for example, argued that bureaucracies develop what he called "functional rationality." According to this view, bureaucracies do not question ends but only increase the precision and efficiency with which those ends are obtained. He goes on to argue that such bureaucratic rationality is frequently inconsistent with individual rationality.

I think, however, that the major problem associated with bureaucracies is not so much that they can very rationally and relentlessly pursue a totally irrational objective (i.e., from society's view) but that the more concentrated power in an organization, the more vulnerable the organization is to senility. The Peter Principle, as you recall, refers to a situation in which people are promoted to their level of incompetence. The Paul Principle, offered as the complement to the Peter Principle, maintains that individuals become incompetent in their positions because the demands of that position, the technologies, the information, etc., develop so much more rapidly than the individual can accommodate to that change. Hence, the person becomes incompetent in his incumbent position.

Bureaucracies are based on the assumption that superiors having clearly defined objectives can simply delegate a line of authority to subordinates. The line is always preserved so that each person can be held accountable for specific duties assigned to him. This presupposes that upper levels of the hierarchy have a set of goals established in advance for subordinates to pursue. The system, then, is a situation in which one level of the hierarchy establishes the objectives for the next lowest level. Each level of the hierarchy in a bureaucratic system feeds up the pyramid to the apex, which is the decision-making center for the organization. That decision maker, the head of the pyramid as it were, sets the goals and directives for the entire organization. The crux of the matter, then, is that centralization of power means centralization of decision making, with all the attendant problems associated with pathological information systems described earlier. When faced with strong adversaries, knowledgeable and powerful peers and subordinates, excesses in inappropriate use of power are subject to scrutiny and redress.

Administrators must recognize that every system, no matter how well intentioned the incumbents, move toward repression of society. Organizations become sluggish, senile and overworked and therefore responsive only to the louder or more threatening constituent groups. Generally the threatening constituent groups are those who represent wealth and privilege in the society, for they are most able to jeopardize a bureaucrat's own position of prominence. The bureaucracy is not independent. It is not a third party, a nonaligned conflict manager, or mediator. Bureaucracies are parties to every conflict within the societal unit. Generally they represent and are advocates for the privileged group. Top-level administrators find facilitating reform difficult because they cannot control their own bureaucracy. They lose control, they do not know what is going on, they cannot weed out incompetents, they are out of touch with reality, and thus they eventually become irrelevant and ignorant. New thoughts, when they do get through the morass of insensate organizational structure, are perceived as heretical or unrealistic. What is needed in any societal unit, be it a church, industrial corporation, or government is a strong people and a smart bureaucracy. We have examined some of the ways in which bureaucracies become stupid and repressive. Let us examine some methods for becoming smart!

Managerial Bureaucratic Procedures

The caveat in all models of conflict management, the law and order model in particular, is the assumption that the bureaucracy (i.e., management, the State, Government, the Establishment, the Administration, etc.) is a nonaligned third party to conflicts. It assumes that the bureaucracy is responding to pressures—from the people, from the wealthy, from the powerful, and is attempting to manage, mediate, resolve, or prevent the inevitable conflicts that develop. The problem, of course, is that the bureaucracy cannot be impartial. Its function is to slow down departures from the status quo and it is responsive to its constituency—that is, it is responsive to the source of its power.

We must shake ourselves of the great person notion that Utopia, or at least one hell of a better situation, can prevail if we can only get the right person into power. The cliché that power corrupts and absolute power corrupts absolutely is true. There are no statesmen. Even the most well-intentioned administrative aspirant will become suppressive and dictatorial. Once he "arrives," he has been shaped by the system. He owes allegiance to the groups that brought him to power. The bureaucratic system he inherits is rigid. He is rapidly over-whelmed by information. No response as a response gains appeal because it is always defensible. Intervention requires constant justification; one is always in the spotlight of powerful critics. No response, in contrast, can be defended on many fronts or, at worst, disasters associated with inaction can be blamed on other parts of or people in the system. What we need is a system to regulate the distribution of resource pools to persons acting in an openly selfish manner—the Chief Honcho included. In short, good conflict management requires that administrators admit that they are a party to conflicts and to design systems which protect them from themselves. What we need is a democratic adversary system. Where conflict is most easily managed, most easily resolved at a low level of violence, is when the adversary is strong rather than weak. A system which encourages self-determination as a major form of social interven-tion and action. Let us consider some things that can be done.

Organized Groups

The central thesis of smart management is that a bureaucracy, recognizing that it is an advocate for certain interests in a society, is best off when it has a strong and well-organized adversary. Bureaucracies always try to keep their adversaries weak. Change, as bureaucrats tend to see it, results from examining the relevant data and, based on the merits of each case, prescribing a course of action.

Administrators must recognize, if they wish to accommodate disciplined change, that all workable governmental systems are adversary systems. Con-flict is good in society provided we know what we are doing with it. Conflict polarizes groups, strengthens groups, makes the issues clearer, sets the bound-aries of protagonist groups, as well as all of the other functions we described earlier.

Strong adversaries are organized. They have legitimate means of harassing unresponsive bureaucrats. Organized groups must have clear issues for groups crumble if goals are not clear or if they represent narrow interests. Strong groups recognized as bargaining agents for a specific delineated constituency are least likely to be forced to rely on guerilla tactics or highly destructive or disruptive forms of protest to force reform. Groups are held together by shared values.

Strong, well-organized groups can bargain. They can enforce agreements by exercising control over their own people. They can exercise self-control and, most important, they can bargain with an organization for the establishment of rules based on shared values. They can exercise rule enforcement in the group. Such rules are recognized as transitory for they derive from a negotiated agreement and such rules serve as the bases for legitimate authority structures.

Smart government, then, is one that encourages strong adversaries. Strong adversaries keep bureaucracies informed and responsive. The overworked cliché that conflict is controlled by opening up communication channels is therefore true in part. It is true if it is done. Bureaucrats cannot be expected to open them up, however. They cannot be expected to keep themselves responsive. Even the most well-intentioned bureaucrat engages in or is party to, the repression of legitimate interests in society. That this occurs because of ignorance, fatigue, inevitable priorities, or what have you, is irrelevant. The opening of channels can be accomplished by encouraging the development of groups that are strong enough to get them open and keep them open.

Community Organizing

I suspect that many readers are surprised to see a section on community organizing. However, smart bureaucracy entails the opening of communicative links within the bureaucracy and with outside groups, the forced delegation of responsibility, and the development or encouragement of strong adversaries. Community organizers, the good ones at least, build powerful groups. In any participatory governmental system, the important power is people or plebeian power. Conflict management, then, is tantamount to harnessing the power of groups to encourage a responsive bureaucracy.

I do not intend to attempt an exhaustive commentary on community organizing for there are excellent books written by such experts as Alinsky (1969) and Kahn (1970) that enunciate its procedures and purpose. In these few paragraphs I shall simply attempt to enunciate some of the more essential features of community organizing. That bureaucracies could encourage community organizing should be obvious. Presently, I suspect churches are generally responsible for raising the starter funds for most community-organizing projects, although some cities have considered bringing in organizers to lay the groundwork for developing several community organizations. The short-term funding of such projects, for after the professional organizers leave the groups should carry on by themselves, I believe to be a step toward smart government.

Community organizers generally require that funding be free of policy-making groups. When a church or a government funds an organizer they must decide on the probity of the organizer's procedures prior to allocating the money. Once the monies are turned over, a point of no return has been reached. The organizers go about their business, without control by the funding agency.

Second, groups should be organized on several issues. Community organizations should deal with recreation, zoning, urban planning, jobs, education, building codes, and whatever else concerns the people. By organizing on several issues, the group's integrity is maintained as a viable political force, regardless of success or failure of particular appeals for change.

Once priorities have been established, the target of the protest must be frozen. The group maintains pressure on the person with decision-making prerogatives until a negotiated settlement is reached. The group attempts to establish itself as the bargaining agent for a constituency and exercises control to prevent subgroups within the constituency from acting on their own initiatives.

Kahn (1970) describes some of the procedures and tactics one can use when organizing poor people. He, of course, is assuming a hostile and unresponsive bureaucracy.

The organizer must be viewed as being aligned with the group he is attempting to organize either by virtue of membership status, similar race, similar background or in terms of common areas of interest. The organizer should also live with the people.

It is also important for the organizer to size up the community effectively, to know the power structure, and to get a feel for the economic conditions in the community. In a poverty-stricken area, it is essential to know whether workers are being exploited by the power elite or by industries that could pay a higher wage and whether the power structure is attempting to attract new industry, or is the area unattractive to industry and poverty structural as opposed to exploitative?

The organizer should also get a feel for those people in the power structure who may be sympathetic to change and those who may be resistant to change, for whatever reason, but should avoid unnecessarily alienating the power structure. It is also important to distinguish between power exercised through a position and power exercised by the position. Frequently, both organizers and power structures attempt to con one another in an attempt to gain confidence. Kahn (1970) states that, when organizers and power structures have tried conning each other, the power structures have very often been the winner, usually because the organizer fails to believe that the power structure can use the same tactics he has been using, and use them as well or better. The good organizer always assumes that the other side uses all the tactics that he does and uses them at least as well.

In an attempt to keep control, the power structure selects its own leaders to represent poor people. Such leaders rarely represented the real interests of the poor in any aggressive fashion. To identify the power structure's leaders, that is, those who have been approved by the power structure, one can simply enquire of the power structure who are the responsible leaders and spokesmen. The emergent leaders in the poor community are likely to be labeled or identified by the power structure as troublemakers, agitators, outsiders, out for themselves, etc.

The power structure's leaders are likely to be those who have found well-paying employment and stand to lose, or conversely, those who have nothing really to gain from any changes within the community that may threaten their positions. In general, this means that the established leaders attempt to support the basic exploitative relationship between the power structure and the poor. Sources of effective leadership in the poor community include (a) those who have nothing to lose and are rejected or found unacceptable by the power structure, (b) those who have income that is independent from pressure from the power structure, such as those on federal pensions of some sort, small businessmen, farmers who own their own land, and so forth.

It is frequently advantageous to have rotating and diversified leadership because this makes it difficult for any Establishment to isolate the driving force and it also helps prevent the Establishment from applying pressure to one or more individuals or attempting to buy them off.

Kahn (1970) suggests escalation as a general strategy for persuading the power structure, proceeding from the least pressure to the greatest pressure. He also suggests reversing the escalating process, in which case maximum pressure is brought to bear on relatively minor problems. The latter tactic is to keep the power structure off balance so that they cannot anticipate a proportioning of means to ends. He also suggests that trying to force the power structures into something that they are not capable of doing may be beneficial to force a confrontation, thus polarizing the community.

A concept that reoccurs time and time again in writings on community organizing is that of giving the opposition a face-saving way out. Kahn talks about creative power tactics that provide a situation in which the power structure can give in without appearing to have done so. In short, power tactics should avoid confrontations or should concentrate on achieving concrete goals. What is more, it is always useful to allow the opposition to believe that they have won whether they have, in fact won, or not. This increases their willingness to yield on future issues.

ORGANIZATIONAL POWER

It is useful now to introduce several additional concepts of institutional power to guide our discussion of power sharing. In the writings addressed to issues of power, we tend to find two traditions. In one tradition they are talking about distributive power, which is the distribution prerogatives that a person has over scarce resources. Hence, such writers as Mills (1956) and Dahrendorf (1959) focus their attention on methods by which the Haves maintain control over the Have-Nots and how the Have-Nots attempt to gain greater access to scarce resources. Parsons (1960), in his critique of Mills, points out that in addition to distributive power, which is rather like the game of two-handed poker mentioned earlier in this book in which the more one person gives away the less he retains, there is a concept of collective power. This refers to the ability of groups of individuals to be able to achieve mutual goals. Now as I indicated in the section on resource pools, the distinction between various forms of power and conflict find their origin in the nature of the resources over which people want to gain access. There are some resource pools that are depletable; hence we talk about distributive power. There are other resource pools however, that require concerted group action to obtain and, hence, we talk about collective power. Of course, all managerial positions involve both types of power and it is people's confusion about the two types of power that gives rise to pseudoconflicts.

The second distinction I think is of importance is that between the power *in* an organization and the power *of* an organization. Within an organization there is a limited amount of time, resources, and decision-making prerogatives available to a fixed number of people. The organization itself, however, represents both a set of goals and the resources to achieve those goals, which is, of course, a definition of power. As Hawley (1963) has pointed out, moreover, all social groups are organizations of power in that they have the capacity to produce results. Now I think it is straightforward to say that organizations gain power when the ability to obtain or achieve shared goals is enhanced. Conflict or power struggles within an organization, however, reduce the size of the power pie. That is, they reduce the ability of the group to achieve goals. The proposal offered in the last chapter is a systematic procedure for structuring the distribution of power in an organization. It is a method for engaging people in group decision making. It is a forced delegation of responsibility procedure. By distributing power in an organization, the total power pie available to the organization expands (i.e., a collective power process). Hence, the total amount of power available to each individual also increases. In short, it is an exchange of one form of control and influence for a greater quantity of another form of control and influence.

We come now to the central issue in the concept of power distribution. The question is, why does power expand in organizations when managers engage in power sharing, or rather, engaged in participatory decision making? There are several reasons for this and we shall take them in order. The first follows from the simplistic notion that power refers to one person's ability to influence the behavior of another person. If a group of people in a social group or organization is involved in true participatory decision making then the participants become simultaneously Sources and Targets. That is, they become both wielders of power and Targets of influence. That this particular explanation for power expansion does not sound very satisfactory reflects only that it is premised on a definition of power that is unsatisfactory. Second, if we consider power an energy as Bertrand Russell did, then we can talk about the motivation or drive of individuals as being a source of that energy. Highly motivated and highly active people are more productive and get more done. The energy potential for the machine, if you like, increases as we charge up our people. There is a carload of evidence indicating that managers are very highly motivated by three structural properties of the job situation, all of which are under direct managerial control. Those three aspects are recognition for achievement, responsibility (i.e., a sphere of influence), and challenge. All of the other things that we commonly think about as motivators, such as money, a good parking space, a plush office, or well-appointed working areas do not in and of themselves increase the energy level (motivational level) of managers. Money, organizational status, and any of the physical accoutrements, such as plush office furniture, have an effect on motivational levels because they are perceived as symbols of recognition. The principle can be well demonstrated in the area of pay raises. Consider, for example, two middle-level supervisors, both doing roughly the same kind of work in the same department or office. Both supervisors are making, say, $12,000 and the time for raises comes; Supervisor A hears that he has been given a raise of $3,000 per year. Of course he is as happy as a pig in mud until he discovers that the other fellow received a raise of $3,020. Companies that have used various status accoutrements for different hierarchical levels of management have also gotten themselves into some hilarious situations. There have been examples of managers purchasing their own special chairs, desk top accessories, etc., which the company normally provides for upper levels of management, and sneaking them in at night. Now, it is not the contention of motivational theorists to argue that these things are not important. They are. Poor pay, poor working conditions, out of date or unattractive equipment, etc., can make the most enthusiastic person working on the most challenging and romantic job dissatisfied with his work situation. These features are similar to what Herzberg (1966) has called the "hygenic factors." They do not motivate anybody but they can certainly make the person extraordinarily displeased with the work situation and hence encourage him to leave. The motivating factors, the ones that generate energy if you like, are job enrichment (i.e., providing challenge), increasing a person's responsibility and sphere of influence, and recognition for achievement.

The more a person participates in decision making the greater is his responsibility, and we have much research to indicate that his satisfaction increases as well as his efficiency and productivity. The above I think are simply byproducts, so to speak, of power distribution procedures in an organization. Power sharing by definition increases the amount of interpersonal influence among members of any participating group. In addition, the increased responsibility, challenge, and recognition for contributions enhances the energy level of the group.

Recall that the definition of an organization is an institution with objectives, goals, resources, and processes for achieving those goals. The greater the potential for achieving those goals, the greater the power of the organization and the greater the power pie. However, goal or objective achievement requires focused energy or focused effort. It is to this property of power sharing that we now turn our attention.

I think it is axiomatic to indicate that sharing power naturally increases the amount of interaction one has with subordinates, which naturally establishes a base for directing the subordinate's activities. It should be added, conversely, that such interaction increases the subordinate's ability to direct your activities also. Second, we again have, I believe, the axiomatic properties that such interactions clarify situations and increase the amount of focused intelligence that one can direct toward the achievement of goals, which again enhances power. The third property, and I think the most important one, is based on the effort–implementation tradeoff which is represented schematically in Figure 5 a and b. In each one of the graphs, the shaded area may be considered as benefit, efficiency, or more generally, organizational power. The vertical axis is implementation, or in more general terms, the amount of focused effort people direct toward putting a proposal or plan into effect. It represents the amount of effort directed to a goal attainment. The horizontal axis represents the magnitude of the goal, objective or, more generally speaking, the magnitude of the plan. The objective of increasing one's sales by 5% next year is under most normal circumstances a far less enthusiastic objective than increasing one's *share* of the market by, say, 25%. The horizontal axis, then, is the scope of the plan and the vertical axis is the degree to which people direct their energies and resources to bringing that plan to fruition.

Now, people work more diligently and more efficiently and with greater satisfaction on proposals and plans that are their own or reflect their influence than they do on plans or proposals imposed on them by others. Even holding the scope or the magnitude of the plan constant, therefore, we can increase the probability or likelihood of an efficient and rapid achievement of goals by

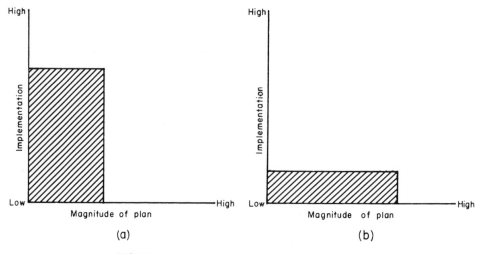

FIGURE 5.   The effort-implementation tradeoff.

intraorganizational power sharing because the implementation of such proposals is enhanced.

Now, with respect to the scope or the nature of the proposal, we also have evidence that plans and decisions reflecting the input of people with different expertise and points of view are of a better quality than those of a single individual. Again, I think we can accept as axiomatic that our organizations are becoming very complex, and are attempting to harness technologies that are developing at a rate far too fast for organizations to accommodate. The day of the great person is over. To run any part of the organization in an intelligent, adaptive, and responsive manner requires the input of many people with different specialities, experiences, and expertise. As stated previously, moreover, the simple overload of information renders the one-person decision center ignorant. Hence, again referring back to Figure 5, participatory decision making can increase both the implementation and the quality of the plan and therefore organizational power expands.

Participatory Decision Making

The bureaucrat's greatest enemy is himself. Once he finds a place where he can hide if he must, his adventurous attempts to keep his bureaucracy responsive and efficient soon flicker out. His values change, his perceptions of situations change, he gets tired and lethargic, he questions whether or not his efforts are worth the result, he slows down. Others in his bureaucracy encourage preemptive moves, delay tactics, and a leisurely pace and discourage, behaviorally or rhetorically, attempts to engage constituencies in the decision-making process. Why open all the potential hassles when one can do things in a traditional bureaucratic fashion? Why ask people to participate in the important decisions that are going to affect their lives? Certainly such participation will expose serious differences, which will only be resolved by difficult and costly negotiation. Why not just move preemptively and defuse the resultant protest with traditional delay and orbiting procedures? Why delegate responsibility when some tedious ass is certainly going to do things the way he sees fit?

The reasons for a bureaucrat not to encourage participative decision making are legion and the logic is compelling. Chances are that defensive management directed at supporting the status quo proves to be the safest course of action, and the most well-intentioned administrator begins questioning the probity of his activities after he has experienced the effort, distress, and personal jeopardy to which he is exposed if he attempts to encourage reform. Every organizational bureaucracy reverts to a sycophantocracy, where power goes to those who support and flatter. Most reform-oriented people in the system simply do not have the extraordinarily high levels of stamina, intellect, and humor to unceasingly harass the arrogant power structure. The risks associated with internecine harassment loom so large relative to the potentially trivial results of one's efforts that inactivity, coupled with the appropriate and approved rhetoric, or even criticism, seems the unmistakable rational choice. People who have initially sought reform in their organizations generally prostitute their values and become weekend radicals—those who complain about the system at cocktail parties.

Recall, from our earlier discussion of conflict strategy, that uncertainty enhances the credibility of any threat. If you can structure your personal bureaucracy so that some part of it is out of your hands, then the means for ensuring some turbulence and responsiveness may be guaranteed. That is, you cannot prevent dissent if you set up a communication channel that you cannot immediately shut down at will. One's control becomes less autocratic, automatically, as it were, if one really does delegate responsibility.

We shall examine some techniques for opening up the channels of dissent and for structuring participative management.

Charettes and Encounters

Several years ago the administration of Columbia University decided that they were going to expand into Morningside Heights. Among other issues, Harlem residents (Harlem borders Morningside Heights) particularly objected to Columbia's proposed gymnasium in a nearby park. Students at Columbia were becoming increasingly involved in social action work with people around the University and many found themselves in direct opposition to the administration's policies regarding not only the community but also other University issues. Students, faculty, and community leaders were unable to influence the administration because none of these groups had meaningful representation in decision-making councils. They were powerless in what has been described as a system of government similar to that of Czar Nicholas II. Hence, violence erupted. The outcome of the Columbia struggle was, I suspect, democratic defeat—everyone who wanted to get involved lost. Turbulence brought some change but no real reform.

Temple University, in a similar situation in Philadelphia, decided to try to hammer out a workable understanding with community residents. They held a charette.

In a Baltimore ghetto, an old high school needed to be replaced. Dissatisfaction with ghetto schools, constructed so frequently without community participation, encouraged the US Office of Education to consider a charette.

Halifax, Nova Scotia, faced with serious economic, social, and cultural problems, held an encounter session to provide a forum for community opinion and outside expert opinion regarding plans and priorities for the city.

The frequency of the use of charettes and encounter sessions for providing effective participatory planning in a variety of settings is increasing. Some are designed to provide workable plans and understandings among various groups who co-reside or are for some reason affected by each other's actions. Others are designed to generate new ideas and reconnoiter public opinion. Others are designed to create the illusion of participatory government or to defuse potential resistance by providing a forum for blowing off steam. We shall examine some of the essential features of charettes and encounteres, mindful that any procedure can be prostituted to serve as a manipulative ruse. The following paragraphs are not meant to provide an operating manual for charettes and encounters but to describe some of the general features of such sessions.

Charettes

"Charette" is a term used in architectural planning. Its literal meaning is chariot or cart, which came to be used to imply nonstop marathon designing sessions of architectural planning teams. The concept of the charette is that of having a mechanism for swiftly circulating information among participants of the project team with the purpose of forcing integration of all phases of planning, consistency of design, and inclusion of all relevant information. Constant feedback of the details of the developing plan is made available to constituents, those people who will be affected by, or who must live with, the design and who have a means for making their desires known. The concept brings to mind a 'round-the-clock brainstorming session where professionals, bureaucrats, and constituents hammer out the details of a proposal so that it reflects both technical excellence as well as the needs and desires of the clients or constituents.

There are differences, of course, in the forms that charettes may take. Charette managers or directors have favorite procedures, but there are some general features common to most such planning sessions. Generally, charettes are used when there is an identifiable focal issue. A university planning to expand wishes to become a good citizen and develop a mutually satisfactory relationship with the community. A high school is to be replaced; citizens, professionals, and city planners work out a school design, a school program, and a community relationship that reflects not only contemporary technology but also the needs of the users and coinhabitants. A community organization, successful in blocking the bulldozer form of urban development, invites the city planners to work out a redevelopment and rejuvenation program reflecting the community's desires.

In a charette there is generally an implied, if not explicit, commitment to carry out the final plan created by the work group. Issues other than the focal issue then become important subjects for the charette to attack. In building a school, the group would undoubtedly deal with the school-related problems in other communities having similar characteristics. They examine curricula, teaching innovations, afterhours use of facilities, parental involvement in the day-to-day activities of the school, expectations of parents for their children, and future needs of students, all of which would force an examination of where society is going.

Therefore, the first steps in a charette are negotiating a mutual understanding regarding the extent of the commitment to implementing the final plan, and recognizing that many issues may emerge that are likely to extend the examination to areas that may be sensitive or under some other group's sphere of influence. A school-planning charette in a ghetto community, for example, may well expand to an examination of welfare systems and recommendations for reform that can accommodate ghetto childrens' education.

Second, the constituency groups must be organized. Commitment to plan means that bureaucrats must acknowledge their ability to act or to include in the charette people or agencies within the administration who do have decision-making prerogatives. Affected levels of government and affected groups within the community are organized or invited to organize, and representatives are elected.

Preliminary training sessions are held to train task group chairpersons, establish working procedures, and develop communication channels, such as intergroup communication, immediate feedback to the constituency groups; as well, they provide a mechanism for rapid input of constituency group reaction. The overlapping decision center model to be discussed, modified slightly, serves as an excellent basic structural framework for charette work groups. During the early training sessions the groups work out some of the basic questions that must be dealt with, the type of expertise required for the planning task, the specific subtasks that must be accomplished, site visits that may be required, sources of information that may be necessary, and so on. In planning a school, for example, some basic questions may include:

1. Who should the school serve: students, families, the community in general?
2. Where will the graduates go? What should they be prepared for?
3. What type of teaching innovations can be anticipated?
4. How does curriculum affect school design and vice versa?
5. What is the relationship of various levels of government to the school?
6. What should the role of business, social agencies, and the like be with respect to the school and its students? How can design or policies affect the relationship in desired ways?

We can think, of course, of many other questions that may be important. The task of designing a school must be broken down into subtasks, the very process of which forces precise problem definitions. Groups must look at recreational needs, equipment needs, space use, curriculum requirements, etc., as well as at the drawing and pricing of the plans.

Once the charette groups have some idea of where they are going and the subtasks that must be accomplished, they can start developing a list of consultants and technicians the process requires. An urban planning charette may benefit from the expertise of architects, landscapers, city planners, economists, social psychologists, sociologists, draftsmen, statisticians, geographers, lawyers, etc., assuming, of course, that one already has a charette manager or director who knows what he or she is doing. The nature of the consulting relationship must be developed, including payment for community residents who are fulltime participants released from their day-to-day jobs for the duration of the session, fees and expenses for consultants, how long each consultant should be available, when they should be phased out and how, technical services and supplies each requires, etc.

The preplanning sessions, which can be scheduled at convenient times (evenings, weekends, and the like), usually begin several months prior to the actual charette. In addition to serving a training function and trial sessions for participants to learn the procedures, the preliminary sessions serve to clarify the issues and provide a general plan for attacking the charette problem.

The charette proper should run nonstop, 12–14 hours a day. The main planning sessions may last for 14 consecutive days, and postplanning sessions may meet every several weeks to see the plan through to implementation. Subgroups, working on specific tasks in conjunction with experts, hammer out preliminary designs that are made immediately available to other task groups. The relevant community constituencies receive continuous information about the development of the plan and various forms of open forums are used to allow the task groups to receive feedback from the community.

Community involvement tends to run high in such charettes and participation generally continues into the plan implementation phase. Charettes can explode if bureaucracies use them to manipulate noisy constituents by giving them the impression of participatory planning.

Encounter Sessions

Encounter sessions are more likely to be used as a ruse. Governments can hold encounter sessions to defuse protest, provide the illusion of participation, create straw men for angry constituents to attack, provide public awareness of dissension to justify inaction, ad nauseam. Encounter sessions can, however, be extremely valuable tools for any societal unit to keep informed and to accommodate needed reform. They can be used by city planners to get information and sample the sentiments from the community and to provide the community with outside expert opinion to point out the imperatives or limitations under which planners must operate. They can be used by upper-level management to get and give information from other levels of management (this procedure generally involves using the consultant experts as a channel for communications moving vertically within the organization). Encounters can be used by any group that wishes to establish a dialog on real issues.

The encounter generally does not involve a simple focal issue, such as a school design, an urban plan, or the like. The rallying issue for encounter sessions are more likely to be long-term continuously changing policy questions, such as the plans for economic development in a community, the future orientation of a corporation, new product developments in a company, the long-term outlook of a growing university, community relations in ghetto border areas, welfare reform in a city, and so on.

Serving a different function from charettes, encounters do not usually involve commitment to proposals emerging from the sessions and therefore no provisions are made for examining recommendations or proposals in detail with respect to cost, technological and social feasibility, social and environmental impact, and the like.

There are two essential features of any meaningful encounter session. First is that of open and publicized community meetings. This can be most important in keeping consultants in touch with the realities of issues and to help them get through the Pollyanna of bureaucrats' descriptions of policies and problems. Second, the encounter group must have what can be called normative subpoena power. The consultants must be able to request meetings with any person or group in the community or the bureaucracy. Furthermore, they must be able to get the desired people to attend the open forums so that people from the community can question bureaucrats directly. The encounter management can obtain the power to encourage cooperative participation by making invitations public information. The force of public disapproval can often encourage the most resistant bureaucrat or industrial fat cat to resist being noncooperative.

Encounter sessions usually are initiated by people or departments within a bureaucracy. Any sessions that are initiated by the community, however, generally have been organized around specific issues and therefore charette-type planning sessions, with mutual commitment to formulate and implement concrete designs, are favored. The encounter session, initiated by the bureaucracy, is most often staffed by consultants picked by that bureaucracy. Community participation is accomplished by having open forums in which community people can speak directly with the panel of expert consultants. A day's schedule focused on secondary education might be as follows:

1. Expert consultants, together with government sponsors, hold a short preliminary discussion on the day's issue. Important aspects of the issue are delineated and relevant sources of information include the school superintendent, teachers' association, parents, students, school principal, school board, such official documents as curricula, disciplinary mandates, rules, early reports, budget, etc. Site visits to look at facilities and observe operations, and talks with teachers and students on the spot are also a source of information.

2. If a site visit is to be included, such as visiting a school or a factory, it generally occurs early in the day.

3. Special sessions with important sources of information are held. For

example, the experts may have a face-to-face meeting with the entire school board.

4. The consultants work independently, in teams or individually, analyzing important aspects of the problems associated with the day's issue. During this phase the consultants identify other sources of needed data, and cooperating bureaucrats attempt to obtain such information. Continuing with the school example, such other sources may be interschool examination results which, for particular subjects, may be valuable.

5. Open public meetings are held in which the consultants give their preliminary findings and assessments of problem areas. This is followed by an open discussion between the consultants and members of the community.

6. On subsequent days, further visits and meetings may be required until the consultants have adequate data to submit the formal analyses of specific problems and recommendations for possible avenues of reform. Summaries of these proposals are again presented to the community, usually in an open meeting, and the community members are invited to question the experts and comment on their analyses or proposals.

As a word of caution, charettes and encounter sessions are likely to have a high degree of personal involvement of active participants. Tempers can run high and people can become extraordinarily emotional. Indeed, marathon encounter sessions, when groups are in close contact for long periods of time, have been used therapeutically for everything from increasing sensitivity to others to working out marital problems. The session manager or director should therefore be someone with training in group interaction. That person structures the sessions to maintain an adequate level of conflict but is careful to keep things under control.

Self-Regulation

We have examined different conceptions of interpersonal power and organizational power and have discussed the beneficial properties of power distribution within an organization. Namely, by distributing power within an organization one renders the organizations more intelligent, increases the potential for change, and also increases the total size of the power pie. However, this does not mean that one simply distributes power in an undisciplined fashion. Managers must know what they are doing. In addition to having a firm understanding of conflict, violence, power, and other features of their day-to-day jobs, it is also important for them to understand how to distribute power and to evaluate what effects such distribution is having on the people for whom they are responsible. The rule of the game is disciplined power sharing. Do not overgeneralize and simply run around helter-skelter trying to give people things to do or delegating responsibility without some absolutely clear structural plan for that distribution. Too much power sharing or unstructured power sharing can have detrimental effects that should be obvious to everyone. Giving away power or distributing power can increase peoples' desire to gain greater power and one must have some method for discouraging, or at least keeping in check, such power-seeking behavior. It is also quite likely that people may not be prepared or capable to exercise the amount of power that you are distributing. They may use the power inappropriately because they have never had experience with exercising or wielding organizational power. Conversely, and probably the most usual experience, people hesitate to use power because they fear the consequences and the responsibility they must accept. An additional consequence of undisciplined or unstructured power sharing is the possibility for developing a cluster of individuals whose goals are inconsistent with organizational goals.

Throughout this book I have been arguing that administrations grow senile, arrogant, and repressive, to say nothing of inefficient, unless they are constantly challenged, attacked, or in other ways shaken up. However, this does not indicate that I am advocating, nor do I think it is possible, that North America do away with most of its institutions and become a place in which we all sit around singing and sipping wine all day. I believe that it was Jerry Rubin who once said that he was glad that the hippies were not running the airlines. It goes without saying, I think, that our institutions, our governments, our services, no matter what form they eventually take, need extremely creative and energetic administrators. We must build systems that are smart, not systems that are stupid or vulnerable to senility. We have talked about some methods for making people strong; we are now going to direct our attention to concepts for making administrations strong.

There is a concept on which I have been working for a long period of time as part of my management consulting work with several large companies and some agencies in the government. It is an attempt to build a system that has a large number of strong components in it. It is a system of management based on the principle that one creates operational systems and organizational systems rather than concerning oneself with managerial styles.

One of the most important parts of any system, be it a managerial system, a process system, a computer system, or what have you, is that it not be capable of developing infinite life. We have discussed the problems of computer systems which become so complex, particularly in terms of the software, that they outlive the intellectual wherewithal of anybody working on it. That is, the programs become so complex that no single individual is capable of fully understanding the total system. Under such circumstances priorities change. New demands on the system are introduced as additions to the existing system or program. Failures in the system are jury-rigged so that the program can be made to work as opposed to examining any long-term policy implications of the system. In short, the very complexity of such systems determines policy because people caught in the system are never capable of standing back and examining the implications of the existing system or program. The same is true of very complex managerial systems and structures. Once activities are launched in such complex systems, points of no return are reached in which the organization is pushed along by technology, inertia, or any of the imperatives of a system operating without intelligence.

When a missile armed with a nuclear warhead goes off course, it is destroyed. It may be destroyed by a ground control center or it may self-destruct. Robots are artificial intelligence machines. And "thinking machines" must also have self-regulatory or self-destruct capability. Should such a device begin an area of activity that is a dead end or wasteful, then it should "recognize" that state and stop or modify its activity. Such artificial intelligence machines normally have built-in activity limiters. Time may be a parameter, for example, so that if a machine has not completed a task within a certain time, it shuts down. Repetition could also be a parameter, so that a specific activity may only be repeated for a fixed number of reiterations. The total amount of mechanical memory used by such a device may likewise be used as a limiting parameter. Should an activity require the machine to remember more than a fixed number of events, the activity is assumed to be inefficient or incorrect, and shutdown or a change in activity occurs.

The development of self-regulatory, self-destruct technology for artificial intelligence systems is fascinating and challenging. Such regulatory systems should be designed so that the machine "learns" from its own activity, preventing recurrence of inappropriate or inefficient activities. The system should not be simplistic in the sense that a human operator simply specifies a few operating parameters, such as time, memory, and the like. Such simplistic systems are not truly regulatory in that the human operator can render them stupid. For example, a missile should not destruct simply because it momentarily departs from a specified trajectory because of some such random influence as air turbulence. It should self-destruct when the trajectory has changed or when it is no longer homing on the target.

Similarly, a computer caught in an insolvable problem of calculation usually terminates the job because it exceeds a time allotment. A human operator can render the computer stupid by constantly increasing the allotted time. Hence, considered as a system, that is, the operator included, the system has limited self-destruct capacity.

The concepts of self-regulation and self-destruction are being extended to social systems. Presently, many of our governmental programs and agencies, as well as most of our private industries and organizations, have few self-regulatory properties. The activities of such societal units continue ad infinitum if not ad nauseum unless encumbered by some external limiting factor, such as reduced funds or death.

Theorists have argued that for society to survive (i.e., not destroy itself), social systems must be developed that have self-regulatory properties. Government agencies, policies, and programs must include provisions that can "automatically" stop the system should certain parameters be violated or exceeded. For example, attainment of objective should bring the activities of many organizations to a halt. Similarly, failure to accomplish an objective within reasonable time or money parameters should force a screeching halt.

The problem with most suggestions for self-regulatory social systems is that they are predicated on the notion of a superadministrator, an elite group of technologists or a supersystem. In most systems someone or some group has to "blow the whistle," or, alternatively, has the option to override self-destruct. To truly be self-regulatory, the system must be, to some extent, beyond the control of any minority.

It is my contention that the only self-destruct system *not* predicated on a notion of a superadministrator or an elite group of technologists, one that is consistent with the freedom and dignity of the person, is a self-destruct system built on autonomous and powerful subgroups. In short, a powerful people forces a smart government, which is a self-regulatory system. Smart administration, similarly, is built on the concept of rapid access to knowledge, full disclosure, the elimination of sanctuaries for the incompetent, and the development of powerful subgroups. The system I should like to propose is called the "overlapping decision center system" and is based on the concept of forced power distribution. It generates conflict that is harnessed.

OVERLAPPING DECISION CENTER SYSTEM

At the time of this writing, I am reality testing. Brought in as the director of an academic unit that has desperately needed restructuring, I am having my memory refreshed regarding the problems of nonsupportive persons under one's direction. People frightened by scrutiny of their activities or hostile toward changing emphases and imperatives of the organization have memory lapses, hysterical fits, and red-faced episodes of principle standing; but more important and more difficult to handle, they develop pathological states of mind. They look for problems or potential problems with every administrative activity beyond sneezing. One can easily deal with people who angrily state that "we all used to be one big happy family" because generally, at least part of the staff react to such statements with genuine shock and disbelief. Hysterical outbursts, unbelievable distortions of perceived reality, irrational refusals to follow directives or to participate in administrative action, despondent forecasts of impending doom, and the carrying about of zombielike facial expressions with the accompanying chanting of "I can't sleep" tend to blow over provided one keeps one's policies and directives clear and offers encouragement to the anxious and the distressed. It is imperative, however, that while you maintain your own sense of humor, for you are finished if you lose it, you do not allow yourself to start giggling, which is the first impulse. Equally important, but less likely if your sense of humor is maintained intact, do not react to anger or stupidity with anger or stupidity.

We want administrative systems that intelligently exploit technology. We want more brain in the brain–brawn ratio, and this can be accomplished by replacing stupid bureaucratic systems with smart ones. We want systems intelligent enough to recognize when ongoing activities must be altered, corrected, or stopped, or when information is needed. Bureaucracies must be capable of rapid starts, abrupt changes, information retrieval, and above all screeching halts.

Let us start with some simplifying, but I believe pragmatic, assumptions. First, a Chief Honcho is a Chief Honcho. That is, the person with the title is the person who is, in the last instance, accountable. He delegates responsibility and authority but retains final accountability. In short, we must assume that any organization we work in is a bureaucracy in which power is concentrated in the hands of a few individuals. Individual accountability is a bureaucratic concept. Although I strongly believe that group decision making and group accountability are not only desirable but also, in the long haul, inevitable, we must start with present realities. All of our establishments are explicitly hierarchical and premised on the notion of individual accountability. Moreover, although such structures encourage buck passing and hiding and stifle self-initiated activity, it is only expedient to assume that any organization one encounters is so structured.

Second, in any area of activity one must expect to encounter halfwits. Although we are stunned by the profound stupidity of people on whom we must depend, including at times ourselves, we must never assume that we shall find sanctuary from stupidity. We must plan for it by maintaining an adequate monitoring system that makes us aware of developing disasters while we can still do something about them.

Third, whenever we find a person for whom we are responsible who lacks initiative, is unwilling to accept responsibility, or in popular terms is poorly motivated, it is most probably our fault. We do not delegate responsibility; we do not give recognition; we try to maintain ourselves as top dog; we are insecure and therefore discourage both insightful suggestions and self-initiated activities; we discourage criticism, encourage sycophancy, and are traumatized by dissent. We structure things so that we hear what we wish to hear by giving recognition to those who support, agree, and praise. Every administrator reading this book probably feels that although he recognizes that other administrators do not really delegate responsibility, he is the exception. It is expedient, efficient, and logical, to say nothing of probably being correct, to assume that you suffer from these same shortcomings.

Finally, let us simply take on faith that you are better off being turned on, motivated if you prefer, by the challenging properties of your work than by impending deadlines or the praise of a superior.

The overlapping decision system is extraordinarily simple. It is based on the concept of delegated accountability and the development of expertise in restricted areas of activity. The system has grown out of recognition that managers spend 70% or so of their time on housekeeping duties. They spend most of their time chasing people to find out what is going on. They are continually attempting to gather information. Consider the following scenario: as part of your budget estimate, which must be submitted in 4 weeks, you ask one of your subordinates who happens to be a close personal friend to work out the details of one of the budgetary items. Let us assume that you want to renovate a part of your plant and that what is required for the budget submission are the estimates of several contractors plus a few details of the renovations. You let your subordinate know that it is imperative for you to have the information within 3 weeks so that you can incorporate these items within your budget and have enough time to finalize the projections. You do not hear anything from the person to whom you assigned the task for 2 weeks and you go down and knock on his door. He responds that, of course, he will have it on time and "Don't worry." Toward the end of the third week, you again go in and ask him about the disposition of the budget estimate and again he smiles and says "Don't bug me" and indicates that "You'll get it when you need it." At the end of the third week you again go down and finally get hold of him. It turns out that he needs another 24 hours and you go bananas.

It is very difficult to supervise the efforts of people with whom you have some affective relationship, either positive or negative. Such people are difficult to supervise because it is tedious to give them admonishments at low levels of your own dissatisfaction. People with whom you have an unfriendly relationship lead you to believe that you are nit-picking if you admonish or correct early. Friends can keep putting you off in a very good-natured way. Given that low-level admonishments or redirectives are avoided, the situation gets out of hand in the sense that the activity or task may have been incorrectly completed or deadlines not met. The situation then explodes and you have both problems of an incompleted task or improperly completed task and a high level of anger and hostility.

Good administrative systems should automate, as far as possible, all house-keeping details. The information flow should be automated and the burden of information exchange should rest on the subordinate, not on the Chief Honcho.

Supervision and Leadership

I think it is most important to recognize that leadership is impossible without supervision. Any system that one attempts to set up should be predicated on the notion that one wants to automate the supervisory requisites of a manager's job. To the extent that one can be relieved of such supervisory and housekeeping details, one can spend ever greater amounts of one's time taking the long-term perspective of where the operation is going. All of our organizations are pulled along by imperatives of technology and the organization itself simply because our senior managers are spending all of their time in day-to-day housekeeping activities required for the institution to run at all. They do not have time to stand back and have a dispassionate view of where the whole operation is going. The system that senior administrators want to set up is one that relieves them as much as possible from the supervisory details, a system that in effect automates these tasks.

To set up such a system, it is important to have a firm understanding of what supervisory behavior entails. In the first instance, supervision and leadership require planning. It is important for the manager to get firm in his own mind some disciplined notion of where he is going and what kinds of tasks are important or essential for the continued operation of his system. Second, supervision requires the full delegation of responsibility, which implies the delegation of authority for tasks. The fact that managers do not delegate responsibility is, I think, the single most critical element in the development of senile and stupid organizations. Third, it is important to establish open communication systems that permit information to flow freely and accurately anywhere in the organization. We frequently confuse communication systems with the notion that documents must be able to flow throughout an organization. What is far more important than the flow of information in any organization is that the system provides some checks on the accuracy of information reception. Frequently, people who receive information within systems interpret it incorrectly. A communication system should provide some method for correcting such error. Fourth, supervision and leadership require constant monitoring and surveillance. It is most important for the administrator to have accurate and up-to-date information about the disposition of any of the tasks or activities of subordinates for whom he is responsible. The monitoring function is by far the most important, for without accurate information it is impossible for the administrator to take corrective action. It is also the activity that occupies most of the administrator's time because he spends enormous amounts of time and energy trying to find out what his subordinates are doing. Finally, the system should provide some mechanism for control. That is, if some task is not going as planned, or is falling behind deadline or schedule, the system must provide for rapid disclosure of the difficulty and must force corrective action. To the extent that we can automate all of these functions with an administrative or managerial system, we can relieve senior administrators of 70% or so of their burden and permit them to increase the amount of brain in the brain–brawn ratio. That is, they become able to do what Chief Honchos are supposed to do.

Imperatives

There are a few guidelines and basics that we want to keep in mind when developing administrative systems. What we are attempting to do is develop a system that encourages the Sherlock Holmes type of management. Good administrators are good scientists. They are observant. They want accurate, up-to-date information. They formulate hypotheses, which are rejected or modified when they prove to be unacceptable because they are either incorrect or not parsimonious. Hence, the most important aspect of any system we establish is that it provide for an accurate surveillance and monitoring system. We must have data; we must know what is going on if we are going to take corrective action.

Related to surveillance is the concept of checks on the system. We want to know immediately as soon as the system is going awry. In short, we want to be able to take corrective, regulatory, or destructive action as soon as it is useful to do so. The first imperative of smart bureaucracy, then, is accurate and up-to-date information. It is also imperative that one automate administrative functions (i.e., make them part of a recurring administrative process). To the extent that one can automate such procedures, the day-to-day activities can rumble along without one's constantly reactivating people or activities.

The Group

The most critical aspect of the system that we are going to discuss is the notion of the power of the group. Managers are motivated by peer recognition, which has been found to be one of the most powerful reinforcers known. Managers are very highly rewarded when their colleagues become aware of the fact that they have accomplished something in a highly efficient and creative way. They are very severely punished or threatened (or destroyed, for that matter) whenever they experience or anticipate that their level of incompetence or lack of effort is going to be made public. In short, the most critical aspect of the use of the power of the group for purposes of controlling one's operation is that managers operate in a wide-open fashion so that everything becomes public information. Although people may know that others within the organization know that they are incompetent asses, public disclosure and discussion of that fact is sufficiently noxious to keep everybody awake. It is important to note that such public disclosure must not be under voluntary control; it must also be automated. The disclosure of competence as well as incompetence must occur rapidly and with certainty.

Recall our earlier discussion of the effectiveness of threats that are, to some extent, beyond the complete control of the threatener. The public disclosure threat becomes highly effective when it is highly credible. It becomes credible because it is certain and not easily stopped. Hence, the threatener cannot be intimidated by threats or promises.

If one is going to make use of the power of the group for the purposes of controlling behavior then, of course, it is perfectly obvious that the group must agree on goals; that is, where it is going. The agreement on goals or objectives of any particular group tends to have the effect of converting all forms of conflict to means conflict. As you recall from earlier sections, means conflict results from disagreements as to how to achieve agreed on goals as opposed to any disagreement about the goals themselves. This does not imply, however, that ends conflicts are not going to be extant in the organization. All people within the system are competing for achievement, authority, and in general, power.

Finally and most critically, one should recognize that in any area of activity there are points of no return. That is, once an area of activity is started there is no way to change the direction of that activity, save for total destruction. As an example, consider something such as negative income tax or baby bonuses as they are called. Such systems, which are government support systems, are systems of no return. For example, one could start a negative income tax system with the payment of $10 a month to people falling below a certain income category. Once that system is started there is only one way to go and that is increasing levels of support. Reducing or discontinuing support would generate unacceptably high levels of disruption. Similarly, in managerial situations there are a great many activities that have the point of no return property. As a Sherlock Holmes manager, one should become skilled at determining when one is likely to become involved in an activity prior to crossing the point of no return.

The overlapping decision system is extraordinarily simple. Again, and this cannot be stated too often, it is based on the concept of the automated and highly certain use of group disclosure. It is based also on the concept of power distribution because the result of this system is the development of powerful and knowledgeable subgroups within one's organization.

Planning

It seems axiomatic to state that one must plan activities and identify the goals or responsibilities of any group for which one is accountable. Although axiomatic, it is staggering, to me at least, when one becomes cognizant of the level of directionless activity of administrators and their subordinates. Planning is the first imperative and simply involves listing the critical recurring tasks one must accomplish to satisfy one's function.

In any organization you have day-to-day operations—the product, if you will. Jobs that are routinely received from other departments or offices in the organization or daily outputs of products as determined by market needs define the extant function for which the department was created. Your product may be service or maintenance functions, such as the treatment of patients or the repairing of television sets, or your output may be the production of steel plates, the writing of speeches, the testing of computers, or the typing of letters. In addition to the day-to-day functions, one has many other tasks that must be accomplished in order to have an intelligent and efficient department or function in any organization. The exact nature of these recurring tasks differs, of course, depending on the situation you are in. If you think back over the course of a year or so, moreover, you can easily develop a list of routine but time-consuming tasks that are recurrent and necessary for the operation of your department. By way of example, consider the functions that must be accomplished to develop and maintain a first-class academic department. In any department one must consider such things as budget, recruitment (i.e., what kind of people are needed and who is available), program and course curriculum development and review, the research and publications output, professional development, space, student training, student evaluation, staff evaluation, supplies, support staff, grievances, and so on. In a sales department, of course, the list would be different. There would be some common elements, such as budget, supplies, professional development (i.e., training), and perhaps recruitment.

Okay, so now you have a list of jobs that must be routinely accomplished to make your operation go. It is important to keep in mind that such jobs are not the equivalent of objectives. The objective may be a certain production rate or a specific proportion of a market. We are concerned here, however, with the tedious but important tasks one must complete in a competent manner to bring these objectives to fruition—the essential ongoing tasks.

Delegation of Responsibility

I have maintained that most managers simply do not delegate responsibility. We simply cannot let go of power and clout. The overlapping decision center organization forces one to both plan and to delegate responsibility. The general procedure is that of forming task groups that meet routinely at scheduled times over the course of each and every year. The purpose of this procedure is to create groups of experts who can deal both leisurely and routinely (and it is hoped creatively), with such critical areas as the budget, training, or what have you.

Consider the schematic diagram of a small department in Figure 6. Let us assume that six critical tasks define the necessary and sufficient jobs that must be routinely accomplished to make the above department go. *After* a deadline has passed and one has dealt with the problem in the routine emergency, bail

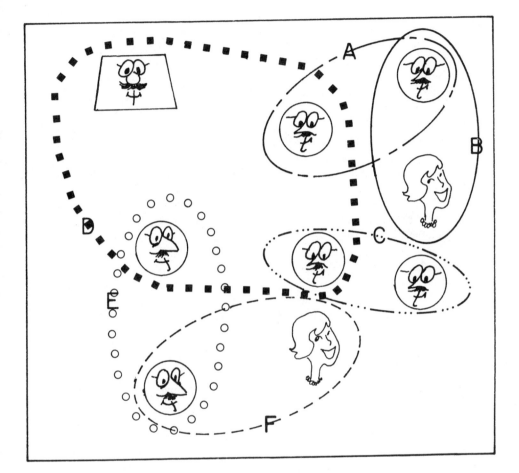

Budget   A —————— — — ——————

Supplies   B ——————————————

Training   C —— · · · —— · · · ——— ·

Scheduling (production)   D ■ ■ ■ ■ ■ ■ ■

Maintenance   E O O O O O O O

Support (clerical and   F — — — — — — —
       secretarial)

FIGURE 6.   The overlapping decision center system.

the boat, put out the fire manner, assign areas of responsibility to specific people in your department. Now, before you can assign anything you must decide how many people should be in the group, who has most to contribute, and who wants to be in it. After you have decided those issues, then establish standing task groups who understand that they are going to deal with the particular task routinely, on a scheduled basis. They must understand that they do not constitute an ad hoc committee but that you wish them to be experts who know more than anyone, including you, about their task. It's their baby! They should be informed that you expect them to deal with the problem on a plan-ahead basis, to consider fine details leisurely—after all, why would you assign the task on March 1 when the deadline is February 15, if you did not want a think-ahead document?

It should be kept in mind that some projects are short lived so that people within the production task group may be responsible for one task for 5 months, another for 2 months, a third for 13 months, and so on. The production of a book or catalog, the evaluation of a project, the filling of special production orders, the forecasting of a specific market, and similar tasks are short-lived projects. They can and must, however, be incorporated into the standard routine operation of one of the task groups. It is also understood that each person in the department contribute to the department's production.

Accountability

Acknowledging the fact that you are the finally accountable person, how do you make others accountable? More to the point, how do you make it bloody difficult for them to hide or find sanctuary? The secret of making others accountable is to make the others responsible for keeping you informed. The procedure is as follows: decide on the frequency of task group meetings that you think is necessary to adequately deal with a task. The budget group may meet once a week, training twice a month, support review monthly, whereas production may meet daily. The critical aspect to this system is that one sets up scheduled meeting times that are *never* altered even if the members meet to reach the consensus that they have nothing to do. Second, and most critical, periodic, presumably weekly staff meetings are held. At these meetings, instead of dealing with the usual trash and having the superhefties report to the lightweights what is happening and what is going to happen, require each task group to report the exact status of their project, to have the working documents available for perusal, and to announce the issue to be considered at the next meeting. The frequency of such reports should be determined by just how up-to-date the senior manager must be kept on a particular issue. Training, for example, can easily be every month, budget perhaps every third week, whereas production should be as frequent as feasible. Reports are made at the scheduled time at the staff meeting (the meeting that includes everyone), even if the group convener reports that he respectfully submits that he has nothing to report. The basic truth of this system, if you will, is that it is immutable. There are *no* exceptions. If the convener cannot report, then some other member of the task group reports. The Chief Honcho never chases anyone.

Wide-Open Management

Now the function that the above system serves is to make everything public information. If one group is not doing an adequate job, not only does the boss know but so does everyone else and, again, the most potent reinforcer or punisher is public recognition of one's accomplishments or shortcomings. Hence, groups keep up to avoid such public disclosure of their incompetence, inefficiency, or laziness. The second, and perhaps the most important feature of the wide-open procedure is that information is always current. If something is not being done or is being handled incorrectly, the situation can be redressed before it gets dangerously out of hand.

The second aspect of wide-open management is that you should let everyone know what you are doing. If you set up this system, have your people read this book. If you set up some other system, clue your staff in too, not only to the processes but also to your purpose for such procedures. There is no need for deception or Machiavellian management. In addition, wide-open procedures increase the self-regulatory features of the system. Your groups of experts can influence your behavior importantly only when they know what you are doing.

Such disclosure happens relatively automatically when one establishes the information system. The manager must make the directives and objectives clear to set up the system in the first place.

Chief Honchos worry about such wide-open procedures. They feel that they become vulnerable when others know all of the details. Remember, however, that disclosure carries clout regardless of the circumstances surrounding such disclosure. The system works as well when everyone knows why you are doing what you are doing, as when they only guess. Most important, however, is that disclosure eliminates your sanctuaries. We want to eliminate the sanctuaries and hiding places for the incompetent, lazy, or senile—and that includes you!

THE BENEFITS OF OVERLAP

The schematic shows that each task group is overlapped with some other group. More specifically, some people in the department serve on more than one task group. Overlapping is important and should not be avoided. Even if one has sufficient personnel to preclude multiple memberships, overlap should be deliberately included. In the first place, communication channels are always open. I do not mean to overwork a nauseatingly overworked phrase but overlap provides check on *incorrectly* received information. If a working document goes from Group A to Group B, the overlapped person(s) provide a check on the received information. Did they get the message? Now, this immediately implies that in setting up these groups one should overlap them logically. Working papers and other documents that logically flow from one group to another should be facilitated by a person in an overlap position. Hence, in the planning, one must include not only tasks to be accomplished but also logical information flow.

The second feature of the overlap is that it provides a logical training system. Our organizations are hopelessly absurd in their promotional procedures. People are promoted into new positions and find, if they are bright, that they know less than the secretary who has come with the job. They have a new set of mandates, entirely different operational procedures and requirements, and virtually no idea of what is going on. In the overlap system people start in a group, presumably a less critical one, in which they are in the company of an expert (i.e., one who has had experience with the task). That experienced person may be overlapped with some other group. When a new person gains experience, he or she can be moved into the area of overlap with the next logical group, depending on where the person is going, where again that person is in the company of experienced co-workers. The process continues, and the person is never placed in a position where there are no experienced people to turn to for guidance.

The system then can accomplish many of the essential aspects of the manager's position. It forces planning; it forces delegation of responsibility; it opens communication networks, and it provides a monitoring and control system. Most important it provides a means for training people and giving them positions of strength and autonomy in the system. They become knowledgeable and capable of importantly influencing the direction of the department or function in the organization. They increase the brain in the brain–brawn ratio.

The overlapping decision center system is not, by any means, the only suitable system for operating our organizations. There are many other good ones. This is the one I sell as a management consultant because I believe it provides for a more intelligent, responsive, and healthy organization.

HARNESSING DISAGREEMENT IN DECISION-MAKING GROUPS

Talking about harnessing conflict and accomplishing it are two very different things. To be an effective chairperson one must conceptualize oneself as a mechanic and the decision-making group as a machine. Your function is to keep that machine operating efficiently and humanely.

All groups go through four phases during the decision-making process. Phase 1 may be called the problem-definition phase, Phase 2 may be called the evaluation phase, Phase 3 is the idea-generation phase, and Phase 4 is the decision phase. Now obviously we should keep in mind that this is a verbal representation of what actually goes on in the decision-making group. It is not a pictorial representation and the lines of demarcation between phases are fuzzy at best. However, it is important that the person responsible for running the group be aware of where the group is in its decision-making process and, second, what is happening to a group if it becomes inefficient and pathological.

The major problem with most groups is that they do not spend an adequate amount of time in Phase 1 activities. Questions are not adequately defined, and hence the questions are not broken down to subquestions. In short, most groups do not adequately analyze the problems to which they are supposed to be directing their attention so that everyone is not aware of exactly what the problem is. By prematurely jumping to the decision-making phase, a characteristic of virtually every group, one finds that the subfactions within the group are in serious disagreement. The reason that these groups are in serious disagreement is that they do not agree on the nature of the problem; hence, one faction may not be able to see the relevance or even the relationship of the proposals being made by another faction to the problem at hand. The results of such lack of mutual understanding of the nature of the problem is that the group constantly goes back to Phase 1 activity. Someone in the group may say "That's not what we're supposed to do, what we're supposed to do is . . . ," and then define his understanding of the problem. This is a perfect cue to the chairperson that conflict is forcing the group to recycle and go back to Phase I activities.

Phase 2 activities frequently go unnoticed but generally take the form of people saying "Gee, this is a very difficult problem," "I don't know why we need a group to settle this issue," "This is really low-voltage stuff," "I don't see why I have to waste my time on this," "I hope we can come up with something that will get us out of this mess," etc. In other words, it is during this phase, after there has been some mutual understanding about the nature of the problem, that individuals express their sentiments about the importance of the issue or, more directly, their feelings about their own participation.

Phase 3 is the most vulnerable of all of the phases. It is the time during which all of the creative work of the group is accomplished. Under such circumstances we have to be very concerned about yielding and conforming behaviors. If somebody has an idea that he feels is weird, unusual, or frowned on by high-status individuals within the group, then the person is very likely not to propose such ideas. All of the influences on individuals to yield and conform or to keep quiet operate most destructively during Phase 3 activity.

Most important however, is that without proper Phase 1 activity, that is, without proper definition and subdivision of the problem, meaningful and productive Phase 3 activity is precluded. One cannot generate ideas that are appropriate to a problem unless one understands the problem. Furthermore, the stigmatization associated with unusual or novel ideas is all the more likely if various groups or subfactions within the decision-making group do not agree as to what the problem is. Hence, an individual proposing an idea relevant to his own definition of the problem may create shock or surprise or feelings that the person is out of touch with reality on the part of another individual, whose definition or perception of the problem is different.

The decision-making phase is simply the putting together of problem definitions and the list of ideas generated during Phase 3 and coming up with the most suitable or adequate solution to the problem. Decision making under such circumstances is not difficult; in fact, one could say that making the decision should be the most trivial part of decision making! For if one has a fully adequate definition of the problem, which is fully shared by all members of the group, and a list of relevant ideas, then pairing them involves finding out what the cost–gains situation is and choosing those courses of action which seem to offer the best ratio.

Now the chairperson of a group is in a delightful position of having the energy of the group at his or her disposal. In the first instance all groups wish to move ahead to Phase 4 activities. Whenever a problem is posed to a group, people immediately propose solutions. Individuals may say "Let's do thus and such," somebody else may disagree and say "No, rather than do thus and such, we should do the following," etc. The function of the chairperson, then, is to hold the group back and prevent it from moving prematurely ahead to later phase activities prior to adequate and mutual definition of the problem (i.e., Phase 1 activity). Now, because the energy of the group is directed toward moving through the Phases 1 to 4, the chairperson must constantly redirect the group back in to Phase 1 activity. If the chairperson does not, then the group goes through the enormously frustrating and endless procedure of recycling from Phase 3 and 4 activities back into Phase 1 activities. Such recycling always gives rise to poor quality decisions because people get bored and tired and have memory problems. High standards for decisions imposed earlier in the decision-making session shift or are forgotten with the result that lower quality ideas and solutions, which would have been rejected earlier, are accepted later. Conversely, good ideas rejected earlier because of an unrealistically high standard are never reviewed again and are forgotten. Furthermore, the group becomes extraordinarily frustrated and angry because it does not seem to be getting anywhere and, of course, it is right. They are going around in an endless circle. Hence, instead of analyzing the problem and making rational decisions, the group makes expeditious decisions in the interest of bringing the terribly boring and frustrating activity to an end.

Harnessing disagreement serves the purpose of holding groups in Phase 1 activity. The function of the chair at this point in time is to encourage minorities to give their full problem definition and problem subdivision so that the potential for communicating these differences of opinion within the group is enhanced. The essential feature of such activity is to determine whether such differences of opinion are real or illegitimate. That is, are they based on real differences in belief structures or preferences, or are they based on misperception of the other person's position?

Once the problem has been broken down and analyzed and differences of values, objectives, purpose, etc., have been communicated, and this is easily said but very difficult to accomplish in practice, then the chairperson allows the group to move forward into later phase activity. It should be pointed out again that the chairperson need not goad the group on; it is the natural drive or orientation of the group to move on to later stages of decision-making activity. Hence, the function of the chairperson is to mobilize the energy that accrues from differences of opinion and conflict for the purposes of gaining a thorough analysis and breakdown of the problem. The chairperson, then, by lifting the gate, so to speak, allows the group to move forward into a later phase activity.

There are several dangers of which all chairpersons should be cognizant. In addition to the tyranny of majority rule or the delusions of consensus, one can get into a situation in which disagreement is valued more than agreement. In such situations individuals are encouraged to be caustic, uncooperative, and disagreeable simply because they feel that this position is more valued by high-status individuals within the organization. Second, you may find that you must stimulate disagreement in some situations because, for any one or more of a number of reasons, individuals are not aware of other orientations or other approaches to the problem. Again, this is easier said than done and one should be cautious that consensus does not really indicate that the problem is trivial and group activity is unwarranted. Some problems should obviously be handled by individuals and do not need the benefit of group decision-making procedures. Recall again that many meetings are held because principals are bored or lonely or are too insecure to make decisions on their own. When you are facing that kind of situation, either because of your own inadequacies or because of those of people around you, then we are no longer talking about the decision-making group as a highly efficient decision-making machine but as a group of individuals who are satisfying other needs.

CONFLICT IS EVERYWHERE

In the song "American Pie" by Don MacLean there is a line that goes "and the players tried to take the field, but the marching band refused to yield." When you set up your marching band you are going to be involved in conflict after conflict after conflict. However, do not make the error of attributing the cause of the conflict to your activities or your methods, for conflict is everywhere. It is true that the more you attempt to do something, the greater your likelihood of encountering resistance. You are going to encounter other people who have other methods of doing things. You will encounter sluggish organizations. You will encounter lethargic principles. You are going to encounter conservatives in the organization who are perfectly content to allow things to continue the way they are. As soon as you act you announce yourself for counterreaction. People who do nothing never get into any trouble. People who tend to initiate programs are those who find themselves face to face with all of the impediments to action that organizations can bring to bear. And we have reviewed a great many of these.

However, I think it is essential to keep our sense of humor about these activities and to recall that life itself is a conflict management or conflict coping situation. You wish to do one thing but must do another. You are having a pleasant conversation but you are late for an appointment. You wish to take in a show but your spouse is tired. You want to shut down a certain area of activity but you find that the people who define that activity as important can marshal very great resources in their attempt to block your efforts. You point out to the principal administrative officers in your organizations that there are certain unconscionable things going on. You find that not only are they distressed by the fact that you are bringing these issues to their attention, for they already knew anyway, but you discover that they further perpetrate the false realities. You sit back in total astonishment that most, if not all, of the high-ranking officials in the organization accept this fiction.

The point that I wish to make in this section is that the purpose or goals of our activities can never be that of attaining quiescence and a conflict-free existence for that means the very termination of life's activities. The critical lesson is that of being realistic about conflict, recognizing it as inevitable, but harnessing the conflict so that it is a constructive vitalizing force rather than a destructive and dehumanizing force. It is not really very important whether we believe that conflict is good or bad but we must recognize that conflict is inevitable and like other ubiquitous forces in life, conflict can be most useful.

It should also be obvious that too much conflict can be destructive. By too much conflict I mean either too many separate decisions that must be rendered or unitary conflicts that reach unmanageable proportions. Although some of the implications of both of these conditions are discussed earlier in this text, I think in this final summing up that it may be well to make a few concluding statements. In the book *The Whore-Mother* by Shaun Herron (1973) one of the principal characters, Powers, an assassin associated with one of the factions in the Northern Ireland flap, states to a less onerous assassin colleague that "When hate's as good as a good fuck, who's for peace?"

You are going to run into people who value conflict, who like fights, who thrive on violence, whose whole orientation to life is one of confrontation and battle. We must recognize that we all have some of these elements in us but it is a question of degree. Some of us are extreme on some of these dimensions, whereas others of us are more quiescent. The point is that, as a manager, you must be able to appreciate the full complexity of the structures with which you are dealing. You cannot, when convenient, attribute serious conflicts to basically deranged personalities or personalities who value violence and brutality.

Nor, conversely, when you are involved in such highly volatile conflict situations can you alternatively attribute them to the structure of the situation. After all you are not a violent person, you do not value brutality, it is not your customary way of dealing with things; therefore, it must be a function of the environment. Hence, although some people may be more "violent" than others or may feel more comfortable within an interpersonal confrontation, the entire system is completely interactive. Conflicts of values give rise to interpersonal violence and the use of force which in turn is both a cause and a result of individuals who take pleasure in such activities. It is very difficult for one to survive without the other. This does not mean, of course, that there are not factors which are primarily personal in nature and other factors which are primarily environmental or structural.

We must be very very careful about attempting to analyze these factors in isolation, however, for we are talking about the real world, and simplistic cause–effect analyses are very likely to give rise to inappropriate models that lead us into further difficulties. Hence, when conflict seems to be getting out of hand, when the level of violence becomes personally intolerable, one must muster all one's analytical capabilities while standing back from the situation, however momentarily, and attempt to analyze the contributory factors, the nature of the conflict process, the nature of the resource pool, and the influence of the individual protagonists.

The second debilitating effect of conflict is that conflict forces decisions. As Trotsky (1973) has pointed out, "War accelerates the various political processes." Every time you are involved in a conflict situation, no matter how trivial, you are involved in a choice situation. As we pointed out in the very beginning of this book, decision making is very difficult and very costly in terms of the decision maker's health and general wellbeing. Decision making, when there is too much of it, and perhaps when there is too little, can render the person both physically and emotionally uncomfortable. It can make us anxious, it can make us neurotic, it can render us helpless, it can affect our gastrointestinal system, it can affect our parasympathetic nervous system. The problem with too much conflict (i.e., too many conflicts) is that we are caught in a situation of too much choice.

Recently I attended a conference on the latency child, children roughly between the ages of 7 and 12 years of age. During this period of time the child goes into a quiet period in which all of the important social learning takes place. The child must learn the various social settings in which he is, and is to be, involved; he must learn a large number of intellectual skills; and he must learn a whole repertoire of appropriate interpersonal behaviors. One of the very great problems that children, in our modern day and age, have during this period of time is that they can have too much choice! There are so many things going on around them and we, as parents, feel that being very democratic, egalitarian, and "modern" requires that we offer the child a whole repertoire of choices among many delightful things and activities. We also pressure the child to some extent, for we feel that with all that is available, why should the child not partake? Frequently, in our efforts to be very helpful and kind and good parents, we render the child emotionally incapacitated because the child simply cannot cope with all of the decisions that he or she is forced to make. Being very confused about the child's behavior we trot off to our friendly mental health worker, who may compound the problem by offering the child some more choices. This is not a book on child psychology, however, although Sam Hayakawa (personal communication) has maintained that political administration should most properly be considered as a subdiscipline of child psychiatry; it is a book on the problems confronting a manager. We can easily see that there may be a syndrome of "too much choice" associated with a child who is faced with such momentous learning situations. Similarly, we should be able to understand that managers may be caught in a situation in which there is also too much choice, and we would also call this the syndrome of too much choice. Managers, depending on their phase of life, enter marriage, experience changes in values, find themselves involved with families, find themselves involved with divorces or separations. They may be experiencing situations in which the entire world seems to be changing at a rate with which they cannot easily deal.

The background of ambient conflicts that people live with, on a day-to-day basis, must always be considered. Involved with skirmishes within an organization one may find that a point is reached at which one can no longer cope. Now one may not be able to cope simply because one is overwhelmed with the amount of information necessary to make sensible decisions. Or one may be overwhelmed by the effects of poorly made decisions, which keep coming back so that each poor decision generates five or six additional conflicts, which in turn means an additional series of decisions that must be made, etc., etc. Finally, the simple anxiety of making decisions in the absence of perfect information and waiting in a level of ambient anxiety for consequences of any particular decisions may also take its toll. Again, given that we are talking about the real world, we are talking about all of these things and they all interact. The important point is that even little conflicts and presumably minor decisions contribute to the choice overload problem.

POWER SHARING: CAVEATS AND CONSIDERATIONS

Assuming that you do not wish to start a revolution, there are a few things about groups that one should keep in mind. The first is that groups are very different from people. This sounds like a trite statement but it is nonetheless important. Many managers frequently make the mistake of assuming that a group is simply a continuation or an extension of the individual. Hence, those properties of people which he thinks he knows something about can be extended and in general made applicable to group function. We must assume that there is a discontinuity between the functioning of an individual and the functioning of the group, and there is good evidence to suggest that this is so.

Wechsler (1971), for example, has found that the intellectual functioning of a group is different from the intellectual functioning of the individuals which comprise that group. That is, the group is something different from simply a collection of individuals; the intellectual properties of the group are in fact different from any combination of intellects of which the group is comprised. Insights and problem solutions do emerge from group effort that could not have been arrived at by individual pursuit. Wechsler points out that this collective intelligence results in part, from the greater amount of information normally at a group's disposal. More important seems to be the fact that group members influence each other's thinking creating a resonance which gives rise to new and different intellectual insight. However, as Wechsler warns and as we have discussed earlier, if there is group intelligence, there is also a group stupidity.

Second, individuals accept greater risk in a group context than when they are individually responsible. When a decision is defined as a group decision, a greater level of risk is accepted than would be the case had any of the individuals in the group been responsible for the decision. That is, there is a shift away from conservatism and toward more risky courses of action. There are, of course, a great many other conditions that are peculiar to groups and that have been reviewed in some detail elsewhere in this book. However, the important point for our present purposes is that the manager or chairperson of the group must consistently keep in mind that all of the insights one may have about individual behavior under decision-making circumstances may have to be modified when the unit of analysis is a group.

No manager would ever maintain that every person can be considered the same as every other person. We would argue, of course, that individuals differ and that the behavior of one individual may be quite different from the behavior of another individual, the capabilities of people differ, their conservatism differs, etc. Similarly, groups have individual characteristics such that a particular composition of individuals gives rise to a unique group character, which can be changed more or less markedly by rather slight changes in the constituency of that group. However, again just as we seek to find generalities applicable to quite different people, similarly we search for generalities that are applicable to very different groups. In the present section we are going to examine some of the dangers associated with power sharing.

The one particular danger is that the group generates an addiction, so to speak, for action, an addiction for power, and an addiction for exercising such power. Hence, as the power base expands through the distribution of decision-making prerogatives so the drive of the group to expand their power base within the organization similarly expands. This is both a problem as well as a benefit to the manager. First of all, it provides a predictable impetus to the group so that the manager can simply attempt to harness this drive in his endeavor to create a responsive and responsible decision center. Second, it is a problem because the manager must always be cognizant of where the group is trying to go and the influence that the group is attempting to have within the organization at large. If the manager loses vigilance, for example, it is entirely possible that the group may run away, so to speak, and generate considerable disruption. This again may be good or bad, depending on the needs and desires of both the group and the manager. However, such things are likely to be very costly if they occur in an undisciplined chaotic fashion. Nevertheless, such drives to expand power bases, to have influence on the organization as a whole, can be a very productive influence if properly channeled and targeted. In this final section we shall review three major problems associated with group functioning under power-sharing conditions.

Intoxication

Machiavelli indicated that the rage of man is always greater when liberty is regained than when it is only defended. We come now to an area in which there is a considerable amount of confusing and contradictory data. However, I think some meaningful generalities can be developed which are applicable to situations of groups that are naïve with respect to the use of power. That problem, of course, is power addiction—the desire to reduce the distance between oneself and other powerful persons within the organization. Mulder (1974) maintains that there is a greater drive to reduce power differences at smaller discrepancies; this is an addiction theory, as opposed to a deprivation theory, in which the drive to gain greater power would be greater at larger levels of power discrepancy. Now, with respect to group functioning I think we can characterize this as the tendency for groups, once they gain greater power and greater influence, not to mind their own business. That is, one of the premises on which this book is based is that at least one method for rendering organizations sensible is to try to create pockets of sensibility within the organization. If you are a manager then perhaps you can develop a meaningful and responsive group among those persons for whom you are responsible. However, individuals who feel that they have set their own house straight look about them and see all of the inevitable senility, unresponsiveness, and downright repression going on about them within their own organization. They then have the tendency to attempt to exercise this greater power that they feel they have. The result, of course, is that they move into other spheres of influence, with the resultant conflict that this necessarily must entail. Now, I am not advocating here that one discipline one's group to mind their own business but I think what is important is to understand the natural tendency of groups to attempt to expand their sphere of influence, to try to institute change in the organization of which they are a part.

Sherlock Holmes once apprehended a criminal because the criminal did not have, according to Holmes, "the supreme gift of the artist, the knowledge when to stop. The inability to leave alone what is already perfect." I think this definitely applies to the manager in the sense that he must discipline himself so that he understands the drive characteristics of decision-making groups and the conditions under which this drive for greater influence should be channeled and disciplined. Otherwise, a group is very likely to run away and no longer be under his influence.

We have a considerable amount of research data indicating that people gain satisfaction from exercising power and that there is a drive to reduce power distance between oneself and others. Combine this with the diffusion of responsibility that occurs in a group because the accountability for action is spread over the entire group, and one has a potentially volatile situation on one's hands. Furthermore, if one happens to walk into a situation in which people have been kept under the thumb in a very strict hierarchical structure, giving individuals greater decision-making prerogatives may well be like giving alcohol to an inexperienced drinker. They become very easily intoxicated and addicted to gaining greater power and influence. Hence, one of the things that one must be cognizant of is the experience that group members have had with the exercise of power. The delegation of greater responsibility must be within the context of a training program so that individuals gain experience with exercising influence. In the individual case the drive to gain greater influence over others or to reduce the power differential between oneself and others is resisted by a counterforce, which is the cost of exercising power. It is costly to exercise power; primarily high is the psychological cost associated with such actions. When one is acting as an individual then one is individually accountable. Under group conditions, in contrast, are situations in which group members feel that accountability is spread across the group. However, you as a manager may find yourself in a situation in which you are held individually accountable for the actions of your group. Hence, the drive and the psychology of the group may be very different from the psychology of the organization. A group that is addicted to power and driven to expand their sphere of influence within the organization by attempting to render change, however admirable and appropriate that change, may therefore do so under conditions in which you as the manager find yourself individually accountable for the actions of that group. You may, in fact, find yourself in a situation in which subordinates have everything to gain from obstruction and very little to lose because of the general protection they derive both from the group as well as from the fact that you as the principal administrative officer are individually accountable for the actions of that group.

The protection that one has against these kinds of things I think is a frank and open discussion with the members of one's group about what are realistic objectives of the group and what one can realistically expect to accomplish. I have been personally involved in several situations in which groups that have gained some modicum of success at attempting to change archaic structures, have taken on challenges that in the clear light of day are totally absurd—situations in which groups have been easily crushed by overwhelming organizational power when even such strategies as publicity and disclosure have been impotent because of the inability of the group to rapidly appeal to a large enough constituency to deter the organization from employing its trump card, which is summary dismissal. One finds, under such circumstances, that when the group has acted on its own initiative and gotten itself into difficulty, all of the potential influence groups, such as professional associations, employee organizations, etc., take a very conservative stand. This, of course, is not unexpected because such organizations have not initiated the action and tend to accept the truism that the action may not have been inappropriate but it has been imprudent. Of course it was imprudent; otherwise one would not have been appealing to such organizations. Under such conditions you find yourself pretty much on your own.

THE CHIEF HONCHO ERROR

Most of our present organizational structures are hopelessly archaic, as becomes obvious as soon as we subject them to systematic "scientific" scrutiny. That our organizations cannot react to change, cannot control the exploding technology for which they assume responsibility, cannot remain responsive to the needs of society, etc., etc. is apparent to most everyone. The purpose of this book has been to examine conflict models, to analyze the problems of regulation of societal units, and to propose the regulatory principle of power distribution. In this chapter the concept of power and independence as a regulatory structural mechanism has been extended to administrative procedure. The book has been written for administrators who want to make their little sphere of influence responsive and intelligent. I, of course, do believe that such regulatory concepts can be applied to large systems but I am also in contact with reality. I am not the president of this university even though I may think I should be.

The fallacy of waiting until you have more influence before you institute change is a perfect indicator of just how flamed out you are. The person who states that he cannot do anything because he lacks power is saying that he has capitulated to the system; or if you believe in the concept of personality you may say that the person is stating that he is a coward. Our systems foster and lavishly reward such cowardliness, so that realistically, if you postpone action, you cannot escape being totally sucked up by the system.

References

Alinsky, S. *Reveille for radicals*. New York: Vintage, 1969.

Atwood, M. *Surfacing*. Toronto: McClelland and Stewart, 1972.

Boulding, K. E. *Conflict and defense*. New York: Harper & Row, 1963.

Brodeur, P. *Expendable Americans*. New York: Macmillan, 1974.

Bronfenbrenner, U. The mirror-image in Soviet–American relations. *Journal of Social Issues*, 1961, **17**, 45–56.

Chadwick, R. W. Power, social entropy, and the concept of causation in social science. Paper presented at the Albany Symposium on Power and Influence, State University of New York at Albany, October, 1971.

Churchman, C. W. *The systems approach*. New York: Dell, 1968.

Dahl, R. The concept of power. *Behavioral Science*, 1957, **2**, 202–203.

Dahl, R. *After the revolution?* New Haven: Yale University Press, 1970.

Dahrendorf, R. *Class and class conflict in industrial society*. Stanford, California: Stanford University Press, 1959.

Deutsch, K. *The nerves of government*. Glencoe, Illinois: The Free Press, 1963.

Durant, W. *The story of civilization: Our oriental heritage*. New York: Simon and Schuster, 1954.

Durkheim, E. *The division of labor in society*. Glencoe, Illinois: The Free Press, 1949.

Eckhardt, W., & White, R. A test of the mirror-image hypothesis: Kennedy and Khrushchev. *Journal of Conflict Resolution*, 1967, **11**, 325–332.

Ellis, A. *Humanistic psychotherapy: The rational emotive approach*. New York: Julian Press, 1973.

Fallaci, O. Indira Gandhi. *The New York Review*, September 18, 1975, p. 14.

Galbraith, J. K. *The new industrial state*. Boston: Houghton-Mifflin, 1967.

Gamson, W. A. *Power and discontent*. Homewood, Illinois: Dorsey, 1968.

Hampden-Turner, C. *Radical man*. Garden City, New York: Anchor, 1971.

Hawley, A. H. Community power and urban renewal success. *American Journal of Sociology*, 1963, **68**, 422–431.

Hayek, F. A. *The road to serfdom*. Chicago: University of Chicago Press, 1944.

Heller, J. *Something happened*. New York: Knopf, 1974.

Herron, S. *The whore-mother*. New York: Signet, 1973.

Herzberg, F. *Work and the nature of man*. Cleveland, Ohio: World, 1966.

Kahn, S. *How people get power*. New York: McGraw-Hill, 1970.

Kelley, H. H., & Stahelski, A. J. Social interaction basis of cooperators' and competitors' beliefs about others. *Journal of Personality and Social Psychology*, 1970, **16**, 66–92.

Kerner, O. (Chairman). *Report of the National Advisory Commission on civil disorders*. New York: Dutton, 1968.

Kittrie, N. N. *The right to be different*. Baltimore: Johns Hopkins Press, 1971.

Mannheim, K. *Man and society in an age of reconstruction*. New York: Harcourt Brace Jovanovich, 1941.

Mills, C. W. *The power elite*. New York: Oxford University Press, 1956.

Mulder, M. Power distance reduction tendencies. Paper presented at the conference: Research Paradigms and Priorities in Social Psychology, Carlton University, Ottawa, July 1974.

Papandreou, A. G. *Man's freedom*. New York: Columbia University Press, 1970.

Parsons, T. *Structure and process in modern societies*. New York: The Free Press, 1960.

Potok, C. *The promise*. New York: Holt, Rinehart & Winston, 1960.

Proshansky, H. M., Ittelson, W. H., & Rivlin, L. G. The influence of the physical environment on behavior: Some basic assumptions. In H. M. Proshansky, W. H. Ittelson, & L. G. Rivlin (Eds.), *Environmental psychology: Man and his physical setting*. New York: Holt, Rinehart & Winston, 1970.

Raven, B. H., & Kruglinski, A. W. Conflict and power. In P. G. Swingle (Ed.), *The structure of conflict*. New York: Academic Press, 1970.

Reich, C. A. *The greening of America*. New York: Random House, 1970.

Rosenhan, D. L. On being sane in insane places. *Science*, 1973, **179**, 250–258.

Royko, M. *Boss*. New York: Dutton, 1971.

Schattschneider, E. E. *The semi-sovereign people*. New York: Holt, Rinehart & Winston, 1960.

Schelling, T. C. *The strategy of conflict*. Cambridge, Massachusetts: Harvard University Press, 1963.

Tannenbaum, A. S. (Ed.), *Control in organizations*. New York: McGraw-Hill, 1968.

Tart, C. T. States of consciousness and state-specific sciences, *Science*, 1972, **176**, 1203–1210.

Trotsky, L. *The history of the Russian revolution*. Ann Arbor: University of Michigan Press, 1957.

Trotsky, L. *In defense of Marxism*. New York: Pathfinder, 1973. P. 21.

Truman, D. B. *The governmental process*. New York: Knopf, 1953.

Vonnegut, K. *Breakfast of champions*. New York: Dell, 1974.

Vonnegut, K. *The sirens of Titan*. New York: Dell, 1970.

Weber, M. *The theory of social and economic organization*. New York: Oxford University Press, 1947.

Wechsler, D., Concept of collective intelligence. *American Psychologist*, 1971, **26**. 904–908.

Zald, M. N. Political economy: A framework for comparative analysis. In M. N. Zald (Ed.), *Power in organizations*. Nashville, Tennessee: Vanderbilt University Press, 1970.

Author Index

Numbers in *italics* refer to pages on which the complete references are listed.

173

Subject Index